PROFICIENCY-BASED GRADING
IN THE CONTENT AREAS

insights and key questions for
secondary schools

wendy **CUSTABLE**

justin **FISK**

jonathan **GRICE**

darshan m. **JAIN**

doug **LILLYDAHL**

eric **RAMOS**

anthony r. **REIBEL**

bradley **SMITH**

eric **TWADELL**

steven m. **WOOD**

edited by

ANTHONY R. REIBEL   ERIC TWADELL

Solution Tree | Press

a division of
Solution Tree

555 North Morton Street
Bloomington, IN 47404
800.733.6786 (toll free) / 812.336.7700
FAX: 812.336.7790

email: info@SolutionTree.com
SolutionTree.com

Visit **go.SolutionTree.com/assessment** to download the free reproducibles in this book.

Printed in the United States of America

Library of Congress Cataloging-in-Publication Data

Names: Custable, Wendy, 1975- author.
Title: Proficiency-based grading in the content areas : insights and key
    questions for secondary schools / authors: Wendy Custable, Justin Fisk,
    Jonathan Grice, Darshan M. Jain, Doug Lillydahl, Eric Ramos, Anthony R.
    Reibel, Bradley Smith, Eric Twadell, and Steven M. Wood ; editors: Anthony
    R. Reibel and Eric Twadell.
Description: Bloomington, IN : Solution Tree Press, 2019. | Includes
    bibliographical references and index.
Identifiers: LCCN 2018050408 | ISBN 9781947604155 (perfect bound)
Subjects: LCSH: Grading and marking (Students)--United States. | Educational
    tests and measurements--Methodology. | Education, Secondary--United States.
Classification: LCC LB3060.37 .C87 2019 | DDC 371.27/2--dc23 LC record available at https://lccn.loc
    .gov/2018050408

Solution Tree
Jeffrey C. Jones, CEO
Edmund M. Ackerman, President

Solution Tree Press
President and Publisher: Douglas M. Rife
Associate Publisher: Sarah Payne-Mills
Art Director: Rian Anderson
Managing Production Editor: Kendra Slayton
Senior Production Editor: Tonya Maddox Cupp
Content Development Specialist: Amy Rubenstein
Copy Editor: Evie Madsen
Proofreader: Miranda Addonizio
Text and Cover Designer: Abigail Bowen
Editorial Assistant: Sarah Ludwig

The authors intend to donate all of their royalties to the Stevenson High School Foundation.

We hope for all students what we hope for *our* students: Kaitlyn, Lauren, Tony, Andrew, Riley, Tristan, Miles, Julia, Carter, Colton, Henry, Charlie, Grace, Jimmy, Alice, Anna, Eden, Brianna, Nathan, Elena, Grace, Bryce, Gabriella, Luke, and Hunter.

Acknowledgments

We are grateful for our friends at Solution Tree who continue to tell the story of continuous improvement that is occurring here at Adlai E. Stevenson High School. Jeff Jones, Ed Ackerman, and Douglas Rife have been especially supportive of our efforts to share the good work that is happening here. Pulling together the thoughts and writing of twelve authors is no easy task, and we are thankful for the words of wisdom and advice of Amy Rubenstein and Tonya Cupp.

Our proficiency-based grading moon shot began seven years ago. While we are, admittedly, not quite there yet, we have made tremendous progress over that period of time. Our administrative team members have worked hard to build coherence and clarity and push the flywheel of continuous improvement in our conversations around instruction, assessment, and grading. We are especially thankful for the service and support of our board of education members: Steve Frost, Dave Weisberg, Terry Moons, Gary Gorson, Sunit Jain, Heena Agrawal, and Amy Neault. Our board of education has been steadfast in its expectation that we never rest on our laurels and that we constantly search for new and innovative ways to improve.

Finally, and most importantly, we must thank the faculty of Adlai E. Stevenson High School, who have led our journey toward proficiency-based grading. Grading reform is not easy work. There is trial and error—two steps forward and one step back (and every other change cliché you can think of). Yet, our teachers realized early on that while the work was significant, the payoff was even more so. Kids are the primary beneficiary. The nature of teachers' conversations with students changed from one of points and averages to one of learning and proficiency. Students started to focus more on their own thinking, reflection, and learning, and less on grades. Parents began to understand that a grade should be more than just a collection of homework assignments and averaged points. This book would not be possible without the hard work and dedication of our faculty, who are embracing the challenge of reform and a commitment to continuous improvement in their grading practices. This is their story. Enjoy.

Thank you to the applied arts teachers for having the vision and the drive to make proficiency-based grading a reality in our division. A special thank-you goes to Sara Lohrmann for inspiring and shaping our work as we strive to achieve success for every student in career and technical education. —Wendy Custable

———————

I would like to thank the teachers of our division of world languages and English language learning for their relentless work to innovate and drive our students' success ever forward. —Justin Fisk

———————

The work of developing, launching, and refining our approach to proficiency-based grading is guided by the hard work and talent of our teachers on the early adoption teams of algebra 1, geometry, and algebra 2. Excellent professional learning communities foster excellent adult learning; teachers are the *first learners*. Through our teams' persistence, innovation, and insights, we have learned to support our students through a new learning lens. All new ideas experience refinement that propels improvement and growth; the mathematics chapter is guided by countless conversations with Eva Lange, Valerie Tomkiel, Tina Nocella, David Irsay, and Eric Goolish. Thank you! —Darshan M. Jain

———————

Our journey toward success for every student in English has always been led by our tremendous teachers here in communication arts. For this brave and thoughtful journey into evidence-based grading, I have nothing but the highest regard and thanks for you all! —Doug Lillydahl

———————

I want to thank the thoughtful and dedicated teachers in the social studies division who are tireless in their development of student scholars, artisans, and citizens. —Bradley Smith

———————

Several science teachers and teams have led our thinking on proficiency-based grading within a science context. They have certainly experimented, learned, retooled, and then taken another shot, much like we ask of our students within this system of assessment and reporting. We are appreciative for the insights, examples, and mindset of the college prep biology and physics teams. In particular, guidance, examples, and insights for the science chapter came from Kellie Dean, Tommy Wolfe, Sara Cahill, Deanna Warkins, and Kristy Wrona. —Steven M. Wood

Solution Tree Press would like to thank the following reviewers:

Sarah Burger
English Teacher
Northwood High School
Northwood, North Dakota

Jennifer Peterson
Director of Academic Services
School District of River Falls
River Falls, Wisconsin

Janna Cochrane
Principal
North Greenville Elementary School
Greenville, Wisconsin

Dawn Proctor
Principal
Benignus Elementary School
Klein, Texas

JR Kuch
Principal
Clinton High School
Clinton, Iowa

Matt Townsley
Director of Instruction & Technology
Solon Community School District
Solon, Iowa

Visit **go.SolutionTree.com/assessment** to download the free reproducibles in this book.

Table of Contents

Chapter 9
Implementing Proficiency-Based Grading in World Languages 251
By Justin Fisk

Epilogue
Building Efficacious Learners 275
By Anthony R. Reibel and Eric Twadell

About the Editors

Anthony R. Reibel is director of assessment, research, and evaluation at Adlai E. Stevenson High School in Lincolnshire, Illinois. He administers assessments, manages student achievement data, and oversees instructional practice. Anthony began his professional career as a technology specialist and entrepreneur. After managing several businesses, he became a Spanish teacher at Stevenson. He has also served as a curricular team leader, core team leader, coach, and club sponsor.

In 2010, Anthony received recognition from the state of Illinois and the Illinois Computing Educators named him Technology Educator of the Year. He is a member of the Association for Supervision and Curriculum Development, Illinois Principals Association (IPA), Illinois Computing Educators, and American Council on the Teaching of Foreign Languages.

He earned a bachelor's degree in Spanish from Indiana University and master's degrees (one in curriculum and instruction and a second in educational leadership) from Roosevelt University.

To learn more about Anthony's work, follow @areibel on Twitter.

Eric Twadell, PhD, is superintendent of Adlai E. Stevenson High School in Lincolnshire, Illinois. He has been a social studies teacher, curriculum director, and assistant superintendent for leadership and organizational development.

Stevenson High School has been described by the United States Department of Education (USDE) as one of the most recognized and celebrated schools in America and is one of only three schools to win the USDE Blue Ribbon Award on four occasions. Stevenson was one of the first comprehensive schools designated a New American High School by USDE as a model of successful school reform and is repeatedly cited as one of America's top high schools and the birthplace of the Professional Learning Communities at Work® process.

Eric is a coauthor who has also written several professional articles. As a dedicated PLC practitioner, he has worked with state departments of education and local schools and districts across the United States to achieve school improvement and reform. An accessible and articulate authority on PLC concepts, Eric brings hands-on experience to his presentations and workshops.

In addition to his teaching and leadership roles, Eric has been involved in coaching numerous athletic teams and facilitating outdoor education and adventure travel programs. He is a member of many professional organizations.

Eric earned a master's degree in curriculum and instruction and a doctorate in educational leadership and policies studies from Loyola University Chicago.

To learn more about Eric's work, follow @ELT247365 on Twitter.

To book Anthony R. Reibel or Eric Twadell for professional development, contact pd@SolutionTree.com.

Introduction

Anthony R. Reibel, Eric Twadell, Wendy Custable, Justin Fisk, Jonathan Grice, Darshan M. Jain, Doug Lillydahl, Eric Ramos, Bradley Smith, and Steven M. Wood

The first question educators usually ask us about implementing proficiency-based grading is, "Because this is a big change, how do you implement proficiency-based grading effectively and maintain its effectiveness over time?" Implementing a grading system that requires a paradigm shift in thinking and practice can easily become frustrating, or worse, it can fail.

The second question educators ask is, "Is *evidence-based grading* the same as *evidence-based reporting* or *standards-based grading*?" Generally speaking, we acknowledge there are quite a few similarities between evidence-based grading and reporting and standards-based grading and reporting. However, as we note in *Pathways to Proficiency: Implementing Evidence-Based Grading* (Gobble, Onuscheck, Reibel, & Twadell, 2017), there are some important distinctions. Both of these new approaches to grading move us away from the collection of points, the percentage system, and averaging. However, while standards-based grading typically focuses on the teacher summatively assessing students' understanding of the larger standards and learning targets, evidence-based grading and reporting emphasizes a collaboratively developed and calibrated proficiency and maintenance expectations based on student evidence.

While we acknowledge that in some settings these differences may be seen as lacking distinction, we believe that the focus on student-produced evidence in relationship to calibrated proficiency expectations helps teachers more effectively provide meaningful feedback and grades. To that end, in this book we use the term *proficiency-based grading* to accent our focus on students' proficiency as the foundation for our grading and reporting practices.

In *Pathways to Proficiency*, we discuss the institutional framework for implementing proficiency-based grading. We go into further detail about how this grading system looks in the classroom in our other book, *Proficiency-Based Assessment: Process, Not Product* (Gobble, Onuscheck, Reibel, & Twadell, 2016). In this book, we will share how to successfully implement proficiency-based grading in different content areas.

A Different View of Formative Assessment

The distinction between summative and formative assessment remains difficult for some educators. Most of the assessments that we call *formative* could be summative assessments in disguise. Some teachers even consider formative assessment as merely practice or as a summative assessment that doesn't count—it isn't graded or marked. Most traditional assessments focus on students' deficiencies and what they don't know. We believe that this is a backward perspective and not how assessments should work. Authors Peter C. Brown, Henry L. Roediger, and Mark A. McDaniel (2014) argue this same point, saying that *massed practice* models simply aren't effective as a practice synonymous with formative assessment.

Formative assessment asks that students "learn how to better assess context and discriminate between problems, selecting and applying the correct solution from a range of possibilities" (Brown et al., 2014, p. 53). In other words, formative assessment is an experience about *development*, not about diagnosis. Some teachers continually overlook this definition of formative assessment. Formative assessment helps both the teacher *and the student* know where the student is and how he or she is growing.

Another challenge to effective assessment is that many teachers position formative assessment at either the beginning or the end of the lesson. This makes it either a pretest or a summative assessment, and neither is particularly helpful for giving students authentic feedback. In a proficiency-based assessment and grading system, formative assessments are not just central to the lesson, *they are the lesson*. Placed as the focal point of instruction, formative assessments can effectively interrupt and even block a student from incorrectly retaining material he or she may have misunderstood. This does not happen as effectively when formative assessment is placed at the lesson's bookends. This placement does not *catch* students before they walk into the summative exams with incomplete or even incorrect learning (Brown et al., 2014).

A typical assessment verifies one level of proficiency, and once students show that competency, more assessments are typically needed. Often teachers see this as valid practice because many traditional assessments are based on achieving outcomes (standards-based grading) instead of developing proficiency (proficiency-based grading). This happens if teachers don't align instruction and assessments with proficiency-based targets, but instead align them with themes and topics. This improper alignment leads us to ultimately assess students on only part of our expectations (Marzano, 2006), making our assessments more of a verifier of learning than a catalyst for learning. The fact that traditional assessment systems struggle to be more than just verifiers of learning leads to many missed opportunities to expose students' thinking *as they engage* in the learning and assessment process.

Data that matter most come from the thinking that takes place *during* the assessment (Schoemaker, 2011). In our experience, reflection-based assessments are very effective, and this concept is at the heart of our proficiency-based assessment process.

We believe that our assessments should be events that assess students on the quality of their thinking, not just the quality of their product or the outcome (Schoemaker, 2011). Such assessments require students to record their thinking during the assessment, state the thoughts that went into the responses, decide between several problem-solving strategies, and even decide how this question relates to all the other questions (Chappuis, 2009). "Thoughts" data allow the teacher to become more aware of student misconceptions and how they developed, and how the teacher can help students overcome them.

We fully acknowledge that creating and sustaining this new culture is not easy, and it will not happen overnight—or even in a year or two. Implementing this work should involve a carefully thought-out approach that places teachers at the center of the professional development and change process. Teachers using proficiency-based assessment practices understand that discovering a misconception's origin is more valuable than interpreting an outcome. The data teachers receive from a reflective assessment helps them design instruction that meets students' real needs and, more important, helps them provide students with the correct feedback to solidify and expedite the learning process.

We assert that the long-standing research grounded in the creative process can guide professional development. Psychologist and author Mihaly Csikszentmihalyi (1990) is one such expert who provides a learning framework that ensures effectively developing initiatives and pedagogy. Csikszentmihalyi (1990) presents this process in five phases that model the way we want to nurture professional growth and positive changes.

1. **Preparation** is being curious about the topics or ideas that interest you or have value to you. This is when individuals are beginning to explore these new ideas or topics and gaining the necessary foundational

knowledge to proceed successfully. Inspiration is an essential part of this phase. It promotes the internal motivation to continue pursuing this learning.

2. **Incubation** is when ideas begin to combine with other ideas and, more importantly, with questions. When someone begins working on a new idea, skill, or topic, new questions emerge, inviting the learner to go deeper or explore new areas of the concept. This stage can last indefinitely as the individual begins to consciously toil with new questions that emerge from his or her subconscious. By letting these new questions incubate, or simmer, unexpected combinations occur. These unexpected combinations form domain-changing breakthroughs.

3. **Insight** is when the individual has a breakthrough realization about the work. The insight stage is where new learning is beginning to cement itself in an individual's cognitive framework. It is similar to the moment a child grasps a new mathematics concept for the first time or suddenly realizes the exact reason he or she couldn't solve the science problem. Insight is when all the incubating concepts come together to illuminate a resolution to the problem. Insights occur only after a lengthy incubation.

4. **Evaluation** is when the individual decides if the insight is worth pursuing. During this stage, insights are scrutinized not only for their worth but for their logical sense. In other words, the individual decides whether to pursue this insight and determines whether it aligns with the desired outcome. If he or she judges the insight worthwhile, the individual will be more motivated to pursue the insight further. If the creator is unmotivated, the work will never become a reality.

5. **Elaboration** is the phase where an individual creates a final product and further nuances and extends his or her learning. Throughout the creative process, pursued insights tend to spark interest and motivate individuals to proceed further. In this phase, work seems more like play, as new insights seem to naturally spark excitement in the learner. During this phase, an individual is continuously growing and improving.

Structure of This Book

Throughout this book, we will outline how each division—the content area or grade level—in our school (Adlai E. Stevenson High School, in Lincolnshire, Illinois) worked with the institutional aspects of proficiency-based grading and, more important, how each division implemented and elaborated on the aspects of proficiency-based grading that should look different in each discipline.

This book focuses primarily on how to implement this initiative in secondary education, although many of these principles and concepts can apply to primary and middle school. Secondary educators have historically struggled with the move away from points-based grading primarily because this transactional grading and learning system is efficient. However, we cannot substitute efficiency for intimacy when it comes to the success of our students. We must promote a mentor–mentee relationship with each of our students and help them develop personal efficacy and discover their own learning identity.

Chapter 1 outlines what decisions should occur at the institution level versus the division or course level, and the seven overarching core beliefs one must hold to begin this work: (1) growth is a central concept, (2) reperformance is essential (where to *reperform* means executing a skill again in the next unit), (3) building students' reflection abilities is essential, (4) homework has a role, (5) communication with parents and the community is key, (6) culminating experiences like final exams have a different purpose, and (7) behavior can be in or out of the grade. Because core beliefs function differently depending on content area, each chapter discusses how those beliefs work within each.

Chapters 2–9 outline how implementing this initiative could transpire in each of the major content areas, from core areas such as English language arts, to electives such as fine arts.

These chapters are organized in the five professional development and learning stages noted earlier.

- **Preparation:** Readers will understand the fundamental commitment that it takes to increase the likelihood of the initiative's success. These commitments act more like the necessary mindsets that one needs to create long-lasting change and promote positive student outcomes.

- **Incubation:** Readers will grapple with the fundamental yet challenging questions that can hinder or even derail the initiative if not explored properly. The section outlines how stakeholders can effectively engage in problem solving around these questions as well as lets the reader see the realities of this change.

- **Insight:** Readers will discover the major "aha moments" that created key realizations and spurred future innovations. Readers will not only understand what these insights were but also read firsthand accounts of the impact these insights had on teacher practice, culture, and most importantly student learning.

- **Evaluation:** Readers will engage with this initiative's key questions— the questions that one must continually ask *during* the implementation process to ensure actual change versus simply the illusion of it. These questions act as guideposts that not only help guide the process of change, but also help promote maximum impact.

- **Elaboration:** This section uncovers the core beliefs that are unique to each content area as it is implemented. These beliefs are the natural by-product of successful implementation, but more importantly, these beliefs can create a lasting culture of innovation.

The book's structure addresses how proficiency-based grading specifically appears in each content area. Each chapter follows the same structure, starting with preparation stages of implementing proficiency-based grading and ending with the elaboration stage. Proficiency-based grading is not a one-size-fits-all practice. Subtleties may appear depending on content area, but implementation phases are the same, which is why the chapters are structured the same—preparation, incubation, insight, evaluation, and elaboration—but each is specific to its content area. You will see that while applying proficiency-based grading may look different in each content area, its core beliefs and general implementation parameters remain the same. Every chapter ends with key points to summarize the main takeaways.

While this book is meant for all educators, teachers will find particular value in reading their respective content-area chapter. Leaders can utilize all areas of the book to successfully lead a specific team or teachers through implementation. This is a book for all educators wishing to make long-lasting reform to grading practices.

Chapter 1

Implementing Proficiency-Based Grading With Fidelity to Core Beliefs

Anthony R. Reibel, Eric Twadell, and Jonathan Grice,

> The organizations that will truly excel in the future will be the organizations that discover how to tap people's commitment and capacity to learn at all levels in an organization.
>
> —*Peter Senge*

Successfully implementing proficiency-based grading hinges on a healthy culture and shared responsibility. Mathematics teacher Eva Lange says she noticed a change in her team: "Outside the classroom, conversations with fellow teachers were often about what problems we were doing in a lesson. Now the conversations revolve around how we can help students make connections with their learning" (E. Lange, personal communication, September 15, 2018).

In our experience, proficiency-based grading's primary benefits are promoting authentic collaboration among teachers and developing student efficacy. In this grading system, the curriculum is not organized around discrete bits and bites of content and skills. Instead, we develop proficiency-based learning targets that focus on transferable skills that help students become more effective learners themselves.

To do this successfully, teachers must share and adhere to proficiency-based grading's seven core beliefs. We fully recognize that these are fundamental shifts in the way that many of us experienced school and from how many of us started in the teaching profession. Grappling with and coming to agreement with these core beliefs in collaborative teams is the most essential first step before a team can proceed to implementing proficiency-based grading.

In our *Proficiency-Based Assessment* and *Pathways to Proficiency* books, we note the irony of authors from Adlai E. Stevenson High School (also known as the birthplace of the PLC movement) not spending a lot of time using the language of Professional Learning Communities at Work. At this point in our PLC journey, focusing on learning, working together collaboratively, and focusing on results (DuFour, DuFour, & Eaker, 2008) is so ingrained in our school's structure and culture that we do not need to rely on PLC acronyms to stay focused on the right work. However, there is no doubt that the fact that we do function as a PLC has made implementing proficiency-based grading more effective. We hope by now that most educators understand the benefits of working together collaboratively. The collaborative teams within a PLC will have a much smoother transition because they are already engaged with one another in collective inquiry. Developing the essential tool of proficiency-based grading—a calibrated proficiency-based expectation—is easier for teacher teams used to working with one another to improve their practice.

We recognize, however, that not all schools choose to function as professional learning communities. It's OK. While it may take a little extra effort, schools that are not working as PLCs can implement proficiency-based grading just as successfully. When teachers are on their own, we encourage finding a colleague to work with, preferably someone in the building. Even if this colleague is not in the building, having a peer to examine your work, ask questions, and help solve problems is extremely valuable and improves the quality of your feedback to students. In addition, we encourage singleton teachers to make sure they have a colleague in their field whom they can informally meet virtually, outside the building, to get additional support (referred to sometimes as *PLCs without walls* or *virtual PLCs*). It is important to develop these relationships and meet at least a couple times per year. Cloud technologies are making it easier to share and provide feedback. Conduct meetings over the phone or with programs or apps like Zoom (https://zoom.us).

The *vertically aligned targets* (that is, the same scale for learning targets in rubrics across courses or departments) should also help the singleton teacher. For example, all visual arts courses may have the same learning targets. Having the same targets helps students understand the consistency of expectations and language across programs. Students and teachers also recognize that the curricular rigor increases over time and as students progress through the program.

When teachers and teams enter the implementation stage at different periods of system refinement, they will seek suggestions, perspectives, or improvements. Leaders must use caution and *not* close the door on improvements that new participants might bring. Proficiency-based grading, like other pedagogical and reform efforts, must be flexible enough to accept refinement. Take caution when considering changes to avoid undermining core beliefs or altering the school's agreed-on vision. To support the potential for innovative changes and adhere to core values, leaders must provide teachers and teams guidelines around the non-negotiables explained in this chapter. Those include the seven core beliefs and what decisions occur at the district level versus the division or course level.

Seven Core Beliefs

The following sections talk in depth about the seven core beliefs. These core beliefs are essential perspectives that we have come to learn through our experience of implementing proficiency-based grading. While they are not an exhaustive list of beliefs by any stretch, they do represent some of the more difficult tension points that arise during implementation.

1. **Growth is a central concept.** Proficiency-based grading is not a growth grading system, but growth is invited and embraced. In this system, you must give students time to grow from, reflect on, and learn from their experiences. Creating a curriculum based on growth is a difficult but essential task.

2. **Reperformance is essential.** If growth is the central concept, then retakes or reperformance is the mechanism that allows this concept to become a reality. It is not enough for students to simply learn from past performances. They must also grow from them. In order to show growth, opportunities for reperformance and an additional performance are essential.

3. **Building students' reflection abilities is essential.** *Metacognition* is not a skill that develops naturally over time. Students need instruction to reflect on their thinking and close any gaps in their understanding and learning. When they receive reperformance opportunities, students begin developing reflective habits that set the foundation for increasing their self-efficacy. By learning how to receive, accept, and react to feedback, a student is poised to be a more independent learner.

4. **Homework has a role.** Homework is not for compliance.
   In proficiency-based grading environments, homework can prepare students for a performance, have them experience a performance,

or be the performance itself. The teacher decides how to use it at a given time. We must move away from thinking that homework is just practice or the opportunity to collect points. Instead, we must see it as another opportunity for students to produce evidence of learning and understanding.

5. **Communication with parents and the community is key.** Consistent, transparent communication about student proficiency and evidence is essential to a healthy grading system. It takes some time for the concept of proficiency to take root. Therefore, it is paramount that teachers communicate how a student is *developing* prior to communicating any *evaluation*. Individual students' body of work must be constantly visible to them and their parents, and the teacher must be ready, willing, and able to converse with students and parents about the evidence of a student's learning.

6. **Culminating experiences like final exams have a different purpose.** As with homework, final exams have a different purpose. While the traditional final exam loses its point value in this grading system, the gathering of final evidence does not. Teachers can decide and communicate how they will collect evidence in the course's last few weeks, in the absence of a summative final exam. Final exams are typically replaced with reperformances for standards in which students are not yet proficient, or, in some cases, teachers talk with students about their evidence.

7. **Behavior can be in or out of the grade.** Compliant behavior should be reported on but not be calculated as part of a grade. In proficiency-based grading, the only behavior included in a grade is when the behavior is a *competence*—a skill the course wants to teach, assess, and develop. Any behavior that manages classroom behavior goes in a nonacademic area of the gradebook.

Each chapter will discuss how each content area can affect certain core beliefs.

Core Belief 1: Growth Is a Central Concept

We want all students to grow in their knowledge and skill to prepare them to be successful in college and careers. To help students build those essential skills, they need student-friendly learning targets scaled for proficiency expectations—what it means to *need improvement* and to *master* a specific skill. Learning, and gaining proficiency, is on a continuum. The scale isn't a scaffold. Instead of asking students to do different things in order, a proficiency-based learning target "offers a gradation of learning within one directed skill" (Gobble et al., p. 6). In this grading system, there are *competencies* (typically known as *standards*), *expectations* (typically known as *proficiency scales*), and *success criteria* (typically known as *learning targets* or *I can statements*). Your school may use these terms interchangeably.

Table 1.1 is an example of the difference between scaffolded and scaled progression.

Table 1.1: Scaffolded Learning Progression Versus Proficiency-Based Scale

Level	Scaffolded Learning Progression	Proficiency-Based Scale
1—Developing Foundational Skills	The student can identify vocabulary terms.	The student can appropriately explain vocabulary terms in a written analysis using simple stated details from class.
2—Developing Proficiency	The student can define vocabulary terms.	The student can accurately explain vocabulary terms in a written format using simple stated details from class.
3—Proficient	The student can explain vocabulary terms.	The student can accurately explain vocabulary terms in a written format using complex stated details from class.
4—Exceeds (Refined) Proficiency	The student can analyze vocabulary terms.	The student can accurately explain vocabulary terms in a written format using creative and unique details.

Source: Gobble, Onuscheck, Reibel, & Twadell, 2017, p. 5.

Students must be familiar with these scales and understand what teachers expect them to know, understand, and do. After and during instruction, students must receive opportunities to practice, take risks, and learn from their mistakes. Their growth takes time, frequent feedback, and self-reflection. As part of our teaching responsibilities, we must give each learner the time and support he or she needs to achieve this goal. Students learn differently and at different rates in all content areas. Classroom work should be tied to feedback, sometimes in the form of detailed rubrics that address learning targets by *scale* or *gradations*. This acknowledges students' growth.

In the gradebook, teachers score the learning targets to clearly communicate to a student if he or she is *exceeding, meeting, approaching,* or *not meeting* the standards. While each student receives a number in the gradebook, the numeric score coincides with written descriptors of the performance level. You can word these levels many ways, including *developing, not yet, mastering, exceeds,* and more. *Pathways to Proficiency* lists the most typical scale structure (Gobble et al., 2017).

- **Refined proficiency (level 4):** Students in this category possess fully mature, rooted competence that is highly refined. Students in this category not only possess the ability to transfer competence between context and concepts; they leverage it in a manner that maximizes impact with high efficiency.

- **Proficient (level 3):** Students in this category are fully competent. Students have a fully mature, rooted competence that is transferable between concepts and contexts.

- **Developing proficiency (level 2):** Students in this category may be ebbing and flowing between competence and incompetence, but overall, they are beginning to build rooted aspects of the desired competence.

- **Developing foundational skills (level 1):** Students in this category may demonstrate basic comprehension or skill development, but show no movement toward competency. What looks like any growth is isolated to discrete knowledge components or skill fragments. Students at this level are still learning the essential criteria that will later develop into a competency.

The goal is not to use the gradebook to emphasize the student's grade, but rather to have the gradebook communicate the student's current state of proficiency and growth toward a *rooted* state of competence (Jain & Reibel, 2018). Trends are evident, as the same targets are scored multiple times. Many students begin by building foundational skills, but as time passes, they gain more experience and confidence with more rigorous material, with scores beginning to reflect some 2s, with more 3s and possibly 4s. This is a typical growth trajectory, and it provides the foundation for the proficiency-based report card.

At the teacher and team level, the proficiency-based report card can support the following.

- Performance analysis

- Student growth tracking

- Individual and team goal setting

- Active steps that support students who are *not meeting* or *approaching* standards

The active steps may include additional time to practice, reteaching, or help outside class time. Proficiency-based grading supports reperforming (see the section

Core Belief 2: Reperformance Is Essential) after the initial assessment so students can continue to improve their learning and performance. Each assessment is formative. This further emphasizes growth and de-emphasizes the grade. It also fosters equity by not penalizing students who take longer to learn.

Some educators may suspect that students will game this grading system by easing up on their effort and waiting until later to perform well. While this can be a temptation for students when they transition away from points accumulation to evidence collection, students and teachers soon realize it is more practical to consistently make their best efforts. Students learn, in fact, that playing the points game no longer works since grades are a reflection of mastery.

Core Belief 2: Reperformance Is Essential

Early in a team's implementation journey, members will recognize the importance of differentiating between *retake* and *reperform*. Clarifying those concepts and solidifying the vocabulary will help smoothen the process. *Retake* means taking the *same* assessment. *Reperform* means executing a skill again in any context. Both are valid practices, although proficiency-based grading relies more on reperformance. Teams should develop norms for when a reperformance is necessary and when a retake may be more appropriate.

We prefer *reperformance* because it captures a more accurate perspective of proficiency development. Reperformance suggests that a student develops proficiency by performing it in multiple contexts and scenarios, not in the same scenario as the word *retake* might suggest. The term *reperform* also helps students understand that while the next unit may have different content, the proficiency skill is the same and that, in general, proficiency targets and scales are enduring skills that have a future value beyond the course and school.

Teams must also be prepared for questions about this aspect of proficiency-based grading. Often, teachers cite students' lack of preparation for the assessment not warranting a retake. This occurs most often when students treat the initial assessment as formative and take action based on feedback to complete the reperformance. The remedy for this is for teachers to ensure numerous feedback moments on student proficiency. When students have time to practice a learning target, they should be able to predict their performance on formal assessments. Skeptics might suggest that reperformance does not mirror the high-stakes nature of the real world and does not accurately reflect knowledge or a skill because the student has already been exposed to the desired performance and has had a chance to adapt.

Teachers will need to consider how to value more recent evidence in light of the overall body of work. Some teachers value recent performance more heavily, virtually eliminating some of the assessment data from earlier in the semester. The *body of evidence*, with special emphasis given to the most recent work, should determine the final grade. Teachers should not eliminate early evidence, but use their own professional judgment when looking at the entire body of work.

Keep in mind that reperformance is not *just* for those who are still *approaching* proficiency. Certainly, these students will need more practice and feedback to move toward proficiency. Similarly, students who have demonstrated proficiency with one learning target or standard will need to demonstrate proficiency while exploring new targets or standards. Reperformance reinforces the importance of growth.

Core Belief 3: Building Students' Reflection Abilities Is Essential

Students are getting feedback from their teachers every day, but that feedback quality may not always be high. We worry that, too often, feedback is evaluative and does not point students in the direction of closing the gaps in their learning. Students sometimes treat teacher feedback like a set of specific directives to check off as they fix errors, but neglect the big picture. Conversely, many students will see lots of teacher feedback and decide it is too intimidating to begin sifting through it to make meaning.

Feedback effectiveness depends primarily on feedback acceptance. If students are not prepared to accept feedback, the feedback has little to no value. A student who can reflect is more likely to accept feedback—from the teacher, peer, or self.

We believe that feedback is not a post-assessment tool, but a tool to utilize during the learning; it should help students reflect on their learning and guide their next steps. When teachers clarify the need for students to pause, reflect, and consider what actions led to improved learning (or distracted from it), students have access to corrective action *before* any cumulative effect on their learning can occur.

To build student proficiency and efficacy, educators must explicitly teach students to reflect on their learning by responding to questions like, How well do I need to know this? How well am I doing? and What will I be able to do if I am proficient? (Gobble et al., 2016). By making reflection a key part of what happens during learning, and by answering these specific questions, teachers help students do the following.

- Understand and use the learning targets and standards.
- Understand and use the proficiency scale.
- Understand and take action to extend or remediate their learning.
- Share a common language with their peers, teachers, and interventionists to achieve the goal.

When they accomplish these things, students become aware of their own abilities and develop the confidence to put them to work. This is a victory for every student who realizes he or she can apply lessons learned to the next assignment, project, or problem. A student may never master all the targeted skills, but learning that he or she controls the pace toward mastery is empowering. Reflection leads students to take more ownership of their learning, more accurately reflect on their performances, and practice self-awareness and self-management. Accurate reflection can also lead to a more accurate appraisal of one's abilities, leading to a more accurate self-perception.

Core Belief 4: Homework Has a Role

In traditional grading, homework acts as an event that supports learning but also as a mechanism to bolster a grade. In many classrooms, teachers still give points for homework completion. Students rely on these completion points to ensure a passing grade, even if they don't perform well in other areas of the course. In proficiency-based grading, there are no points, so what purpose does homework serve? Will students do homework if it's not for points? By stripping away points for homework completion and similar tasks (participation, extra credit, good behavior, or even bringing classroom supplies), teachers can ensure grades reflect academic performance and proficiency. To make homework function appropriately in a proficiency-based grading model, teachers must keep in mind several things.

- Homework is tied to a learning target.
- Homework is about feedback.
- Homework is considered evidence of learning.

Homework can be practice, proficiency development, or even proficiency evaluation. With experience, teams will get more purposeful and adept at assigning meaningful homework explicitly linked to developing skills that lead to proficiency. When homework is specifically connected to a learning target, it can play a bigger role with in-class discussions. For example, if students write a few paragraphs describing their weekend, the in-class conversation—both around the content and around competency evidence—is infinitely richer than a rote worksheet review.

However, different homework for different students is essential for learning. Homework should always be differentiated for each student based on his or her current proficiency level. A student who is currently at level 1, or still developing, should get homework that invites him or her to level 2. A student who is at level 3 should get homework that encourages development toward level 4. Differentiation is hard work, but is essential to ensuring that students get what they need to close their learning gaps.

Teachers must continue to interact with students' work and provide meaningful feedback. While posted solutions and tutorial videos are instructive, they do not provide the specific, eyes-on-the-work feedback that links teachers with their students in reflective, trusting, and interdependent relationships. Just as students need feedback on their work, teachers need to know where each of their students are in relation to the course expectations and growth trajectory. The lack of graded and recorded homework does not deter its completion; rather, it is the lack of differentiation of a one-size-fits-all independent practice that mutes its value. Students seek affirmation and crave feedback; while teaching students to learn to use digital (posted homework) platforms for assessing their work, it cannot substitute a teacher's interpretation of his or her students' work.

We have found that some teachers may worry that if students aren't held accountable for doing homework (by receiving points for it), they won't do it. However, there have always been students who don't do homework. When creating a culture of learning centered on *student efficacy*, "an individual's belief in his or her capacity to execute behaviors necessary to produce specific performance attainments" (Forsyth & Carey, 1998), and clear, actionable formative feedback, students will view homework not as an act of compliance but as a form of reflection and feedback (Bandura, 1997).

Teachers can continue to chart students' homework completion in a separate log to inform students, parents, and other teachers of a student's effort and outcomes. When retakes or reperformances occur, teachers can point students toward missed practice opportunities in their homework log as a first step in intervention.

Finally, students often demonstrate proficiency through a variety of performance events—however, this doesn't eliminate the need for independent practice. Teachers still provide supportive guidance so students can demonstrate proficiency. This supportive guidance will still primarily take the form of homework.

Core Belief 5: Communication With Parents and the Community Is Key

Research supports the widely held belief that communication with parents and guardians is essential for student learning (Kraft & Dougherty, 2013). Communicating with parents, guardians, and the community (school counselors, social workers, tutors, coaches, and so on) also helps ensure support when implementing a proficiency-based grading system. Effective, clear communication with parents and guardians is just as vital once proficiency-based grading is the ingrained practice.

When using proficiency-based grading as the tool for communicating performance and growth, students should become experts in their learning progress. However, parents and the community will want to know how students are progressing, and they will ask teachers to confirm or revise feedback they get from their children. The gradebook is accessible to interested stakeholders, but teachers may have to explain that the gradebook reflects the students' performance over the course of the trimester, quarter, or year.

It is important that we explain the new system proactively, using numerous points of contact with stakeholders, including written communication, forums on open house nights, and online school resources. Communication in a proficiency-based grading system can be easier and help reinforce the larger goal of developing academically conscious learners schoolwide. The syllabus should list the scaled learning targets and the success criteria behind them. Teachers should send these criteria and targets home with students and post them online. Teachers and school personnel better communicate a small number of standards—usually one, but sometimes two to four—with a few targets on a single common proficiency scale. Here is an email from our teachers to our community discussing the proficiency they are developing that week.

> Students are continuing to develop the ability to read and comprehend grade-level text proficiently (proficiency level 3). We will continue developing this skill during our next unit, mythology. Students were assigned their trimester two independent reading project yesterday. They need to read a mystery book and complete questions related to mystery genre literary components to ensure they are reading at an appropriate level. These questions are due at the end of January. Then, students will be asked to reflect on their comprehension ability.

Parents and guardians are used to such scores, but teachers will need to educate them on the ideas surrounding this method. The continual focus on a few targets and the lack of points can be confusing. Keep messages simple and bold, and only go into the supporting details as needed. Parents want their children to master each of the skills, and they see that when a student falls short, it is fair to receive a reduced grade. When teachers consistently show the same learning targets to parents and then log progress toward target proficiency, there is a great deal more clarity than saying "Your child got a 75 percent on *The Great Gatsby* discussion." While the 75 percent is clear, it is not clear what the student's actual proficiency is. Did this student get a 75 percent because he didn't know one small detail and that had a cascading effect on the exam? Did he not understand most of the text? Or did he not know the content or have the necessary reading skills?

Teachers must decide which behaviors represent compliance—turning in homework, being prepared for class, paying attention—versus competence—collaborating, participating, contributing. Compliant behavior is never included in proficiency-based grading because compliance simply maintains an orderly learning environment. It has no bearing on a student's proficiency in the course skills. *Behavioral competencies* (some schools call them *academic behaviors*) can be included in the grade if the teacher commits to directly developing them in the students. For example, preparedness—being able to prepare oneself for class—is a self-reliance skill. Teachers would set criteria for this skill, assess it, instruct it, and give feedback on it.

Some parents question how well this system prepares students for college. One response is that the school doesn't want to continue a grading system it doesn't think is best (or simply to keep things the same). Students will also need to adapt to numerous grading systems, given the range of postsecondary institutions. Truly preparing students for college and the workplace is best done by providing grades for their *learning* of identified skills with clear *success criteria*, the parameters and requirements to achieve proficiency.

Be patient with parents during this process, and realize that in most cases, the parents who reach out with the most questions and concerns are typically very committed to their child's learning and long-term success. This is particularly important for high-achieving students and their parents, since they have found comfort and success in traditional grading systems.

Ultimately, teachers have an intimate connection with parents through their students. Teachers can actively help parents who are new to or hesitant about proficiency-based grading understand this shift by recognizing and empathizing with parents' primary concerns: Whatever the change, will teachers form connections with my child? Whatever the change, will teachers know how to help my child when he or she struggles? Whatever the change, will my child be able to understand it and still succeed? Only after addressing these primary concerns will parents be receptive to the logistics and benefits of proficiency-based grading.

Core Belief 6: Culminating Experiences Like Final Exams Have a Different Purpose

Final exams have traditionally played a key part in teachers assigning grades, and there can be value in having students consolidate and synthesize their learning at the end of the semester. When implementing proficiency-based grading, teams should take the opportunity to consider the function of final exams, or an equivalent culminating learning experience, and how best to position these exams to align with the course proficiencies. Some teams may view the final exam as a summative exam. Advanced placement (AP) teams may choose to extend students' academic exposure to relevant content that the College Board does not formally assess. Other teams may use final exams as opportunities for a final period of reflection and goal setting for students. Other teams may use final exams as an opportunity to validate (or revalidate) the breadth of learning evidence over the semester and compare this body of work against recent growth patterns. As part of the reflective process, teams can provide students a choice to reperform in an area of relative weakness even after a final exam. Students who have displayed mastery across all targets can use final exams as a chance to show performance that extends beyond mastery.

With this in mind, it is up to each course to decide whether a final exam is necessary. If one is not, the teachers can choose not to administer a final exam. It is important to see the final exam as a season instead of a moment. This means that teachers should do the following.

1. Build a body of evidence in each standard of the course during the semester.

2. End the semester earlier than the final exam day.

3. Use the last few days or weeks to have students reperform standards if they are not proficient, extend standards for students who are proficient, or talk about evidence with the students.

Core Belief 7: Behavior Can Be In or Out of the Grade

Behavior should not impact determining student proficiency toward an academic skill. However, to develop a fully rounded skill set for an academic subject, a teacher may need to factor behavior into the final course grade and, therefore, into the teaching and learning process. The following steps support that decision and process.

1. **Separate behaviors from academic skills.** For example, consider whether a daily reading quiz shows a reading habit or a behavior compliance. Regardless, teachers must agree that the quiz result is an imperfect measure of academic reading—it can't be the driving force behind a student's grade.

2. **Determine if the behavior or habit is an act of compliance or competency.** If it is the latter, teachers can include it in the grade calculation. For example, a team may decide that a reading habit is part of English language arts competency. Then, teachers may reintegrate

the measure of the habit—a longitudinal log of reading completion, for instance—as a success criterion for a learning target.

3. **If behavior is included in the grade calculation, then the team commits to instructing it, collecting evidence on it (assessing), and providing feedback to students about it.** For example, the team could develop norms for nurturing and supporting reading habits by providing students with a regular location, adequate lighting, and a regular time for practicing it, plus encourage habits of mind (Costa & Kallick, 2008) for when encountering challenging text while reading alone. If students don't read regularly in class and the success criteria teachers identify are not observable, this student behavior should not go into the gradebook. There has to be a cycle of expert teacher feedback to help develop student reflection and learning.

If a behavior is deemed to be a course competency, then it can be considered for inclusion in a grade. Ensuring that these competence behaviors are taught is difficult. When teachers plan these lessons that develop social-emotional and behavioral competence, students engage in the lesson to learn the behavior.

When a compliant lesson masquerades as a competence lesson, students don't learn the behavior; they learn the content, and behavior essentially becomes a set of norms for the classroom discipline. A compliance lesson puts teachers in a supervisory role, checking and verifying the learning is on track. Since the teacher is verifying the learning, it relieves the student of responsibility. When lessons build behavioral *competence*, teachers can nurture and seed self-reliance skills and supportively coach students to become personal agents for their own learning.

District-Level Versus Division- or Course-Level Decisions

One of the bigger chicken-or-egg questions we get is, Should implementation guidance come from the district level or the school and grade levels? Our answer is, Both. No single point of school leadership is responsible for making these changes—we all are. For example, each content area implements aspects of proficiency-based grading that the entire school should implement or vice versa. Some decisions are more appropriately decided at the school or district versus the faculty level.

To avoid potential pitfalls, use the accountability method in table 1.2 to ensure proper assignment of responsibilities of proficiency-based grading.

Table 1.2: Essential Decisions of Proficiency-Based Grading

Decide at Institution Level	Decide at Division or Course Level
Self-regulatory learning and efficacy vision	Self-regulatory learning and efficacy building
Grading policy	Grading conversations
Learning target structure and scales	Learning target rigor and success criteria
Growth-focused feedback	Classroom-level learning feedback
Rubric criteria (template only)	Rubric structure
Instructional design	Instructional delivery
Gradebook structure	Number of assessments and amount of evidence

The following sections further discuss what school leaders should decide at the institution level and what teachers should decide at the content area or course level.

Decide at Institution Level

As shown in table 1.2, school leaders such as principals, superintendents, or boards of education should make decisions about the following things for the institution: self-regulatory learning and efficacy vision, grading policy, learning target structure and scales, growth-focused feedback, rubric criteria (template only), instructional design, and gradebook structure.

Self-Regulatory Learning and Efficacy Vision

When implementing a proficiency-based grading system, it is important for school leaders to outline why the change in grading practice is being done. Without the correct vision and purpose for the work, schools run the risk of proficiency-based grading appearing to be nothing more than a grading change. A vision of grading that centers on scores, marks, and rubrics (instead of student learning) is faulty and will lead to a lack of stakeholder buy-in and teacher motivation to implement.

A vision based on self-monitored and self-guided learning provides a solid foundation for effective proficiency-based teaching, learning, and grading to blossom. The goal of proficiency-based grading systems (as well as school in general) should always be to promote personal efficacy for all students—in other words, to teach students how to grow themselves in both academic and social arenas.

Grading Policy

The grading policy for proficiency-based grading is and always should be professional interpretation of student-produced evidence (Guskey, 2015). Interpreting evidence is always more accurate than averaging marks or points to arrive at a grade. This is because the absence of grading scales and averages allows the teacher and student to talk directly about the learning (or lack of) demonstrated in the student's work.

> You continue to develop your ability to accurately explain historical events and figures. This week, you will explain Gandhi and his life. We discussed the effects of noncooperation and the many forms of protest Gandhi supported. We also discussed the history of India since its independence from Britain. With this knowledge base, you can more accurately explain the impact these events had—and still have—on society. Because this skill is something you are still struggling with, consider visiting our class website to reperform and submit more evidence of your development.

A grading policy based on evidence can simply become to what degree the student is or is not meeting the learning expectations. Here is an example of a proficiency-based grading policy.

A: Scores of 3 or 4 in all academic standards

B: Score of 2 in one academic standard, with other standards 3 or 4

C: More than one score of 2, with no scores of 1

D: One or more scores of 1, regardless of other academic scores

F: More than one academic score of 1, regardless of other academic scores

If the semester's culminating evidence shows that a student is competent in *all* skills, then the student can receive an A. Here is how the traditional letter grades align with competency.

A+: Highly refined competence in all skills

A and A-: Competence in all skills

B+, B, B-, C+, C, and C-: Developing competence in all or some skills

D+, D, D-, and F: Lacking competence in certain skills

If a student produces a body of work that shows proficiency in each of the course's expectations, then the student deserves an A. If the student produces a body of work that is approaching proficiency but not quite there, he or she earns a B or a C. If the student is producing work but making no growth, then the student earns a D or an F. Essentially, both the teacher and the student review the student-produced evidence during the entire semester and determine the degree to which the student has met or not met the course expectations.

Typically, there are four to six course expectations throughout the entire semester. These are usually teacher-outlined *transferable skills*—skills students can apply across units of study or even across courses. In the absence of points, these expectations serve as the primary mechanisms teachers use to grade students.

Teachers avoiding assigning zeros also diverges from traditional grading. Assessment expert and author Thomas R. Guskey (2015) explains why they should do so in *On Your Mark: Challenging the Conventions of Grading and Reporting*: "When combined with the common practice of grade averaging, a single zero can have a devastating effect on a student's percentage grade" (p. 31). Zeros sap student motivation for learning and do not show what a student truly knows and is able to do. An alternative to entering a zero into the gradebook is to assign an incomplete. Most gradebook systems use an *I* to indicate incomplete or insufficient evidence. A teacher-assigned *incomplete* communicates to a student that to earn a final grade he or she needs to produce the missing evidence through an approved development plan. In addition, an incomplete communicates that not completing a project is unacceptable (in the workplace and in the classroom).

Since point accumulation does not exist in a proficiency-based grading system, there is no need for extra credit. Teachers no longer need to help students collect extra points to earn the desired grade. If a teacher requires additional evidence about a student's proficiency on a particular learning target, the student gets an extra learning opportunity. Additionally, proficiency-based grading has no percentages or averages, so grades are not weighted in the traditional sense. All standards and expectations are of equal importance.

Learning Target Structure and Scales

Many different schools and teachers continue to define learning targets or course standards, which makes it hard to collaborate around them. Teams should outline and implement a common learning target structure and formula for creating proficiency scales at the institution level. Learning targets or learning standards teachers use to grade students must be about transferable skills that last the duration of a student's schooling.

"Write arguments to support claims in an analysis of substantive topics or texts, using valid reasoning and relevant and sufficient evidence" (W.9-10.1; National Governors Association Center for Best Practices [NGA] & Council of Chief State School Officers [CCSSO], 2010a) is an example of a transferable skill: argumentation. This skill is equivalent to Standards of Mathematical Practices, Next Generation Science Standards, social studies inquiry standards, or the three modes in world languages.

This argumentation standard is written in a way that makes it a skill applicable to learning in multiple courses, including English language arts, science, social science, and even some mathematics. Teachers can make targets more transferable by rewriting them with language that represents broader competencies that can be leveraged across content areas.

When the learning target is a transferable skill, not isolated components, you can more successfully implement proficiency-based grading. The broad, transferable skills provide a manageable communication framework that sets the foundation for curriculum development and, ultimately, grade determination. Trying to implement proficiency-based grading with isolated, discrete success criteria only, teaching, grading, and reporting would be far too cumbersome to benefit students.

Growth-Focused Feedback

Proficiency-based grading is not a growth grading system; teachers do not assign a grade based on how much growth a student has made. In a growth-based grading system, a letter grade of A represents that a student grew *toward* proficiency in the appropriate manner, amount, and speed. A student in a proficiency-based grading system earns a letter grade of A only if he or she is truly competent in the skills, regardless of how much he or she has grown. Proficiency-based grading will always remain a competency-based system, which means there is a level of competence that must be obtained and maintained in each standard or learning target to earn a grade. However, proficiency-based grading invites and permits growth. It does not penalize students for rocky starts or late blooming. Instead, proficiency-based grading gives students time to develop and learn how to grow themselves.

Teachers should center their feedback on growth—meaning not giving feedback about how confident a student is right now, but rather suggesting what future competencies may be on the horizon based on the student's current work. Seminal research by Albert Bandura (1986) confirms that growth-based feedback connects directly to the vision of self-regulated and efficacious learning and must be an essential part of conversations with students. An example of non-growth feedback is "You need to work on vocabulary. The required works aren't correctly included. Your message was somewhat clear." Growth-based feedback sounds like "Vocabulary is an essential aspect of a clear message. The way you used vocabulary in this task did not give a clear message and may continue to be unclear. What are some ways you can add to your vocabulary application to enhance your message?" Always face your feedback forward. This forward projection provides clarity, direction, and purpose.

Rubric Criteria (Template Only)

The rubric structure is relatively straightforward—it should include a proficiency scale, criteria, and a reflective component for both the teacher and student to comment about evidence. Each team can create a rubric structure for each learning target with these three components in generally any form. However, there are two aspects to proper use of criteria in proficiency-based grading.

1. There are never separate criteria for each level of the proficiency scale. The criteria should only relate to the scale's level 3, or proficient level. The three other points in the scale always reflect a relation to the proficient 3.

2. The proficiency scale should be a four-point gradation, but the related success criteria should be a descriptor, such as a word or a short phrase that outlines the content knowledge and prerequisite skills needed to become proficient. *Only* the proficiency scales should have evaluative language; success criteria should not. For example, a teacher would *not* list the following as success criteria: *I can use vocabulary effectively and accurately.* An appropriate phrasing is *Vocabulary use.*

Criteria remain the tools students use to create and demonstrate proficiency.

Instructional Design

Instruction in proficiency-based grading classrooms must deliberately develop student proficiency in the course expectations. This is typically a shift from what we know about traditional classrooms, where short-term learning of isolated content and skills components is the primary goal. In traditional classrooms, proficiency is usually seen as a by-product of learning massive amounts of content and performing skills in a rote and repetitive manner.

In proficiency-based grading, proficiency in the core standards and, further, the ability of students to create, monitor, and be confident building their own proficiency, is the primary goal. Breaking standards into student-friendly learning targets and then proficiency scales aids student proficiency; reflection helps students gain confidence.

Content and skills are means to an end, with the end being proficiency in all core standards. Therefore, it is important for teachers to center instructional design on the development of a student's ability to grow toward course expectations. This creates a paradigm shift that can cause apprehension for some educators and strain the successful implementation of proficiency-based grading.

Essentially, teachers must adopt instructional design at the institutional level in a *student does first* rather than *teacher does first* model. In this model, students can develop the skills they need for self-initiated growth and efficacy by *experiencing* first and *instruction* second. Learning can't be maximized if there is not some experience first (Brown et al., 2014). Students should start riding a bike. As they ride, we teach them about the pedals, handlebar, spokes, and brakes. In other words, experience the competency you want from students and then, as they engage in the competent performance, teach them the content.

Gradebook Structure

Teachers must also implement an institution-level gradebook structure. In order for students to get an equitable learning experience, the grading structure—the way the gradebook looks to students—should be the same no matter the course. All teams structure the proficiency-based gradebook the same way, as in the following.

- **A section for growth:** In other words, are students making growth toward the proficiency expectations of the course?

- **A section for competency or proficiency:** This section communicates how the students are demonstrating proficiency on each assessment or event.

- **A section for behavior:** Behavior reporting is essential to maintaining an effective classroom environment. However, unless it is behavior directly related to course competence and students receive instruction, assessment, and feedback about it, behavior is not included in the grade. Behaviors are separate from academic skills.

The gradebook structure in figure 1.1 is a helpful view for teachers, parents and guardians, and students alike.

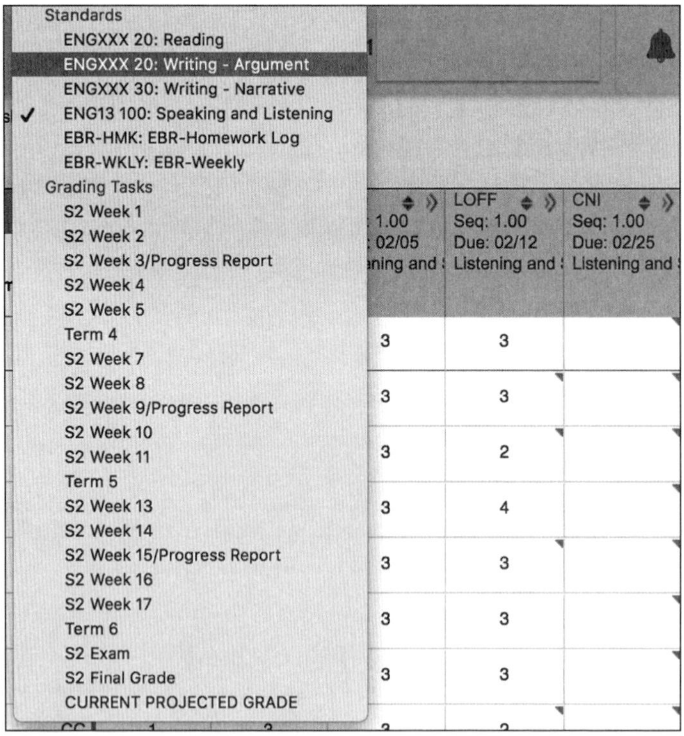

Figure 1.1: Gradebook structure.

At Stevenson, we always display a drop-down menu, and transferable skills (standards) appear in cells at the top of the screen. This allows students, teachers, and parents to select the standard they wish to view. In each drop-down menu lives a category (Standards) and the corresponding events (Grading Tasks). Anyone can review each standard separately or review all standards together to determine a grade.

Figure 1.2 reflects a proficiency-based gradebook for a single student (with scaled scores and separate behaviors), and figure 1.3 (page 29) reflects a traditional gradebook using points.

Semester One Writing Detail

Category: Character Analysis, Scene Study

Name	Due Date	Assigned Date	Score	Comments
Information	10/31/2016	10/25/2016	2	Excellent script example highlighting actor's objective at the scene beginning. Consider how your physical choices can further express motivations to audience. Please provide another script quote that highlights how the relationship changes between the characters in this scene. Actor use of "moment before" isn't fully imagined; lacks clarity and theatrical structure. Some evidence of planning, but lacks a sense of rehearsal. Let's meet to discuss your next steps
Structure	10/31/2016	10/25/2016	3	
Authenticity	10/31/2016	10/25/2016	2	
Punctuality	10/31/2016	10/25/2016	3	

Category: Post-Scene Performance Analysis

Name	Due Date	Assigned Date	Score	Comments
Information	11/18/2016	11/14/2016	2	
Structure	11/18/2016	11/14/2016	3	
Authenticity	11/18/2016	11/14/2016	3	
Punctuality	11/18/2016	11/14/2016	3	

Figure 1.2: Proficiency-based gradebook for an Acting 2 course. continued →

Category: Object Character Post-Performance Analysis

Name	Due Date	Assigned Date	Score	Comments
Information	10/27/2016	10/21/2016	2	
Structure	10/27/2016	10/21/2016	3	
Authenticity	10/27/2016	10/21/2016	3	
Punctuality	10/27/2016	10/21/2016	4	

Semester One Ensemble—Social-Emotional Detail

Category: Ensemble Behaviors 2

Name	Due Date	Assigned Date	Score	Comments
Adopting Routines of the Actor	10/21/2016	09/26/2016	3	
Adopting Rituals of the Actor	10/21/2016	09/26/2016	4	
Creating Community	10/21/2016	09/26/2016	4	

Category: Ensemble Behaviors 3

Name	Due Date	Assigned Date	Score	Comments
Adopting Routines of the Actor	11/29/2016	10/24/2016	3	
Adopting Rituals of the Actor	11/29/2016	10/24/2016	4	
Creating Community	11/29/2016	10/24/2016	4	

Category: Object Character Final Draft Performance

Name	Due Date	Assigned Date	Score	Comments
Technical Requirements and Preparation	10/24/2016	10/07/2016	3	
Character Development	10/24/2016	10/07/2016	4	

Copy of Actor Immersion	10/24/2016	10/07/2016	4	

Category: Final Draft Scene Performance				
Name	**Due Date**	**Assigned Date**	**Score**	**Comments**
Technical Requirements and Preparation	11/14/2016	11/07/2016	3	
Character Development	11/14/2016	11/07/2016	3	
Relationship Communication	11/14/2016	11/07/2016	3	
Actor Immersion 1	12/13/2016	11/17/2016	4	
Actor Immersion 2	11/14/2016	11/07/2016	3	

Visit **go.SolutionTree.com/assessment** for a free reproducible version of this figure.

	Blindfold for Exercise	Independent Title in Class	Family Improv. Scene 2	F/S Production Response	Family Improv. Scene 3 Performance	Marvin's Room Photo Copy of Scene	Marvin's Room Scene Memorizations	One Acts Response Extra Credit	Improvisation Workshop Extra Credit	Marvin's Room Scene Analysis	Marvin's Room Character Analysis	Marvin's Room Character Research	Marvin's Room View Guide	Marvin's Room Post Analysis	Final Exam Scene Analysis	Final Exam Character Analysis
Points per Assignment	**5**	**10**	**10**	**0**	**10**	**10**	**20**	**0**	**15**	**32**	**20**	**15**	**15**	**25**	**15**	**30**
Student 1	5	10	10		10	10	18		12	31	17	14	15	24	12	26
Student 2	5	10	9		10	10	15		12	30	19	13	11	23	13	28
Student 3	5	10	10		10	10	20		14	25	8	11	15	22	14	28
Student 4	5	5	10		10	10	20		15	28	18	13	12	25	14	30
Student 5	5	10	10	10	10	10	20		15	32	17	13	15	25	15	29

Figure 1.3: Traditional gradebook for an Acting 2 course.

Decide at Division or Course Level

As shown in table 1.2 (page 21), teachers or discipline-level leaders should make the following decisions at the division or course level: self-regulatory learning and efficacy building, grading conversations, learning target rigor and success criteria, classroom-level learning feedback, rubric structure, instructional delivery, and number of assessments and amount of evidence.

Self-Regulatory Learning and Efficacy Building

At the division level, each content area must provide activities, assessments, and processes students will use to develop self-regulatory capabilities. It is detrimental to the successful implementation of proficiency-based grading if a school attempts to outline or mandate how to achieve the vision. Each content area is different and has its own nuances (as you will see in the following chapters); therefore, teachers or teams must retain responsibility for creating an environment that creates the type of learner they aspire to grow. While individual departments develop a future scientist, a budding artist, or an eventual engineer, the vision of developing self-reliant learners is shared. School leaders set the vision for self-regulation and efficacy, but it is the teachers who are responsible for helping build this in each student.

Curricula should be organized proficiency first, content last. Content should take a supporting role in learning. When teachers create proficiency-first curricula, they create transferable and enduring learning expectations that students can experience throughout their academic career. When students continually experience, self-assess, and get feedback on skills that endure, they can build self-efficacy and self-appraisal.

Grading Conversations

While the grading policy is the same across the school, the structure of teacher–student grading conversations must always be the responsibility of the course teacher. The school should outline norms of grading conversations with students, but the way a course teacher structures or reacts in these conversations is completely up to him or her. An example norm might be *If we believe in students acquiring mastery over specific skills as identified by the team's rubrics and applied to key or common assessment moments, then we will teach students to reflect and own their growth by tracking their progress.* This principle is the same for the teachers, but how each teacher carries out this principle is up to the individual.

However, we believe there will never be *one* correct way to talk to a student about grades. This means that interpreting evidence and ultimately determining a grade remains the teacher's responsibility, not the school's. This includes deciding between a B or a C, a D or an F, or an F and an Incomplete. These can be difficult conversations, but in order to be effective, the teacher must retain the ultimate authority as well as develop the ability to give a grade.

Learning Target Rigor and Success Criteria

Too many times, the implementation of proficiency-based grading fails due to teacher confusion about learning target rigor. Standards and learning target *structure* must be consistent across all courses. However, the *rigor* (the skill's difficulty and complexity) and *criteria* (course content and skills) are solely up to the teacher or team. The criteria and rigor outlined in the proficiency scale are typically what delineates courses. The difference between a regular chemistry course and an honors chemistry course is not the structure of the proficiency scale but the rigor and criteria.

Classroom-Level Learning Feedback

When teachers give feedback, it should always center on the proficiency scale, learning target, or standard. At a school level, all proficiency-based courses should use the proficiency scale as the teacher's feedback script for talking with students about their growth.

While this should be a universal application among all courses, the feedback to each individual student about his or her proficiency is the responsibility of each teacher. While the schools should foster this mindset, teachers should explore methods and practices to promote clearer, more effective conversations with students about evidence. Well-conceived rubrics help with this. Common feedback mistakes to watch for include making it deficiency based (focusing on what students can't or didn't do) or diagnostic (focusing on the current state of learning). Feedback should always be positive (concentrating on what the student can do), prescriptive (focusing on current and future states of learning), and mutual (inviting the student to provide insights; Gobble et al., 2017).

Rubric Structure

Rubrics should contain a proficiency scale, the success criteria, and space for reflection. Along with the gradebook, the proficiency-based rubric remains the main tool for students to understand how they are performing in a course.

Teachers typically use rubrics to evaluate learning. They rarely use them to *create* learning. We consider rubrics a conversation with students about their developing proficiency, acting as the main portal through which teachers communicate with students about evidence, thinking, and growth. Therefore, it is essential for teachers to provide rubrics to students at the onset, not at assessment time. It is easy to confuse rubrics with proficiency scales, but several components are necessary to make something a rubric. A proficiency-based rubric's structure is important because the interplay between scales and criteria is essential for students to initiate their own learning and monitor their own growth.

Instructional Delivery

Sometimes in proficiency-based grading implementation, it can appear that the school is attempting to make all teachers teach same way. However, this is simply not true. While we suggest the design of instruction remain the same across content areas, the delivery of instruction should always remain the responsibility of the teacher.

Number of Assessments and Amount of Evidence

All teachers must adhere to quality assessment practices, which means reperformance opportunities, feedback, reflective post-assessment activities, fair and student-friendly question structures, and assessment timing and pacing, among others. However, assessment creation and how much evidence teachers collect can vary.

The amount of evidence that efficiently shows how a student is progressing is always relative to each course competency outlined in the proficiency scales. For example, citing textual evidence may require many small assessments that produce many instances of potential for evidence collection. On the other hand, writing may require only two or three essays—but both those amounts may be enough to determine the student's writing proficiency.

When teachers ask how many assessments or how much evidence is enough, we simply state, "You need as little as you need but not any less." As you read the content-area chapters, keep in mind that this grading system focuses on proficiency development and the proficiency-based grade in each standard.

Key Points

To ensure full understanding, review the following key points from this chapter.

- Institution leaders must have a very clear research-based vision of the grading system. Once the leaders communicate this vision, they must solicit and offer all stakeholders a chance to communicate their perspectives. Collective reflection on the vision can bolster buy-in and boost the initiative's long-term success.

- Successful implementation of proficiency-based grading depends on shared responsibility and collective decision making. Teachers and leaders alike must not only be held accountable to the principles of the initiative but also be given the freedom to make role-appropriate changes and decisions.

- Decisions about pedagogy must remain the discipline leader, teacher, or team's responsibility. If pedagogical decisions are not allowed to organically grow from the teachers' actions and reflections, you run the risk of confusion, low morale, or initiative failure.

Wendy Custable, EdD, is the director of applied arts at the award-winning Adlai E. Stevenson High School in Lincolnshire, Illinois. She has been in education for twenty years, beginning her career as a technology education teacher.

In her current role at Stevenson, she leads career and technical education and driver education teams in professional learning, curriculum and instruction improvement, formative assessment, proficiency-based grading, and social-emotional learning.

In addition to her teaching and leadership roles, Wendy has been involved in coaching volleyball and softball and is a member of many professional organizations, including Learning Forward and the Association for Supervision and Curriculum Development.

Wendy earned a bachelor's degree in industrial technology education from Illinois State University, a master's degree in educational leadership from Northeastern Illinois University, and a doctorate in educational leadership from Loyola University Chicago.

To book Wendy Custable for professional development, contact pd@SolutionTree.com.

Chapter 2

Implementing Proficiency-Based Grading in Career and Technical Education

Wendy Custable

High school students need to be lifelong learners who are prepared for the changing and "flattening" global economy, no matter their career and education goals.

—Alisha Hyslop

Career and technical education (CTE)—agriculture, business, family and consumer sciences, technology, and health sciences—tends to have a diverse population of learners. Some learners know exactly what career they intend to pursue after graduation, while others hope to be exposed to a variety of learning experiences. Some learners view school as a path to a flattening global economy, while others struggle to see the purpose of going to school at all. Because CTE teachers want to prepare their students for success in the work world, giving them access to the knowledge and skills to succeed in college and career is more important than letter grades.

Within Csikszentmihalyi's (1990) phases, it is important to note that successful implementation hinges on the common understanding and use of *standards*, *learning targets*, and *success criteria*. Although there is some guidance for established CTE standards through Advance CTE (www.careertech.org/cctc), no official standards similar to Common Core State Standards (CCSS) guide curriculum development for CTE content. This responsibility falls on individual states, districts, schools, or CTE teachers.

This chapter explains the reasons to implement proficiency-based grading in CTE courses through five phases: (1) preparation, (2) incubation, (3) insight, (4) evaluation, and (5) elaboration (Csikszentmihalyi, 1990).

Reasons to Implement Proficiency-Based Grading in CTE

When considering proficiency-based grading in CTE classrooms, teachers often worry changes will undercut their teaching values of appropriately preparing students to be successful in college and career. Concerns around how it may change CTE instruction, content, and grading workload are also common. Questions like, Can I still teach the projects that attract students to this course? or I teach five different courses, so how do I find time to make all of these changes for each one? are common. As CTE teachers learn about proficiency-based grading (which *sounds* valuable, but so unfamiliar), they begin to understand the deeper rationale—the *why*—and their concerns diminish.

The following sections address how proficiency-based grading fits naturally in CTE, builds confident CTE teachers, builds student efficacy, improves CTE programs, and promotes collaboration on CTE teacher teams.

Proficiency-Based Grading Fits Naturally in CTE

On any given day in a CTE classroom, teachers and students discuss the knowledge and skills required to change the oil in a car, read a recipe, or manage a business. And the traditional grading system has not matched most CTE teachers' instructional methods. CTE courses teach problem solving and skill development, and grow students who are not afraid to fail. To support students in their growth toward mastering these skills, CTE teachers provide a continuous stream of information to students about their learning progress via rubrics, checklists, and verbal feedback based on a predetermined set of course standards. This is proficiency-based grading.

Because CTE teachers rely heavily on rubrics already, proficiency-based grading is a natural fit. (Read more about rubrics in the section Unexpected Question 2: How Do Assessments Align With CTE Course Learning Targets? [page 45]). Rubrics tell students academic and behavioral expectations and the skills they need to thrive in the workplace. Proficiency-based grading rubrics provide the structure for grading and reporting that CTE teachers needed when they used a traditional grading system. For example, all manufacturing courses have rubrics for assessing students' ability to operate shop equipment. *I can safely and efficiently operate shop equipment to produce course projects* is the kind of learning target that appears on a scaled rubric in a proficiency-based grading system. When CTE courses have scaled learning targets that align with course standards, students will interact differently with their new knowledge and skills and make better end products (including computer-aided design [CAD] drawings, marketing plans, and well-balanced meals) when learning (not grades) is the focus.

Proficiency-Based Grading Builds Confident CTE Teachers

Some teachers might be skeptical about the prospect that a grading system can make a CTE teacher a more confident professional—but it is quite simple. When CTE teachers know exactly what they want their students to know and be able to do, they can link the lesson's purpose to student interests and communicate clear expectations for student learning. For example, being able to present a product to an audience is a skill many CTE teachers want their students to learn. Presentation skills, like many employability skills, are challenging to teach, collect evidence of, and provide feedback on. Establishing a presentation skills standard with an aligned learning target of *I can communicate information and ideas to multiple audiences using a variety of media and formats* means teachers articulate exactly what they expect of students. Once teachers know what they want the students to know and be able to do, they can design purposeful instruction and assessments that connect to student interests.

Being specific about skills and expectations, and having to articulate that to students, develops confidence in teachers about the proficiency-based grading system, which leads to competent instruction and assessment. Researchers say—and it makes common sense—that teacher competence increases student achievement: "There lies a solid relationship between teacher ability and viable learning outcomes" (Allen & Fraser, 2007, as cited in Sultan & Muhammad, 2014, p. 11).

Creating scaled rubrics is sometimes challenging for CTE teachers because it forces them to use a critical eye on loved curriculum. For example, how does a welding teacher know if a student proficiently performs an arc weld? Is a student proficient if the weld holds two pieces of metal together only, or does the weld need to look a certain way or be applied within a certain amount of time? The impact of knowing exactly what is expected of student learning on curriculum, instruction, assessment, and teachers' competence has the potential to foster successful CTE teachers and teams who are confident in their curriculum, instruction, and assessment practices.

Proficiency-Based Grading Builds Student Efficacy

CTE teachers want their students to not only learn course-specific skills, but also learn transferable skills—how to think critically, solve problems, and innovate. To help students gain these vital workplace and life skills, CTE teachers must teach students how to reflect on their own learning (core belief 3) and how to provide feedback and support to their peers. In addition, CTE teachers must have an established classroom culture and a set of procedures that empowers students to own their learning. A proficiency-based grading CTE classroom creates what educator George Couros (2014) describes as *a culture of empowerment* where students "explore and make meaningful connections to the content to deepen their learning" (p. 99). Students can do this because they know exactly what is expected of them and the path to get there.

Consider the following questions when designing a proficiency-based grading CTE classroom that builds student efficacy.

- "Am I scaling learning targets so my course is rigorous and requires critical thinking, problem solving, and innovation?"

- "Am I teaching how and providing time for students to self-reflect and give feedback to their peers?"

- "Am I creating a culture for learning that communicates to students that they have the capacity to do anything they set their minds to do?"

- "Am I providing opportunities for students to own their own learning in the classroom by using the learning target to reflect on what they know and do, as well as what they still need to learn?"

If the answer to any of these is *no*, figure out what next steps you might need to begin building student efficacy through proficiency-based grading.

Proficiency-Based Grading Improves CTE Programs

I challenge you to find a CTE teacher who has implemented proficiency-based grading and did not see a significant impact on student learning, classroom culture, program advancement, and professional growth. Just as proficiency-based grading requires student reflection, teacher reflection is just as essential. First, turning a critical eye to your current grading system and how it affects your instruction, assessment, and student achievement requires serious reflection. Effectively implementing this new approach requires further reflection. As teachers implement, they will ask themselves a lot of questions, including those in the section Evaluation: The Key Questions of Proficiency-Based Grading in CTE (page 53).

Proficiency-based grading provides a lens for CTE teachers to continually reflect on their professional growth, which ensures that the intended learning goals are clear. This grading system improves classrooms and programs, resulting in a positive, successful learning experience for all students (Conti, 1989, 2015; McCaskey & Crowder, 2015).

Proficiency-Based Grading Promotes Collaboration on CTE Teacher Teams

Teaching a practical, relatable subject that students choose to take as an elective because it connects to their interests is a positive. When a teacher is the only person in the building (or district) who teaches that elective, it can be a negative. When it is time to meet in collaborative teams to reflect on student data and learn from each other, these elective teachers are either doing the work alone or required to meet with other singleton teachers who may be unfamiliar with their content.

In traditional grading practices, when singleton teachers meet, they might struggle to find much in common. Proficiency-based grading's focus on students mastering identified skills—and not on specific content—makes finding commonalities between courses much easier. For example, many CTE courses also cover the Common Core State Standard that asks students to "Integrate and evaluate multiple sources of information presented in diverse formats and media (e.g., quantitative data, video, multimedia) in order to address a question or solve a problem" (NGA & CCSSO, 2010a). Measuring, analyzing data, presenting, and communicating are other skills that transcend a program or department.

Further, with the focus on skill development, teachers of courses in career pathways can align and articulate what they want students to learn and be able to do at the conclusion of the programs. For example, all courses in a culinary arts program could have common scaled learning targets for safety and sanitation, recipe innovation, and culinary techniques. A culinary arts program has learning targets similar to those in table 2.1.

Table 2.1: Culinary Arts Program Standards and Learning Targets

Standard	Learning Target
Safety and sanitation	I safely handle knives, tools, equipment, and both raw and prepared food in the lab.
Recipe innovation	I apply reading strategies to recipes before cooking and correctly follow recipe directions.
Culinary techniques	I demonstrate a variety of culinary preparation and cooking methods while incorporating food science principles.

Source: Adapted from Adlai E. Stevenson High School, 2018.

Preparation: The Commitments of Proficiency-Based Grading in CTE

CTE teachers and teams make certain commitments to successfully implement this improved assessment and instruction. Staying committed can be difficult because teachers often have very personal and intense attachments to specific resources, curricula, instruction, and assessment. When a teacher or team prepares to do this work, there will be worries about losing autonomy and the challenge of adapting teaching and assessment within this new system. This will be most visible for CTE teachers when revising rubrics to align with course standards and learning targets.

Similar to the transferable skills that CTE teachers hope to teach their students, teachers will need flexibility, communication, and collaboration skills to work with their colleagues to learn, employ, and refine this new grading system. As a result, remaining dedicated to the following commitments will allow CTE teachers to support each other on the road to success: (1) teach CTE content through transferable skill development, (2) value learning, not collecting points, and (3) develop rubrics that assess what students should master in class to be successful in the unit, the next unit, the next course, or college and career.

Commitment 1: Teach CTE Content Through Transferable Skill Development

According to the Association for Career and Technical Education (n.d.b), to be college and career ready, students need academic knowledge, technical expertise, and employability skills. CTE curriculum is constantly changing to ensure students are ready to apply these skills in a changing economy. Whether it is the software they are learning to use in an engineering course or the latest fashion trends they are studying in a clothing and design course, the content and skills are fluid. Therefore, it is in the students' best interests to learn specific content as they develop transferable skills so they can adapt to a world yet to be defined. As examples, table 2.2 lists three CTE course standards and learning targets and how they support transferable skills.

As stated at the beginning of this chapter, CTE teachers are committed to teaching students the skills necessary to be successful in college and career. For students to reflect on their proficiency toward these transferable skills, CTE teachers need a method for communicating to students their learning strengths and areas of growth. This method is proficiency-based grading.

Table 2.2: CTE Learning Targets and Transferable Skills

Learning Target	Transferable Skill
Culinary Arts	
I can demonstrate proactive methods for selecting and planning nutritious meals.	• Read food labels • Evaluate the nutrient density of a recipe
I can demonstrate cost-effective and conservative methods for shopping for and preparing food.	• Manage a budget • Minimize food waste and recycle • Plan a meal
I can list a variety of dietary needs, describe a reason for the need, and choose appropriate foods for an individual or adjust recipes as needed.	• Understand the reasons for a variety of dietary needs • Plan a meal based on unique dietary needs, such as vegetarianism or food allergies
Consumer Education	
I can apply business professionalism when working with peers in class.	• Apply work ethic • Make ethical decisions • Work collaboratively • Embrace diverse perspectives
I can communicate my ideas to achieve a designated purpose.	• Use oral communication • Use written communication
I can use various forms of technology to share information, communicate my ideas, and manage work.	• Analyze data • Enter data • Manage projects
I can use critical thinking skills to generate ideas and solve problems.	• Solve problems • Create and innovate
Introduction to Engineering	
I can accurately calculate all statistics and create visual representations from collected data.	• Calculate a data set's mean, median, mode, range, and standard deviation • Visually represent a data set • Describe patterns observed in a data set
I can accurately measure objects within the second allowable tolerance using measuring tools.	• Read accurate measurement • Use appropriate measurement tools • Communicate correct units

Source: Adapted from Adlai E. Stevenson High School, 2018.

Commitment 2: Value Learning, Not Collecting Points

A student will not obtain and maintain a successful career because he or she earned an A in a CTE course. Knowledge and skills are not learned by collecting a designated number of points for assignments and projects. A student will obtain and maintain a successful career because he or she learned the academic knowledge, technical expertise, and employability skills from that CTE course.

To help students gain mastery of the necessary skills to earn an A, CTE teachers must do the following as they implement proficiency-based grading.

- Determine and clearly communicate to students what they must know and be able to do by designing courses that have scaled, proficiency-based learning targets with success criteria.
- Align projects and assessments with course learning targets.
- Establish a culture for learning that puts students in charge of their own learning by providing self-reflection and peer assessment opportunities.
- Allow for students to reperform skills to prove proficiency.
- Eliminate compliance behavior assessments and extra credit.
- Work with building and district colleagues to collaboratively develop and align standards and learning targets that transcend programs or departments.

Incubation: The Unexpected Questions of Proficiency-Based Grading in CTE

As teachers progress toward using proficiency-based grading, they will uncover some wonderful questions that drive inquiry and implementation. During this second stage, several adopted practices may be working, but teachers may pay a lot of attention to the items that seem to threaten work or that have provided new challenges. With so much new information, it can be hard not to worry that some challenges will never be overcome. The following questions are representative of the incubation stage challenges that require patience and persistence.

Unexpected Question 1: How Will Assessments Change in CTE Courses?

The National Board for Professional Teaching Standards (2014) asserts, "using assessments that connect academic instruction with real-world experience" supports CTE teachers' goals of teaching the transferable skills that are so important to students' success in college and career (p. 6). Ensuring that CTE course assessments address and accurately assess the right skills, teachers must ensure that current assessments and assessment practices align with the course learning targets and standards. For example, trying to assess students' skill development using equipment safely in a construction course by only looking at the finished house will not provide the evidence teachers need to know if a student can operate equipment safely. To assess this skill accurately, CTE teachers will discover that within a proficiency-based grading system, they need to develop new performance assessments that can be used to determine whether students are safely using equipment.

As stated earlier in the chapter, CTE teachers regularly use rubrics to assess students while they are doing something (safely operating a table saw) and to assess a final project (wooden bookcase or computer program). The difference between the rubrics we know and love and a proficiency-scaled learning target is that the latter includes the success criteria for mastering the *learning target*—the *skill*—the teacher is assessing, not the project itself. That assessment is discussed in the section Unexpected Question 2: How Do Assessments Align With CTE Course Learning Targets? (page 45).

In addition to revising assessments to align with course learning targets, CTE teachers must change the following practices when transitioning to proficiency-based grading: (1) no longer assess compliant behaviors, and (2) grade less and provide more feedback.

Not Assessing Compliance Behaviors

Is the behavior a *compliance* you want your students to follow—or is it a *proficiency* you want your students to gain? Examples of compliant behaviors are arriving to class on time with a positive attitude and following the established classroom procedures. Despite CTE teachers designing their classroom culture to promote these traits, which employers want employees to possess, the traits are difficult to teach and even harder to provide feedback on learning to students.

Table 2.3 (page 44) provides a few examples of compliance versus proficiency behaviors.

If you can teach the behavior and provide feedback to your students on their growth toward that behavior, then you can assess it. For example, whether it is a business education course that requires collaboration skills or an early childhood development course that requires time management, the teacher or team that wants to assess these skills needs to (1) have a scaled rubric that communicates the knowledge and skills necessary to be proficient in working with others to develop an idea or product, (2) teach the skills required for someone to work collaboratively, and (3) provide feedback to students on their progress toward proficiency of that skill.

Table 2.3: Compliance Versus Proficiency Behaviors

Compliance Behaviors	Proficiency Behaviors
• Turning in work on time • Arriving to class on time • Following classroom procedures • Having a positive attitude	• Working collaboratively with teammates • Planning and efficiently managing time • Using technology • Operating shop equipment safely • Safely handling knives • Safely handling raw meat • Properly preventing the spread of blood-borne pathogens • Using critical thinking skills to solve problems • Establishing a schedule and plan to meet customers' needs

These steps are especially important in CTE courses where students must learn how to work safely within a lab setting. Courses in the health science, manufacturing, engineering, agriculture, and food science in particular need to have curriculum, instruction, and assessment practices that teach students how to be safe in a lab.

Grading Less and Providing More Feedback

CTE teachers who change their grading practices to proficiency-based grading find out quickly they were grading too much. When using a proficiency-based grading model, you do not need to grade everything students do in class or for homework. The purpose of assessing is to ensure students' grades reflect their proficiency of the identified learning targets, not the accumulation of points for completion. Therefore, you only grade the evidence you (and students) need in order to know where they are in their learning.

Observing, questioning, critiquing, and reteaching students is a daily occurrence in a CTE classroom. Providing feedback that supports students is an instructional tool that CTE teachers tend to feel comfortable using. Feedback for a graphic arts student who is approaching mastery on designing a page layout for her notepad project might read something like *You use some layout techniques to produce this graphic design document, including the use of appropriate tool type and placement of images. However, you need to improve your skills of selecting and placing high-resolution images to reach mastery of this learning target.* This feedback clearly states what she is doing well and the skills she has yet to master based on the course's learning target.

Once CTE teachers feel comfortable teaching and providing feedback within a proficiency-based grading system, many take feedback to the next level and establish a collaborative culture within the classroom where students regularly provide feedback to each other while learning. Of course, proficiency-based grading requires students to reflect on their own learning. Well-designed scaled learning target rubrics that reflect the success criteria will be a vital tool.

Unexpected Question 2: How Do Assessments Align With CTE Course Learning Targets?

Assessment and grading guidelines require teachers to create learning targets. This means breaking standards into individual components that teachers can instruct on and assess. As mentioned, there is no singular source for curricular standards that all CTE courses are required to follow. However, this does not mean that CTE curriculum should not align to standards. It just means that CTE teachers have some flexibility when defining the standards they align to. Check with local, state, national, and global CTE organizations, as well as Common Core State Standards, for guidance when establishing learning targets.

After establishing learning targets, CTE teachers must scale those learning targets to communicate what students must do to master those targets—their success criteria. Use rubrics to break out the *scales*, or *gradations*, students will show as they master a skill. After deciding on the learning targets and success criteria, the CTE teachers align assessments and design methods for communicating that learning.

Therefore, instead of using a rubric for each assignment, project, or presentation, there are scaled proficiency and success criteria for each assessed learning target. Again, a *learning target* is a measurable, clearly stated goal that students are to achieve by the end of a lesson, semester, or year in order to achieve mastery. Figure 2.1 (page 46) shows an example of a scaled learning target to assess student presentation skills. Notice three elements.

1. The scaled learning target uses positive language.
2. The verb remains the same in each level. In figure 2.1, the teacher or team uses the verb *communicate* in all four levels of the learning target.
3. The proficiency levels correspond with the success criteria.

Figure 2.2 (page 47) is an example of a scaled learning target that teachers use to assess operating shop equipment, specifically the table saw.

Standard: I can communicate information and ideas.			
Learning Target: I communicate information and ideas to multiple audiences using a variety of media and formats.			
4—Refined Mastery	**3—Proficiency**	**2—Approaches Proficiency**	**1—Still Developing**
I communicate and engage multiple audiences with information and ideas using a variety of media and formats.	I communicate information and ideas to multiple audiences using a variety of media and formats.	I communicate information and ideas to an audience using assigned media and formats.	I attempt to communicate information and ideas to an audience using assigned media and formats.
Success Criteria: • All necessary components are included as outlined in the assignment description. • Digital media, data, charts, and examples enhance understanding and add interest. • Presentation preparation and prior practice is evident through group member responsibilities, correct spelling and grammar, content knowledge, and meeting time requirements.			
Reflection on learning:			
Teacher feedback:			

Source for standard: Adapted from Adlai E. Stevenson High School, 2018.

Figure 2.1: Scaled learning target for presentation skills.

*Visit **go.SolutionTree.com/assessment** for a free reproducible version of this figure.*

After identifying course standards and learning targets, and scaling proficiencies with success criteria for mastery, you will align projects and assessments with those elements to create robust instruction that engages students with the knowledge and skill you want them to learn. Figure 2.3 (page 48) is an example of a robust instruction and assessment plan that aligns with a learning target for an engineering or a building trades course.

Standard: I can safely operate shop equipment.			
Learning Target: I can safely and efficiently operate shop equipment to produce course projects.			
4—Refined Mastery	**3—Proficiency**	**2—Approaches Proficiency**	**1—Still Developing**
I demonstrate safe and advanced operations of shop equipment to produce course projects.	I demonstrate safe and efficient operations of shop equipment to produce course projects.	I demonstrate safe and efficient operations of shop equipment with support from my teacher or peers to produce course projects.	I have not yet demonstrated safe and efficient operations of shop equipment to produce course projects.

Success criteria to *exceed mastery* for table saw operation:

Supports or teaches peers how to operate shop equipment safely and efficiently

Success criteria to show *proficiency* for table saw operation:

- Uses push stick, stop block, and all other safety features of the machine
- Keeps clean work area
- Makes proper height and angle adjustments
- Wears proper safety gear, including glasses
- Focuses on task when using equipment
- Follows prescribed start-up and shut-down procedures

Reflection on learning:

Teacher feedback:

Source for standard: Adapted from Adlai E. Stevenson High School, 2018.

Figure 2.2: Scaled learning target for operating shop equipment.

*Visit **go.SolutionTree.com/assessment** for a free reproducible version of this figure.*

Learning Target	Lessons When Taught	Reteaching Plan for When Students Do Not Master Target	Enrichment Activities for Students Showing Mastery	Formative Assessment Moments	Summative Assessment Moments
I accurately measure objects in the second allowable tolerance using measuring tools.	Imperial (U.S. customary) measurement system	Reteach in small groups using simple shapes	Provide more challenging objects (such as a stapler) from the classroom for students to measure	Measuring practice one	Measuring assessment one
				Measuring practice two	Measuring assessment two
	Using dial calipers to measure	Provide additional objects to measure		Measuring practice three	Project one
				Measuring practice four	

Instruction and Assessment Calendar					
Day one: Deliver instruction	**Day two:** Develop learning and provide reflection time	**Day three:** Deliver instruction	**Day four:** Develop learning and provide reflection time	**Day five:** Determine proficiency and provide feedback	**Day six:** Deliver instruction
Instruction on imperial measurement system	Measuring practice one	Reteach imperial measurement system (to the whole class or a small group)	Measuring practice two	Measuring assignment one	Instruction on using dial calipers to measure
Day seven: Develop learning and provide reflection time	**Day eight:** Determine proficiency and provide feedback	**Day nine:** Deliver instruction	**Day ten:** Develop learning and provide reflection time	**Day eleven:** Determine proficiency and provide feedback	**Day twelve:** Determine proficiency
Measuring practice three	Measuring assignment two	Reteach using dial calipers to measure (to the whole class or a small group)	Measuring practice four	Apply knowledge and skills of measurement to project one	Student self-reflection, peer assessment, or both; teacher assessment

Figure 2.3: Measurement learning target instruction and assessment plan.

Figure 2.4 shows an example of a learning target and assessment alignment plan. Both it and the instruction and assessment plan are important tools for building a proficiency-based grading system.

Learning Targets	Planned Assessments
I can demonstrate professionally competent cardiopulmonary life-saving resuscitation skills.	Adult CPR assessment
	Infant CPR assessment
	Basic life support check—primary
	Basic life support check—secondary
I can competently provide immediate care response that maximizes the chance of a positive patient outcome.	First aid assessment
	O_2 assessment
	Splint skills assessment
	Bleeding control quiz
	Suture skills assessment
I can apply medical and anatomical terminology in correct context.	Basic life-support assessment
	Splint application skills
	Medical interpretation test
I can critically evaluate a program, skill, or topic.	Career exploration project
	Weekly whole-class debrief
	Teacher observations

Source: Adapted from Adlai E. Stevenson High School, 2017.

Figure 2.4: Learning target and assessment alignment plan example.

*Visit **go.SolutionTree.com/assessment** for a free reproducible version of this figure.*

Insight: The Essential Insights of Proficiency-Based Grading in CTE

As teachers begin to move beyond the initial fears and roadblocks and gain insight, it is vitally important to take some time to look back on and appreciate how the team has passed some intimidating hurdles thus far. Teams should have a clear enough idea of how proficiency-based grading works, and they can play to its strengths as they teach and plan. They begin providing proficiency-based grading with more power instead of just trying to get their balance.

At this point, CTE teachers might have the following insights: (1) CTE teachers weave formative assessments and feedback throughout instruction, (2) CTE teachers might need to give up loved projects or lessons to align curriculum with learning targets, and (3) CTE teachers must differentiate instruction while aligning with learning targets.

Insight 1: CTE Teachers Weave Formative Assessments and Feedback Throughout Instruction

CTE teachers love long-term real-world projects that let students apply their content knowledge and skills. For example, in an introduction to business course, students might design marketing campaigns for a local restaurant. In a foods and nutrition course, students might learn the food pyramid to craft a balanced meal plan for a client. In a multimedia design course, students might create promotional literature for a family business. In addition, CTE teachers like engaging students in collaborative design challenges—bridge-building contests, chili cook-offs, and emergency drill simulations—where students experience what it might be like to work in their chosen career.

Over the years, many teachers became confident designing assessments that communicate to students what they are expected to learn and do while engaging in assignments and projects. Teachers check students' progress and provide guidance along the way. Then, they grade the final product. Although this traditional approach—(1) providing direct instruction on a new topic or skill, (2) assigning students a real-world project to do for a few weeks, and (3) assessing the final project to check if students learned—*probably* engages students in the physical work, it omits valuable learning and assessment opportunities. As assessment experts and authors Kim Bailey and Chris Jakicic (2017) state in their book, *Simplifying Common Assessment*, "To truly know where individual students are in their learning, teachers must intentionally and systematically implement in-class formative assessments" (p. 10).

Figure 2.3 (page 48), figure 2.4 (page 49), and table 2.4 illustrate how to weave in formative assessments and provide frequent feedback to students on their proficiency of the learning targets throughout instruction within a CTE course. When teachers purposefully plan formative assessments into lessons, it engages students in the work and, at the same time, encourages deeper learning of the intended learning targets.

Table 2.4: CTE Instruction in a Traditional Classroom Versus a Proficiency-Based Grading Classroom

Instruction in a Traditional CTE Classroom	Instruction in a Proficiency-Based Grading CTE Classroom
Step 1: Teacher identifies topics for students to learn in the course.	Step 1: Teacher identifies learning targets for students to learn in the course.
	Step 2: Teacher finds out what students already know about the learning targets and provides students an opportunity to engage in that work.
Step 2: Teacher provides instruction about new knowledge and skills.	Step 3: Teacher provides instruction about new knowledge and skills as they relate to the learning targets.
Step 3: Teacher assigns a real-world project, possibly providing students a rubric or checklist.	Step 4: Teacher assigns a real-world project, and collaboratively the teacher and students review the rubric's scaled learning targets and success criteria for that project.
Step 4: Students do projects—sometimes independently, sometimes in a small group.	Step 5: Students begin project—sometimes independently, sometimes in a small group.
	Step 6: Students self-reflect or peer assess on progress toward learning target mastery.
	Step 7: Teacher formatively assesses students' progress toward learning target mastery and provides feedback.
	Step 8: Students adjust their approach based on self-assessment and feedback from the teacher and peers.
Step 5: Teacher grades the project, referencing a rubric or checklist.	Step 9: Teacher provides additional instruction to individuals, small groups, or the entire group based on formative assessment information.
	Step 10: Teacher and students repeat formative assessment cycle, if needed.
	Step 11: Teacher uses scaled learning targets with success criteria to assess students' proficiency on the learning targets.
Step 6: Teacher may or may not allow reperformance to provide students another opportunity for a better grade.	Step 12: Teacher allows for reperformance to provide students another opportunity to show their proficiency of the learning targets.

Insight 2: CTE Teachers Might Need to Give Up Loved Projects or Lessons to Align Curriculum With Learning Targets

There are moments when CTE teachers must ask themselves, "Am I ready to give up pet projects that do not inform me or my students about the growth they are making toward an identified learning target?" Constructing a bridge out of toothpicks or baking cookies for a school fund-raiser might engage students, but the projects themselves do not provide information about students' growth toward mastering identified learning targets. Perhaps there is a way to reframe or tweak the projects to align with learning targets. If not, let the projects go. Letting go of some of those fun projects that students love might be hard. However, keep in mind the purpose for transitioning to a proficiency-based grading system—you want your students to be independent learners who take initiative and will be successful in the work world. For students to do this, they need to be clear where they are in their learning at all times. Therefore, realigning assignments, projects, and assessments to the course learning targets is necessary.

Insight 3: CTE Teachers Must Differentiate Instruction While Aligning With Learning Targets

CTE teachers have a lot of experience with diverse learners in their classrooms. A diverse classroom might have *stacked* classes (when there are two or more content or rigor levels occurring during the same period). Because of this, many CTE teachers do not spend a lot of time lecturing about a topic. However, they are not really guides on the side, either, because they still need to provide some instruction.

When proficiency-based grading is embedded into a CTE classroom's daily routine, teachers are ready to react to any individual or group learning needs. These needs, which may require reteaching or other learning supports, could fall into one or more of three categories: (1) content knowledge, (2) process learning, and (3) product development. For example, in an engineering course, one student might require relearning how to use a 3-D software program before he begins his project. Another student might require the directions for the same project to be broken into smaller steps. Still another student might need help physically completing the project.

When aligning differentiated instruction to proficiency-based instruction, CTE teachers should keep the following guiding questions in mind.

- Do I have clearly articulated course standards and learning targets that students know and understand?

- Do I have criteria-based scaled learning targets—rubrics—that students and I can use to formatively and summatively assess proficiency?

- Do I have a system for assessing proficiency behaviors, and do I have an established classroom culture that fosters compliance behaviors?

- Do I have a differentiation system in place to provide students the knowledge and skills they need to move toward mastering the identified learning targets—reteaching particularly challenging content or breaking a project into manageable steps?

- Do I have a system to extend students' knowledge and skills when they achieve proficiency—a free-choice project that aligns with the learning targets and student's interest?

Evaluation: The Key Questions of Proficiency-Based Grading in CTE

Implementation's beginning stages bring a perspective of evaluation. While professional growth never takes one path, reaching this point allows teams to set a goal of reaching regular practice and to confidently look into ways that the system impacts feedback and grading. Evaluation can lead CTE teachers to ask the following key questions: (1) "How do teachers determine student grades for a CTE course?" (2) "How are grading practices different in CTE courses using a proficiency-based grading system?" and (3) "How do CTE students learn how to reflect?"

Key Question 1: How Do Teachers Determine Student Grades for a CTE Course?

Nancy Hoffman, senior advisor at JFF, a workforce and education nonprofit organization that promotes economic advancement for all, has advice for teams changing their CTE program. Teams must ask if their program's outcomes are "measured according to appropriate criteria" (Hoffman, 2018).

When using this system, focus is no longer about students completing a product— a webpage, a birdhouse, cupcakes, or a business plan—but on students' demonstration of proficiency of the learning targets. Projects and assignments are the vehicles for students to learn and display evidence of their proficiency. For example, in a residential architecture course, the teacher might assess and give students feedback on their growth toward proficiency of a learning target such as *I can develop a final design document that includes all criteria*. Making proficiency the focus, instead of the project itself, fundamentally shifts how a teacher approaches instruction and assessment. Instead of grading the final product, the teacher assesses the student's proficiency through the final product. The final grade for a course is determined by evidence collected for each learning target.

Key Question 2: How Are Grading Practices Different in CTE Courses Using a Proficiency-Based Grading System?

For most CTE teachers who are versed in using rubrics and have the mindset that it is more about learning than points accumulation, grading in a proficiency-based system is not too different from grading in a traditional system. With that said, curriculum and instruction in a traditional grading system are usually centered on the cool projects students complete. Proficiency-based grading, however, is much less about the final product and more about the learning targets students master while *doing* those cool projects. As illustrated in table 2.4 (page 51), a steady stream of formative feedback from teachers and peers supports students on their journey. Then, at the conclusion of the course, the final letter grade is a culmination of evidence and determined by the teacher's professional judgment of each student's body of work.

Further, in a proficiency-based CTE classroom, teachers and students spend more time reflecting on learning and providing feedback than ever before. With a proficiency-based grading system, feedback and reflection are a crucial part of reporting and grading.

Key Question 3: How Do CTE Students Learn How to Reflect?

To successfully implement proficiency-based grading systems in CTE, students must be able to reflect on their learning. When asked, students should be able to articulate the success criteria they learned, are learning, and have yet to learn as it relates to identified learning targets. This can be a challenging skill for anyone to master. However, with purposeful time built into lesson plans (like that in figure 2.3, page 48, and table 2.4), structured learning activities that use reflection tools, and tools to reference, students can learn how to reflect on their progress toward the learning target. In addition, teachers must model reflective practices by posing questions that get students thinking about their thinking, so students begin asking themselves the following questions.

- "What success criteria have I mastered? What evidence do I have that confirms this thinking?"

- "What is some of my most powerful learning regarding this learning target so far?"

- "What steps do I need to take to achieve the success criteria I have yet to master?"

- "Where do I still need to grow in relation to the stated success criteria?"

- "Why do I think this skill is important to learn, and how does it connect to the real world?"

Elaboration: The Core Beliefs of Proficiency-Based Grading in CTE

Teachers at the elaboration phase of implementation have reached a mature and clear perspective of using a proficiency-based grading system. They have discovered that the system does not push them out of valued projects, simulations, or other assessments and activities they know help students learn; instead, they see there is depth to be gained from such work, with an underlying and clear focus on skills. With their comfort in this system, teachers are resources for their colleagues and on the cutting edge for new ways to provide more support for and collaboration with their students.

Teachers who successfully implement proficiency-based grading adhere to all seven of the core beliefs explained in chapter 1 (page 9): (1) growth is a central concept, (2) reperformance is essential, (3) building students' reflection abilities is essential, (4) homework has a role, (5) communication with parents and the community is key, (6) culminating experiences like final exams have a different purpose, and (7) behavior can be in or out of the grade. The following sections, which reflect the core beliefs' original numbering, explore the core beliefs that CTE teachers in particular should never lose sight of.

Core Belief 2: Reperformance Is Essential

During my first year as a CTE teacher, my mentor told me to allow my students to reperform assignments, projects, and even exams to improve their grades. Her rationale for reperformance was that as CTE teachers, it was our responsibility to ensure students learn our course knowledge and skills. If students did not learn something the first time, they needed another opportunity to learn it and prove that they learned it. This is my team's mindset. The rationale for reperformance is the same as for reassessment in a proficiency-based grading system. Students' learning is deeper when they have multiple opportunities to try, receive feedback that tells them what they need to change or improve, reflect on their work and the feedback, try again, and then reassess to show proficiency. As education author Tom Schimmer (2016) writes in his book *Grading From the Inside Out*, reassessment "lies at the heart of the notion of giving students full credit for what they know or understand" (p. 64).

Establishing a culture of reperformance is essential to proficiency-based grading in CTE courses because in most cases, there is rarely just one right answer. There are many different ways students can make a stir fry, design a single-family home, and market a new product, for example. To truly learn in a CTE course, it is essential for students to have opportunities for reperformance.

Core Belief 4: Homework Has a Role

Homework in a CTE classroom is an interesting concept. Because many CTE courses are hands-on and require equipment that may only be available at the school, teachers tend not to assign a lot of homework. With that said, because CTE courses do play a large role in preparing students for life after high school, work to be completed outside of the school day—job shadowing, interviewing professionals, collecting data, and so on—is sometimes a necessary part of achieving a learning target. In a proficiency-based grading CTE course, teachers use this homework seldom as evidence toward students' proficiency of learning targets, but typically as an instructional tool. In the rare cases that homework is used as evidence toward proficiency, it is assessed and weighted the same as any in-class projects or assignment.

Core Belief 5: Communication With Parents and the Community Is Key

It can be difficult to communicate to students, parents, and the community about this new grading practice, especially when you are first learning how to implement it into your CTE curriculum. With students and parents, be transparent about your assessment process. Furthermore, be transparent and humble about learning this new system. Acknowledge that you understand everyone's need to know where students are in their learning at all times and work hard to keep them informed.

Communicating this new grading practice to the community should be a much easier process. The companies and local businesses that host students for internships and shadowing tend to care less about a student's letter grade and more about his or her abilities to work collaboratively with others, clearly communicate ideas, and take initiative—all skills that are communicated using a proficiency-based grading system.

Key Points

To ensure full understanding, review the following key points from this chapter.

- Success in the workplace and in life is not about where people started, but about where they end up. CTE teachers want all students to be successful in their programs. To make this happen, CTE teachers must establish a grading system that aligns with the outcomes they want to see in their students' performance in the classroom. The purpose of proficiency-based grading is to ensure students' grades are reflective of their learning of the learning targets, not an accumulation of points.

- When using a proficiency-based grading system, the focus of student achievement is no longer on completion of the product (for example, a webpage, a birdhouse, cupcakes, or a business plan); instead, the focus of student achievement is on demonstration of proficiency on the learning target. The project acts as the vehicle for students to learn and display evidence of proficiency on the learning target.

- Using a proficiency-based grading system in their classrooms provides a lens for CTE teachers or teams to continually reflect on their professional growth regarding their instruction of the course content and their assessment practices to ensure clarity of the learning. This work results in the creation of a positive and successful learning experience for all students.

Doug Lillydahl is director of communication arts at Adlai E. Stevenson High School in Lincolnshire, Illinois. He guides literacy interventions and staff development, oversees English language arts assessment and achievement data, and supports curricular and instructional evolution in the division's professional learning communities.

Doug has worked in education since 1993, mostly as an English and American studies teacher. In addition to teaching at Stevenson and in Germany for two years, Doug spent six years as department chair at Mundelein High School in Illinois, raising overall pass rates in reading—and among Latinx students in particular—to school records. He is a former curricular team leader, award-winning swim team coach, and activity sponsor.

He is a member of the Association for Supervision and Curriculum Development, National Council of Teachers of English, Learning Forward, International Literacy Association, and Illinois Principals Association.

Doug earned a bachelor's degree in sociology and organizational behavior from Stanford University, teaching certification (with English endorsement) from the University of Washington, and a master's degree in administrative leadership in education from the University of Wisconsin-Milwaukee.

To book Doug Lillydahl for professional development, contact pd@SolutionTree .com.

Chapter 3

Implementing Proficiency-Based Grading in English Language Arts

Doug Lillydahl

> It's no use going back to yesterday, because I was a different person then.
>
> —*Lewis Carroll*

The case for using proficiency-based assessment and instruction in English language arts (ELA) classes is, happily, strong. From common base courses (such as seventh-grade English) to the outlying specialty high school electives (such as creative writing, journalism, or media studies), this discipline has several advantages when it comes to making this transition including a rich history of writing instruction embodying reflection and rubric-based instruction. While at first glance this does not make the pathway more obvious or less disruptive in the eyes of the average ELA teacher, it does mean those who start this journey can easily begin discussions with others with a clear, resonating *why*.

This chapter explains the reasons to implement proficiency-based grading in ELA courses through five phases: (1) preparation, (2) incubation, (3) insight, (4) evaluation, and (5) elaboration (Csikszentmihalyi, 1990).

Reasons to Implement Proficiency-Based Grading in ELA

When considering proficiency-based grading in ELA classrooms, teachers often worry about changes that would undercut values they hold around teaching literature deeply. Concerns around how this change may affect ELA instruction, content, and grading workload are common. As teachers learn about this grading method (which sounds valuable, but so unfamiliar), they begin to understand the deeper rationale—the *why* behind proficiency-based grading—and their concerns diminish.

The following sections address how proficiency-based grading promotes valued ELA skills, changes the conversation around reading and writing, promotes alignment of ELA expectations, supports best practices for teaching ELA, supports co-constructed learning of ELA skills, and makes visible students' thinking about reading, writing, thinking, and speaking.

Proficiency-Based Grading Promotes Valued ELA Skills

The starting point for the *why* discussions is recognizing how a seed of success in writing instruction and assessment can grow into improved student learning across ELA. Specifically, skill-based learning targets in writing instruction have successfully increased effective communication and reflection in students—a key proficiency-based grading starting point (Stiggins, 2008). The near-universal use of writing rubrics invariably lays out the desired skills and content. Success has been seen in rubrics that often clearly lay out the expectations (for focus, organization, support, and language conventions, for instance). ELA students study the teacher feedback, realize their areas of strength and weakness, and set their minds to improve.

When I ask ELA teachers to use similarly clear and standards-focused rubrics for other valued literacy skills—reading, speaking, listening, and viewing—they often look down and falter. "We have been too busy to get there, but we want to" is a typical, honest answer. Bringing the same clarity and openness in writing instruction to the internal world of reading instruction and the fast-paced world of discussion is the responsible thing to do. Proficiency-based grading helps ELA teachers do more than encourage students to *read more carefully* or *participate more*; it actually turns students toward self-regulation based on clear learning targets and focused assessments.

Proficiency-Based Grading Changes the Conversation Around Reading and Writing

The recursive nature of the CCSS for English language arts promotes proficiency-based grading–empowered conversations with students to change the discipline to include a more balanced literature and skills instruction philosophy (National Governors Association Center for Best Practices [NGA] & Council of Chief State School Officers [CCSSO], 2010a). The ongoing arc of the umbrella standards (such as for argumentative writing) runs from kindergarten through senior year, and this time provides students the opportunity to grow and experiment throughout the entire arc. Indeed, teachers can guide students to reflect on the similarities of writing an argument in multiple modes (such as in a letter, an editorial, an essay, and a speech). Conversations with students change as the repeatedly revealed targets use increasingly familiar vocabulary and concepts. Teachers are able to help build student reflectiveness and self-efficacy as they take aim at each stable target.

Proficiency-Based Grading Promotes Alignment of ELA Expectations

Proficiency-based grading helps ELA teachers recognize inequalities among classrooms. Many English departments or middle schools have a teacher who is known for having students write early and often, while another has the reputation for using project-based learning, and a third has students read the classics. Which teacher would I want for my own child? A thoughtful combination. Of course, teachers may develop these differences because they follow their strengths, but all students deserve the chance to develop each target fully.

The good news is that proficiency-based grading doesn't explicitly separate ELA teachers from their favorite modes of instruction. This system doesn't change day-to-day interactions in the classroom as some teachers fear it will. It aligns student growth to teacher expectations in the specific skills that make those students better readers, writers, and speakers. Teachers know what mastery of a specific skill looks like, share that with students, and then tailor both whole-class and differentiated instruction to achieve a common expectation that no longer varies from teacher to teacher and classroom to classroom.

Further, ELA teachers' love of literature can tempt them to narrowly focus on literal comprehension or recall so students understand the great literature. While all teachers want students to read their assigned texts effectively, how does a student—or a teacher for that matter—make sense of a five-point quiz? Such point-driven feedback from an annotation check or a literal reading quiz of the previous night's reading provides a warped message to students about the course skill goals. Proficiency-based grading filters out the white noise around assessment and places the targeted literacy skills center stage for all.

Proficiency-Based Grading Supports Best Practices for Teaching ELA

When talking with successful teachers about benefits of proficiency-based grading, many point out how so many of their best innovations align with the philosophy. However, this alignment makes these teachers question how worthwhile this additional journey is. They ask, "If I can just give 50 points for essay number one and 150 points for essay three, doesn't that show the desired additional consideration to the most recent learning, and can't we just skip this difficult proficiency-based grading transition?"

Removing the inconsistencies in instruction and assessment between the different literacy skills is best practice. Proficiency-based grading aims to treat reading, speaking, and listening as thoroughly and precisely as writing. In addition, teachers should recognize the frequent inconsistencies between how and how often different teachers apply these proficiency-based grading-like patches, such as allowing students to revise final essays after receiving additional feedback but not focusing on learning targets during instruction. Although teachers may be approaching some of the same goals, doing the real thing with fidelity across an entire English course or department will benefit all students.

Proficiency-Based Grading Supports Co-Constructed Learning of ELA Skills

Students can own their learning and learn to self-reflect accurately and productively about even naturally low-visibility literacy skills. Quite often, successful ELA students are already quite adept at internalizing new grading models and receiving feedback in a very authentic, holistic environment (Hattie, 2009). However, it is the students who struggle to recognize and integrate the moves that expert readers, writers, speakers, and listeners use. Students can spend years of their schooling stagnating despite the best efforts of teachers. To students, these professionals simply understand a text the first time they encounter it.

No longer can extra effort spent memorizing vocabulary lists or doing homework on time mask shortcoming in the essential skills that produce success criteria. There are students who become frustrated and near tears when grading methods that previously earned them As do not prepare them for reliable success when pursuing skill targets. While uncomfortable at times (for both teacher and student), such situations provide opportunities to refocus these learners on the learning they need to master, and only by doing that do teachers give them a chance to move forward.

Proficiency-Based Grading Makes Visible Students' Thinking About Reading, Writing, Thinking, and Speaking

Proficiency-based grading exposes and places even the mostly hidden, complex literacy skills center stage. It's important to note that many teachers and students have only just begun to think about speaking and listening (or even reading) as learnable skills with procedures. Also important is eliminating students' beliefs that teachers and accomplished peers have some sort of magical ability to read perfectly on the first try or to provide thoughtful rebuttals as they speak. Instead, by comparing the specific moves that appear in student work, such as the transitional expressions in a paper, with the specific success criteria in a rubric, students can see that their writing provides a record of their thinking. Side by side, the teacher and student then explore alternative phrases. This discussion and clear focus on the student work reinforces how writers, including each student, follow processes of experimentation and consideration when they write or think.

There is plenty of work to do around developing teaching strategies and laying bare the skills and success criteria for these skills. However, as teachers develop the ability to convey a student's progress along these paths, there are huge benefits ahead. Ultimately, students more accurately assess their own progress, and take increasingly control of their learning progress through metacognition. Technology has clearly been a partner in providing some new windows into reading, speaking, and listening. Teachers should continue to experiment with these new tools that empower students and lead to their future success. The new generation of applications that allow students to share and peer review work holds promise, and with recording devices in so many students' hands, the realm of speaking and listening holds much higher opportunity for students to self-reflect over small-group discussions and even edit a highlight reel of their best moments of driving the discussion forward.

Preparation: The Commitments of Proficiency-Based Grading in ELA

Teachers and teams make certain commitments to successfully implement this improved system of assessing and instructing. This can be difficult because teachers often have very personal and intense attachments to specific resources, literature, other curriculum, instruction, and assessment. When a team of teachers is preparing to do this work, there will be worries about losing autonomy and the challenge of adapting teaching and assessment in the near future. That is when making a series of commitments will allow teachers to support each other on the road to success.

The following commitments are discussed in subsequent sections: (1) literacy comes first, (2) standards reflect ELA skills, (3) understand ELA success criteria and essential standards, and (4) transferable ELA skills are key.

Commitment 1: Literacy Comes First

Primarily, a proficiency-based grading system will not yield results until teachers make a commitment to teaching literacy skills. Reading, writing, speaking, and listening must use texts and other content to spark engagement and provide the playground for literary experimentation and learning (Fisher & Frey, 2014).

Teachers who require students to learn the plot or theme of *The Great Gatsby* (Fitzgerald, 1925) will be pulled away from looking at transferable literacy skills. Both students and teachers often struggle to interpret multiple choice or short recall questions that amount to a confusing lump of memory, literacy, behavior, and plot summaries. Committing to literacy, to students growing as readers and communicators rather than simply as memorizers, is an undeniably important goal.

Commitment 2: Standards Reflect ELA Skills

ELA teams tend to use a fairly common set of standards and core values, although some evolution still occurs. Teachers value reading, writing, speaking, and listening skills and adopt them in most proficiency-based grading courses; it is no accident that these skills are consistently reflected in the CCSS and other standards. Indeed, standards are the backbone of proficiency-based grading. It could not effectively exist without them.

A consistent question that arises is whether to subdivide these skills in various ways to reflect the breadth of ELA. For example, some teams adopt argument writing as the primary representative of the writing skill. Other teams explore the inclusion of narrative writing or even creative writing to embody the artistic and articulate the importance of storytelling. Teams might also consider whether a reading should contain standards of literal and then inferential reading or even break down the reading to differentiate between fiction and informational texts—a valid line of action. Further, teams generally keep a standard of combined speaking and listening to reflect that skill area, but teams may wonder whether it is important to develop a standard for both listening and speaking individually.

A final area of value—*process*—reflects the value ELA teachers place on the writing process, inquiry process, and reading process, something that crosscuts previous value areas.

Commitment 3: Understand ELA Success Criteria and Essential Standards

One of my team's tougher transitions to proficiency-based grading occurred when we were replacing traditional writing rubrics (which we scaled for focus, organization, development, and language) with a single scaled learning target, *argument writing*. Teachers are accustomed to assigning a rating and a score for each skill (in this case, focus, organization, development, and language) and reluctant to move away from doing so. In fact, in our first implementation attempts, some teams kept each of those as targets, as well as added seven targets for reading. However, these pseudo-targets were so narrow and numerous that team members found the bookkeeping overwhelming. It further became concerning that teachers were providing a professional judgment not on one of the core ELA skills, but rather on a narrow subskill. Those judgments often did not translate into an accurate appraisal of a student's ability to reliably apply the entire learning target. So many individual subskill judgments implied each one—instead of the actual skill we sought—was an end in itself: argument writing. We don't want students to think that an end goal is to be an effective claim writer, but rather want them to see that it is just part of the required package of subskills needed to reach the finish line of argument writing.

By providing feedback on each subskill (which we have since accepted as success criteria), we were in fact muddying the waters for our students. Students were unclear as to whether they had reached the truly valued portions of our curriculum, and having so many standards brought up the temptation to average grades again, a practice we wanted to leave behind. After all, if students have fifteen learning targets, can they be expected to master them all? Or just show an average of mastery? It became confusing and frustrating.

But through this process, teachers came to grips with a wider vision for the discipline. As Adlai E. Stevenson High School teacher Edgar Aguirre remarks, "For the sake of clarity and of your students, you can't do this half-heartedly. It takes a lot of dialogue and decision making to lay out what makes sense to your team" (E. Aguirre, personal communication, September 10, 2018).

Commitment 4: Transferable ELA Skills Are Key

Teachers must ask for transferability of the learning targets. Teams must look at the instruction and assessment surrounding each skill and commit to requiring a diverse and demanding array of performances from students. It may, for instance, be easiest to assess speaking and listening targets repeatedly in a full-class Socratic seminar format; however, this format provides a limited perspective for what speaking and listening entails, and demands less rigor for students who can mindlessly repeat their performance in a familiar task. The teachers and teams who want to know whether a student is proficient in speaking and listening skills need to also create ways to assess and challenge students with small-group, partner, and online discussions. Furthermore, the discussion settings might include role playing, community participation, online forums, or a school board meeting. Can the students transfer their learning? Ultimately, that is our goal. Committing to such innovation as a team seems risky and too difficult for those used to autonomy, but students must be able to apply their learning outside classrooms.

Incubation: The Unexpected Questions of Proficiency-Based Grading in ELA

As teachers progress toward proficiency-based grading implementation, they will uncover some wonderful questions that drive inquiry and implementation. During the incubation stage, several adopted practices may be working, but teachers may pay a lot of attention to the items that seem to threaten time-consuming work around providing students co-constructed feedback or designing new practice opportunities. With so much new information, it can be hard not to worry that some challenges will never be overcome. The following questions are representative of the incubation stage challenges that require patience and persistence.

Unexpected Question 1: What Is the Right Evidence for Showing Proficiency Development in ELA?

As ELA teams re-envision gradebooks, rigorous conversations around feedback and recordkeeping follow. The current diversity of gradebooks and what goes in them threatens equity for students. A prime example is the variation over what teachers count as so-called *homework points*. One teacher gives reading quizzes, another annotation check-offs, and a third no reading homework but weekly vocabulary quizzes. Which of these give clear feedback to students on a particular target? The answer is probably none. And so, with proficiency-based grading, teachers must refocus on standards and feedback to get students to reflect and grow. Simply put, teacher feedback should use rubrics that provide a *scaled* target. That means each target is restated to describe the four levels of achievement—(4) refined mastery, (3) proficiency, (2) approaching proficiency, and (1) still developing.

Additionally, the success criteria describing each narrower skill in a learning target helps guide teachers and students to reflect on the criteria that define mastery of the full learning target. For example, in figure 3.1, the overarching skill is clearly stated as the learning target, and the teacher shares with students the success criteria most appropriate for supporting growth at each level of development. Presentation and participation (delivery) includes specific, practical skills students can learn, practice, and transfer to new situations. As in this rubric, teachers or teams can replace the sample feedback (*Articulate an appropriate point in response to the questions or tasks with a clear and polished expression*) with language tailored to fit the students' progress toward that success criteria.

Learning Target: I share information so that the delivery, content, and structure are appropriate to the task.			
4—Refined Mastery	**3—Proficiency**	**2—Approaches Proficiency**	**1—Still Developing**
I share information by integrating the delivery, content and structure, and it is suited to an unfamiliar task.	I share information so that the delivery, content, and structure are appropriate to the task.	I share information so that the delivery, content and structure, are sometimes appropriate to the task.	I share information when prompted or echo what others have said.
Success Criteria	**How Well I Am Doing (Student Self-Reflection)**		**Teacher Feedback**
Preparation			Read carefully and prepare a variety of texts or tasks in relation to the topic. Construct thorough and organized notes (including annotations and questions) to support work.
Presentation and Participation (Delivery)			Articulate an appropriate point in response to the questions or tasks with a clear and polished expression.
Use of Evidence			Provide relevant, varied, and appropriate evidence for the task. Demonstrate knowledge of and flexibility with a range of evidence (from the beginning, middle, and end of the text).

Figure 3.1: Speaking rubric.

*Visit **go.SolutionTree.com/assessment** for a free reproducible version of this figure.*

Assessments are the next consideration. Will teachers only accept full essays, full discussions, or fully explained reading interpretations? If teachers wait for such fully developed items, they will discover their feedback is too infrequent to meet the needs of students and other stakeholders. It is reasonable to ask whether homework provides meaningful and frequent-enough feedback. For example, how might an exercise such as writing five possible claim statements play a role in assessment?

While easier to give frequent feedback to, individual success criteria such as *Use of evidence* from figure 3.1 (page 67) does not represent enough of the learning target to be a meaningful indicator of the student's ability to reach the full target. Such individual success criteria belong in an ungraded, no-stakes homework log. Such a narrow success criteria assessment will tell students what proficiency level they are at in their daily work habits and whether they have mastered this single skill. Educators know transfer of a skill to new and authentic situations is the ultimate test of learning, so looking at even a collection of these narrow homework items does not add up to the actual, complex target.

A helpful analogy for understanding the assessment pattern and practices ELA teachers use is based on the sports or theater experience (see table 3.1). Daily isolated drills for practicing a single skill allow for focused, precise feedback. These drills are like success criteria for achieving a literary learning target (for example, drawing inferences, writing a claim statement, and listening accurately). However, since drills for practice are so far from a true game experience, coaches can't use them to judge the athlete on his or her complete sport skill.

Table 3.1: Helpful Analogy for Assessment Patterns and Purposes in ELA

	Purpose	Sports or Theater Analogy	ELA Application
Proficiency Evaluation	To provide a current judgment of ability	The game or performance	Assessments that demand using a full, complex target: essays, debates, projects
Proficiency Development	To provide a current judgment on development to aid reflection and growth	A scrimmage or dress rehearsal	Demand at least multiple success criteria from a learning target: the first three paragraphs of an essay, an outline of debate ideas, a step in a project (or fully formed essays, debates, projects)

Supporting Assessment	To teach a particular skill or move that can be later transferred to the full target	A practice drill or running lines backstage	Pulls attention to a narrow skill for development: write three possible claim statements or collect ten pieces of evidence to support your debate topic

Source: Adapted from Reibel, 2018.

Teachers respond by providing proficiency development evidence early in the semester that incorporates two or more of the success criteria for a particular standard. For instance, writing claim statements should only be in the homework log, but if a teacher asks a student to generate a claim and then provide corresponding evidence to support it, teachers can interpret the student's progress toward full target mastery and include it in the early semester feedback. That early feedback is systematically overwritten as more recent evidence goes into the gradebook.

Unexpected Question 2: What Role Does Multiple Choice Play in ELA?

Proficiency-based grading implementation requires teams to re-examine multiple choice reading assessment. High-stakes state and college entrance testing still relies on multiple choice questions to assess reading, yet often, little is revealed about the student's thinking process in an incorrect multiple choice response. If the goal is to help students reflect on their process and learn to improve their work, teachers need to expose that thinking.

It is common for teams looking at multiple choice reading test data to wordsmith the stem and choices repeatedly in order to correct unclear or unfair wording. Teams need to recapture as much of that time as possible for discussion around instructional responses to the data. The focus needs to be on skills instruction, not by rewriting questions to ensure the number of points per multiple choice question aligns to a one-hundred-point scale.

To maintain balance between the test format and the information test data provide teachers and reflective learners, teams can experiment by having students provide a written rationale for their multiple choice selections either in the moment (by adding space on the test) or on reflection later. Teams should not apply this strategy to every question, as it would be tedious, but it will help clarify student needs.

A next step in maintaining a balance between test format and test data is to closely consider what level of performance a particular question represents in a particular standard. The *scattershot approach* is not enough; teachers can't trust that if they ask fifty questions, enough of them will address the success criteria in both literal and inferential reading to allow them to accurately assess skill development. More important, teachers cannot trust that a learner reflecting on such feedback can draw accurate conclusions about his or her current performance and the next steps toward mastery. (At my school, teachers do not allow a student to demonstrate a *refined mastery* performance via a multiple choice test.)

Other teams at my school experimented with a short-answer reading inventory based on the work of University of Chicago education professor George Hillocks (2011). Without having to guess at a student's rationale for multiple choice answers, these teams have been able to more directly ascertain the thinking and skill development behind student answers. This aids them in guiding students toward their next learning steps.

On Hillocks's (2011) reading inventory, the first three of the seven questions all focus on comprehension skills ([1] basic stated information, [2] key details, and [3] directly stated relationships), while the final four questions delve into inferential skills ([4] simple implied relationship, [5] complex implied relationship, [6] author's generalizations, and [7] structure). Taken together this set of questions allow teachers to isolate where student skills may break down on their way to reaching standards such "Analyze how complex characters develop over the course of a text, interact with other characters, and advance the plot or develop the theme" (NGA & CCSSO, 2010a). Teams may decide, as my school's ELA teams have, to include literal comprehension skill as an individually assessed target in the first semester, while using answers to the inferential skill questions to identify any remaining students struggling with literal comprehension in the second semester (Hillocks, 2011).

Unexpected Question 3: Is There Enough of the Right Evidence to Show Proficiency?

In ELA, the right evidence is all around, but not necessarily organized into student- and assessment-friendly ways. Accustomed to having enough assessment data on various criteria and skills, our team had to develop and ensure a thoughtful, organized assessment plan (see figure 3.2, page 72).

Then, the team must review that assessment plan to ensure it provides early, low-stakes opportunities for teacher feedback for students. As English teacher Edgar Aguirre notes, "The skills are so recursive in ELA, so we are able to truly track proficiency and skill development throughout the semester. It is not just one-and-done summative assessment. It really makes sense" (E. Aquirre, personal communication, September 10, 2018).

For example, in the past, the team might have produced a grade that included input and feedback on student inferential reading of a text, creation of a claim, collection of evidence and detail, grammatical expression, peer critique in the writing process, and then focus, organization, support, and mechanics of an essay. Team members felt that with everything taken together, credit was probably given where it was due across this broad target range, and the team gave some feedback at various points to help students where needed.

In proficiency-based grading, this type of assessment occurs under a single learning target (or two), and the target is part of a deliberately timed pattern aimed at the student journey to and beyond proficiency (see figure 3.3, page 73). In this case, the argument essay would be one of a series of argumentative writing learning target efforts dispersed over the semester. Team feedback on the success criteria is deliberate and directly addresses the most important next steps, but it doesn't hide the complex end product sought in this assessment—*argumentative writing*.

Because of its process orientation, this assessment is an early and midsemester effort to support learning while providing feedback on the target. Later in the semester, the team asks the student to produce similar efforts in class, with less teacher or other support. That allows the team to provide a more accurate assessment of what the student has learned and can transfer to new tasks independently. Of course, the team is also mindful of the text and task complexity as part of the arc of the semester. Synthesis argument writing is not covered until students have had an opportunity to hone their argumentative writing, and the team might ask students to base their arguments on simpler scenarios or texts before moving them into writing a research paper or basing their writing on something complex, like *A Tale of Two Cities* (Dickens, 1859).

In ELA, a temptation to guard against is waiting too long to provide feedback on a particular learning target because the teacher feels he or she is still laying the groundwork of individual success criteria through narrow instruction and assessment of them. These targets are complex. While the team may feel it's too early to grade a student on his or her ability to read inferentially (and thus determine and defend theme or character change insights) because the teacher has not taught all of the moves one makes while doing so, students need teacher feedback early to set their sights on the ultimate goal.

With proficiency-based grading, the first-effort grade is low or no stakes. Teachers or teams then update that first effort with more recent efforts as long as the assessments contain multiple success criteria (and not *all* of them until later in the semester). As long as teachers ask students to simulate the full target by negotiating their way through a few success criteria, teams will use their professional judgment to provide the trajectory of progress toward the full target. This voids long gaps in feedback and student reflection on learning targets.

Reading

Assessment Format and Text	Short story short answer from "White Circle" (Clayton, 1957)	Excerpt of short answer from *The Tempest* (Shakespeare, 1973)	Excerpt of short answer from *A Tale of Two Cities* (Dickens, 1859)	Final exam reperformance opportunity	Final proficiency evaluation score
Purpose	Literal and inferential score	Literal and inferential score	Literal and inferential score	Optional reperformance based on student reflection	Teacher professional judgment summary
Timing	Week seven	Week twelve	Week sixteen	Week eighteen	Week eighteen

Writing

Assessment Format and Text	*Lord of the Flies* (Golding, 1954) essay	*The Tempest* (Shakespeare, 1973) process essay	Reperformance opportunity	*A Tale of Two Cities* (Dickens, 1859) essay	Final proficiency evaluation score
Purpose	Argument score	Argument score	Optional reperformance based on student reflection	Argument score	Teacher professional judgment summary
Timing	Week six	Weeks eleven to thirteen	Week fifteen	Week eighteen	Week eighteen

Speaking and Listening

Assessment Format and Text	*Lord of the Flies* (Golding, 1954) class discussion	"What is freedom?" essential question discussion	Literary analysis and focus discussions on *A Tale of Two Cities* (Dickens, 1859)	Final proficiency evaluation score	
Purpose	Speaking and listening in discussion score	Speaking and listening in discussion score	Optional reperformance based on student reflection	Teacher professional judgment summary	
Timing	Week four	Week ten	Week sixteen	Week eighteen	

Figure 3.2: Example proficiency evaluation assessment pattern for accelerated ninth-grade ELA.

Visit go.SolutionTree.com/assessment for a free reproducible version of this figure.

Learning Target: I write consistent arguments to support claims in an analysis of substantive topics or texts, using valid reasoning and relevant and sufficient evidence.

4—Refined Mastery	3—Proficiency	2—Approaches Proficiency	1—Still Developing
I write effective, insightful arguments in varied contexts to support claims in an analysis of substantive topics or texts, using valid reasoning and relevant and sufficient evidence.	I write consistent arguments to support claims in an analysis of substantive topics or texts, using valid reasoning and relevant and sufficient evidence.	I write partial or inconsistent arguments to support claims in an analysis of substantive topics or texts, using valid reasoning and relevant and sufficient evidence.	I write incomplete, illogical, or unsupported arguments.

Success Criteria	How Well I Am Doing (Student Self-Reflection)	Teacher Feedback
Focus		You should have an opening that moves from general to specific, and a clear, complex claim. Stay on topic throughout the piece.
Organization		Make sure your subclaims support your central claim. Check your transition phrases—Is there an organizational pattern suggested by them?
Development		Use specific textual evidence from the beginning, middle, and end of the piece. Explain your evidence. Make sure you address a counterargument to your claim.
Language		Work on combining sentences effectively. Remove grammatical errors. Try to use rhetorical strategies such as questions, repetition, and use of metaphor, simile, or both.

Source for standard: NGA & CCSSO, 2010a.

Figure 3.3: Sample argumentative writing rubric from accelerated ninth-grade English.

*Visit **go.SolutionTree.com/assessment** for a free reproducible version of this figure.*

Insight: The Essential Insights of Proficiency-Based Grading in ELA

As teachers begin to move beyond the initial fears and roadblocks and gain insight, it is vitally important to take some time to look back on and appreciate how the team has passed some intimidating hurdles thus far. Teams should have a clear enough idea of how proficiency-based grading works, and they can play to its strengths as they teach and plan. They begin providing proficiency-based grading with more power instead of just trying to get their balance.

At this point, ELA teachers might have the following insights: (1) ELA teachers provide space for students to engage actively in learning and insight, and (2) ELA teachers consistently provide space and opportunity for students to find success through skills refinement.

Insight 1: ELA Teachers Provide Space for Students to Engage Actively in Learning and Insight

One of teachers' most common observations at the beginning of proficiency-based grading implementation is they already have students reflect about their own progress and on their peers' progress. Indeed, my years of observing the teachers has shown a strong strand of reflection and goal setting in the typical English classroom.

Transitioning to proficiency-based grading and adopting rubrics that support the philosophy has interwoven this element into classrooms, instead of just being available. By making few learning targets, students better understand them. By bringing scaled learning targets to speaking, listening, and reading, students must reflect across ELA skills, not just primarily writing. Finally, students feel ownership when there is no averaging of rubric elements. The need to at least master each learning target skill brings the bar for success to a clear and delineated space. Students—even those motivated by the ultimate grade—focus on their own success criteria weakness, not points. English teacher Edgar Aguirre agrees, saying:

> It just makes sense to look at writing and reading holistically; the targets allow us to look at a work and judge it clearly. We are able to say whether a student has mastered this skill without parsing out all these minute details percentage point by percentage point. (E. Aguirre, personal communication, September 10, 2018)

Insight 2: ELA Teachers Consistently Provide Space and Opportunity for Students to Find Success Through Skills Refinement

Teams lay out semester assessment patterns with the knowledge that students will receive multiple opportunities to reperform the recursive set of skills in ELA. Supplemented by retakes as necessary, students are always in a state where they know and have reflected on their current performance level, and are being met by the teacher with intervention and instruction based on their current level of achievement.

Portfolios are a related idea. By collecting work and reflecting on it, students see their current state and gather the feedback necessary to take the next steps forward. The twist that proficiency-based grading provides for a reading portfolio, for example, is that the targets are few and powerful, and the desired state—the mastery level—is central to their reflection and action. It is not simply "Do your best" or "See if you can improve." Those are worthy goals, but lack the urgency or focus of trying to reach mastery and, if you fail, of plotting how you can do it! Proficiency-based grading draws the student's focus upward.

Evaluation: The Key Questions of Proficiency-Based Grading in ELA

Implementation's beginning stages bring a perspective of evaluation. While professional growth never takes one path, reaching this point allows teams to set a goal of reaching regular practice and to confidently look into ways that the system impacts feedback and grading.

Evaluation can lead ELA teachers to ask the following key questions: (1) "Is ELA feedback planned and frequent?" (2) "Do teachers agree on ELA grading feedback?" (3) "How do teachers help students identify next steps in reading, writing, speaking, and listening?" and (4) "How can teachers balance sufficient, timely evidence and feedback with grading papers?"

Key Question 1: Is ELA Feedback Planned and Frequent?

Teams must commit to providing frequent feedback to help students reach the targets. The concern is about not just the teacher gathering timely information, but *both* the teacher and student doing so. English teachers know guiding students through the composition process and then grading essays can result in a long assessment–feedback loop. ELA teachers work very hard tackling stacks of essays; however, it is not enough to let a preferred assessment method (such as essay writing) determine feedback-cycle timing. No, teachers must consider the timing and feedback that will help students reflect and grow, and then innovatively plan to provide that feedback.

Key Question 2: Do Teachers Agree on ELA Grading Feedback?

Teams committing to and developing a common and reliable interpretation of assessments is also important. There can be no more "tough" teacher, teacher who provides loads of feedback (or virtually none), or teacher who never gives a top score on the first essay of the year. Instead, teams must use professional judgment by collaboratively using student work and team discussion to link the rubric's proficiency scales to anchor papers and exemplars early in the year. For example, when proficiency assessments for inferential reading populate a gradebook, individual team members must have a shared performance expectation they can refine with their students.

Key Question 3: How Do Teachers Help Students Identify Next Steps in Reading, Writing, Speaking, and Listening?

Rubrics should help students develop a plan for improving the moves they make in pursuit of a skill. Traditional rubrics categorize a student's performance, but the student needs to interpret his or her classification to know the next rungs on the ladder to improved performance. Including descriptions of common next steps in success criteria and adjusting the phrasing of preloaded success criteria feedback can help students achieve this understanding (Wollenschläger, Hattie, Machts, Möller, & Harms, 2016). This is especially helpful when looking at the skills around speaking and listening, where the elusive nature of discussion leads teachers to give feedback that too often amounts to simply counting a student's number of contributions to a discussion rather than providing quality, skills-based feedback.

Key Question 4: How Can Teachers Balance Sufficient, Timely Evidence and Feedback With Grading Papers?

At this point, most teams have grappled with the admirable goal of giving students as much low-stakes practice as possible. Students need time to experiment and grow without the pressure of counting points or final exams. This is a fertile time for teaching students the social-emotional skills (persistence and goal setting) that will make for healthy, lifelong learning beyond any particular class.

In theory, during the last couple of weeks in a semester, a teacher gathers enough evidence (from perhaps three quality assessments) to feel certain of each student's proficiency level for the course. The catch is to do this for each learning target in a course—for example, five assessments for each student over the final two weeks of the semester. Clearly, the projected number of assessments (fifteen) is unmanageable. In fact, for many teams, gathering evidence from assessments during even the final six or nine weeks proves problematic since ELA assessments tend to be items like essays, graded discussions, and short-answer responses to reading questions. Is it possible for teachers to provide students with low-stakes practice time without sinking themselves?

A team's response should center on the concept of *enough of the right evidence*. This concept helps teachers refocus on what it will actually take to give an accurate, professional judgment of student achievement on a learning target—not more or less evidence. And this amount may even vary between learning targets.

So, while teachers might seek proficiency evaluation of student narrative writing once and offer reperformance opportunities to students who do not meet proficiency, they may ask for five higher-stakes demonstrations of inferential-reading proficiency. Teachers may spread out these five assessments over the relatively wide window of the semester's final ten weeks, finding the time necessary to integrate these more thorough or project-based assessments. Meanwhile, students get the feedback and reflection opportunities they need to grow and then display their learning.

Elaboration: The Core Beliefs of Proficiency-Based Grading in ELA

Teachers at the elaboration phase of implementation have reached a mature and clear perspective of using a proficiency-based grading system. They have discovered that the system does not push them out of valued projects, simulations, or other assessments and activities they know help students learn; instead, they see there is depth to be gained from such work, with an underlying and clear focus on skills. With their comfort in this system, teachers are resources for their colleagues and on the cutting edge for new ways to provide more support for and collaboration with their students.

Teachers who successfully implement proficiency-based grading adhere to all seven of the core beliefs explained in chapter 1 (page 9): (1) growth is a central concept, (2) reperformance is essential, (3) building students' reflection abilities is essential, (4) homework has a role, (5) communication with parents and the community is key, (6) culminating experiences like final exams have a different purpose, and (7) behavior can be in or out of the grade. The following sections, which reflect the core beliefs' original numbering, explore the core beliefs that ELA teachers in particular should never lose sight of.

Core Belief 1: Growth Is a Central Concept

Once teachers move away from using content-based reading tests to determine a grade, growth can assume the driver's seat in the ELA classroom. For example, no longer is reading simply a matter of marking a checkbox *yes* or *no*, from which there is no growth and where the teacher's job is to simply record whether reading occurred. Rather, proficiency-based grading sees reading as a set of moves and skills students learn, display, and improve on *as they read*. Of course, the same holds true of the discussion and writing that go on in any class.

The reward of this reframing is that a student's growth in ability unlocks new doors of meaning and purpose in reading texts, discussing texts, and then writing well-considered responses. Over time, this promotes a mindset of empowerment and growth. Teachers do not need to demand perfection of students to start the semester, nor do they need to assign reading or tasks that are easy so students can still gather points at a 90 percent or greater rate. Students begin an honest journey toward developing skills as they read, write, and discuss the world around them.

Core Belief 2: Reperformance Is Essential

When determining learning targets and ensuring they represent skill mastery, teams at my school bolded the language drawn from state standards in the rubrics' success criteria. Teams also reaffirmed that while biology may require students to know certain content about photosynthesis before they can move on to effectively study ecosystems, the ELA content did not hold the same prerequisite value for students. Although teams know reading quality literature and studying great speeches supports the growth of solid citizens, these content activities are not as direct as knowing how to participate in democracy. That approach strongly influenced how the team looked at the next two concepts: *retake* versus *reperformance*.

If a student wants to retake an essay assessment, won't he or she complete the reflection, targeted learning, and rewritten essay just about midway through the next essay and accompanying instruction? Would that be manageable for the student and teacher in the context of the course workload and focus? Likewise, having a true group or class discussion serve as a speaking and listening assessment retake means logistical issues, such as what to do when a single student needs to retake a discussion or when awkwardness occurs because students from different classes who don't know each other are grouped together as a retake. These concerns might be overcome or overlooked periodically, but as a systemic method, they seem disruptive to good assessment.

Thus, while there is a role for retakes if there is very small class size or a student is sick leading into the end of a semester, more potential lies in *reperformance*. Illinois state standards for ELA are so recursive (with the same standards tracing from first to twelfth grade), a reperformance in the next unit does provide an equal opportunity to demonstrate growth toward the standard. For example, the teacher can assess a student's use of inference to determine theme and how he or she supports that determination with evidence from the text as easily in Golding's (1954) *Lord of the Flies* as in Shakespeare's (1973) *The Tempest*. The student does not need to master these skills using *Lord of the Flies* before moving on to *The Tempest*. In fact, the teacher's time between assessments is better spent responding to a student's areas for growth rather than losing time to retakes. Thanks to reperformance, students can regain time for learning, *and* teachers can see the transferable nature of the skills.

Core Belief 4: Homework Has a Role

ELA homework often takes on the role of classroom preparation; if students read twenty pages or write three pages at home, then the classroom is a more productive and interactive place. With this time-tested model, teachers still face the prospect that some students will come to class without having done the work. To counter, teachers need to make their classrooms places where coming prepared makes students feel involved and inspired—and where not being prepared leaves students wishing they were (yet not punishing them by cutting them off from learning until they catch up while reading in the hallway). The bottom line is homework must be part of the daily practice and growth of students in the classroom—because the skills practice matters.

A common initial worry for teachers in proficiency-based grading classrooms is that removing the homework reading quiz will result in students simply stopping reading and coming to class unprepared to learn (and, even worse, deciding they do not need to read). Our team uncovered a few insights about this potential problem. First, all team members agreed that it is important (and a high priority) for students to read (and do other prerequisite work). However, team members did accept there is some level of reading refusal or false reading (where students either accept consequences openly or use friends or online resources to cover their nonreading tracks). Proficiency-based grading is not going to create or completely solve this issue.

In proficiency-based grading, it is acceptable for teachers to continue giving reading quizzes or other feedback to students, parents, and school support personnel. This feedback is part of the story of student growth and helpful data when students don't progress as they should. However, what appears in feedback should not be confused with a student's ability to reach the targets and standards. A traditional gradebook readily mixes the behavior of reading on a schedule with the skills of reading; teachers must be certain not to confuse the two.

After implementing a proficiency-based grading system, my school's students have read at a similar rate as prior to implementation, so the questions of homework reading go back to best practices around encouraging students to read. Some of these best practices include the following.

- Conducting supportive prereading activities such as opinion questionnaires or previewing exciting passages

- Framing inquiry through teacher-developed essential questions

- Allowing student choice

- Incorporating peer discussion

- Integrating second and third readings of selected passages in class

- Considering whether the assigned texts authentically engage students

Key Points

To ensure full understanding, review the following key points from this chapter.

- Build on the success of ELA writing rubrics to guide your efforts to expand the practice of proficiency-based grading to areas that have traditionally not been skill or rubric based.

- To gather enough of the right evidence in ELA, teacher teams must experiment and learn from their evidence collection. Teams need to explore how quickly they can turn around focused written assessments, how to allow reperformances for discussions, and how to collaboratively identify what behaviors represent effective reading. Patience and a long-term vision are keys to success.

- Literacy skills are the primary objective for ELA teachers. The lessons from literature and the beauty of writing are the hooks for gaining the interest and devotion of students, but teachers must also assess by pushing students to achieve skill levels that unlock these treasures.

Jonathan Grice is director of fine arts at Adlai E. Stevenson High School in Lincolnshire, Illinois. Previously, he served as the fine arts department chair and visual arts teacher at Riverside Brookfield High School in Riverside, Illinois.

Stevenson is one of the first comprehensive schools designated a New American High School by the United States Department of Education as a model of successful school reform. It is repeatedly cited as one of America's top high schools and the birthplace of the Professional Learning Communities at Work® process. The fine arts division at Stevenson High School has a long tradition of excellence and has been recognized for its high standards and accomplishments at a regional, state, and national levels. The division is regarded as one of the most exemplary high school arts programs in the country by some of the most prominent colleges, universities, and professional organizations.

At Riverside, Jon helped lead the school in becoming a PLC. Riverside was also recognized as a School of Distinction in Arts Education by the Illinois Alliance for Arts Education. In 2017, Jon was recognized by the National Art Education Association as the Western Regional Supervisor/Art Administrator of the Year. In 2016, he earned Art Administrator/Supervisor of the Year from the Illinois Art Education Association. He has presented on a number of topics, including PLCs, standards-based grading, unpacking standards, and response to intervention, and is currently coauthoring *The New Art and Science of Teaching: Art and Music* (2019) with Robert J. Marzano and Mark Onuscheck.

Jon holds a master of arts in educational leadership from Concordia University and a bachelor's degree in visual arts education from Northern Illinois University.

To learn more about Jon's work, follow @SHS_FA_Director on Twitter.

To book Jonathan Grice for professional development, contact pd@SolutionTree.com.

Chapter 4

Implementing Proficiency-Based Grading in Fine Arts

Jonathan Grice

Assessment, of course, is a continuous process in arts education. The day to day formative judgments made by teachers to assist students' progress towards their learning goals play a central role in any successful art education program.

—Douglas Boughton

This chapter prepares educators to implement proficiency-based grading in the fine arts classroom. Broadly speaking, fine arts include the subjects of dance, media arts, music, theater, and visual arts. These areas offer a range of classroom experiences that might include the studio, nonperformance and performance settings, and different tools, equipment, and supplies to support these enriching educational experiences. While there is great variety in these subjects, our commitment to proficiency-based grading remains unified. Our attention to place the learning at the heart of our curriculum, instruction, and assessment cycles only further supports our developing dancers, musicians, actors, and artists.

This chapter explains the reasons to implement proficiency-based grading in fine arts courses through five phases: (1) preparation, (2) incubation, (3) insight, (4) evaluation, and (5) elaboration (Csikszentmihalyi, 1990).

Reasons to Implement Proficiency-Based Grading in Fine Arts

When considering proficiency-based grading in fine arts classrooms, teachers often worry about changes that would undercut values they hold around teaching. Concerns around how this may affect fine arts instruction, content, and grading workload are common. Teachers often wonder how grading fine arts might change their students' overall experience and grades. Including effort in the fine arts gradebook is the tradition. Furthermore, teachers may rather emphasize the fun, enriching, and engaging environment fine arts experiences provide students, rather than implementing new assessment and grading processes altogether.

As teachers learn about this grading method (which sounds valuable, but so unfamiliar), they begin to understand the deeper rationale—the *why*—behind proficiency-based grading, and their concerns diminish. Teachers should consider three questions at this phase of their journey: (1) What is the essential learning that takes place in my fine arts classroom? (2) How can our assessment practices promote creativity, experimentation, and risk taking? and (3) How can students receive ongoing feedback to further support learning and growth as fine artists?

The following sections address how proficiency-based grading is more authentic to fine arts than traditional grading, promotes accurate feedback in a fine arts classroom, is about students' growth in fine arts, puts learning at the center of fine arts instruction, promotes rubrics-based fine arts assessments, and validates fine arts as rigorous academic subjects.

Proficiency-Based Grading Is More Authentic to Fine Arts Than Traditional Grading

The first implementation phase in my department was to reflect and study fine arts teachers' current grading and assessment practices. When doing this, teachers immediately realized some practices were flawed and, at times, questionable. This primarily related to the lack of alignment among fine arts teachers, scoring practices that penalized students and potentially limited creativity, and uncommunicative gradebooks.

When they opened their gradebooks and observed their practices, teachers immediately recognized that they were not aligned. It was clear the fine arts teachers had the same assignments worth different values, different weighted categories for overall grade determinations, and different policies for deducting points for missing class, not participating, or turning in late assignments. Most notably, fine arts teachers learned that student grades were often unable to recover when they assigned zeros for late or incomplete work. They began to recognize how their grading practices were penalizing students.

The teachers also began recognizing that in many cases fine arts novice learners had had points deducted because the performance quality demonstrated emerging skills, while our traditional grading system rewarded students who previously had fine arts experiences. This led the fine arts teachers to wonder if their traditional grading system using points might also prevent students from experimenting and taking artistic risks due to a fear that their grades may suffer.

In other cases, fine arts teachers struggled to articulate the reasons why a student earned an 87 percent on a performance assessment versus another student earning an 84 percent on the same assessment. Teachers began recognizing that if we were unable to explain the differences between these different percentages, a student or parent would also struggle to know what needed to improve. They recognized that a single numeric value in our gradebook lacked descriptive feedback for students and their parents.

Finally, the fine arts teams began to think differently about the use of averaging and recognized that averaging grades was creating the problems. On one hand, a student who earned high scores at the beginning of the year could mentally check out at the end of the semester because the student had already accumulated enough points to earn a certain grade without doing much more work. On the other hand, a novice fine arts student may not have the experiences or foundational skills to initially perform at the proficient level at the beginning of the year, but as the student gains new knowledge and experiences through engagement and practice, the student grows over time. In a traditional grading system, this particular student is often penalized when the teacher averages the lower scores from earlier in the learning process despite the student growing and meeting class expectations by the end of the course.

Discussing these issues together, fine arts teams began to recognize that traditional grading using points, percentages, and averages was not an authentic grading system they had hoped to use. They began to realize that the traditional way of grading had some severe issues, and that moved our fine arts teachers away from accurate and honest feedback around the essential learning and performance goals of their classes. Once fine arts teams determined these issues, it was a goal to utilize a more authentic approach to teaching, learning, and assessing in fine arts classrooms. This allowed us to de-emphasize the grade and focus solely on our students' technique, process, performance, expression, growth, and ability to give and accept feedback. By reflecting on the evidence created by students, the feedback process became rich and focused on helping students grow as artists and human beings. What we came to realize was that proficiency-based grading was more authentic and met student and teacher needs much more than traditional grading ever did.

Proficiency-Based Grading Promotes Accurate Feedback in a Fine Arts Classroom

Prior to proficiency-based grading, fine arts teachers used points or percentages to determine their students' grades for assignments, terms, and end-of-semester grades. The fine arts team now recognized that this approach provided an unclear picture without specifics of what students were doing well and needed to improve. They acknowledged that students and parents understood the traditional grades of A, B, C, D, and F and the coinciding percentages of 90, 80, 70, 60, and below. However, proficiency-based grading offered a comprehensive approach to instruction, assessment, feedback, and grading that was more authentic to the fine arts.

Often, fine arts grade sheets included the key topics and skills teachers identified as important and often listed additional criteria related to these key topics and skills. Depending on the importance, or weight, of each topic related to the overall unit of study, a numeric scale represented the range of scores a student could earn depending on how well he or she performed. Rarely did the teachers include clear descriptors for each point value. The teacher would then evaluate the student's work or performance and calculate a single grade to enter in the gradebook. This numeric value would calculate into a percentage easily translated into a letter grade of an A, B, C, D, or F.

For example, previous grading practices for the box and ball drawing assignment in visual arts included assigning points for a student's ability to observe and render a sphere and box realistically using pencil. In this example, a student could earn a maximum of twenty points. Ten points were assigned to realism, including realistic proportions, perspective, highlights, and shadows. Another ten points were assigned to the shading, including using a drawing technique that was expected to be smooth with the full range of values, while excluding bold contour lines to separate forms or distinct value changes.

When teachers determine grades using poorly defined performance standards and criteria, those grades are inaccurate. What the fine arts teachers came to realize was that despite the verbal and written feedback teachers gave their students, the earned numeric value entered in the gradebook did not provide a clear picture of what the students did well or needed to improve. The singular numeric value did not explain how well students were meeting or not meeting the essential learning for the fine arts class. The numeric value was vague and required students and parents to make assumptions about the students' performance and achievement in the class.

Parents and students sometimes challenge teachers' grading practices and their professional judgment. At times, parents do not understand the academic nature of the fine arts and assume their children deserve an A for their hard work. After all, as professor of art and education Douglas G. Boughton (2016) explains, "It is a common misconception that determination of the quality of student artwork is a subjective process" (p. 8). Understandably, students and parents had questions when they tried to understand what fifteen out of twenty points truly meant. These occasional instances led to unnecessary confrontations between parents and teachers as parents asked questions such as "How can my child earn a 75 percent or C on a drawing assignment?" While the teachers would go out of their way to explain the rationale behind a student's scores and grade, in some cases parents continued challenging the teacher's evaluation and the high expectations established in the fine arts curricula. At the time, the fine arts rationale for these interactions seemed appropriate. At the time, our grading system seemed valid and reliable, but in hindsight, the numeric values had numerous issues. Most notably, the numeric values lacked the descriptive feedback that truly advances student learning and performance. The fine arts teachers recognized there was a better system.

With the shift to proficiency-based grading, fine arts teachers began to develop and create proficiency-scaled learning targets reflecting the essential skills in the classes. Re-evaluating the learning targets meant defining what it means for students to (4) exceed standards, (3) meet standards, (2) approach standards, or (1) not meet standards. The teams also established clear, observable success criteria related to each learning target to further emphasize the quality desired. The rubric in figure 4.1 (page 88) has a number of important components that are essential to proficiency-based grading, including standard and skill identification, the scaled proficiency (which includes the learning target at level 3—meets standard), the coinciding success criteria, space for teacher feedback, and space for student self-reflection.

Standard: Idea development			
Skill: Artistic voice			
4—Refined Mastery	3—Proficiency	2—Approaches Proficiency	1—Still Developing
I convey personal meaning and visual intent that is sophisticated, sensitive, and evocative.	I convey personal meaning and clear visual intent.	I convey meaning that is intended or implied.	I recognize meaning and visual intent in art.

Success Criteria:

- Individual interest
- Connecting
- Expression
- Artistic style
- Artist statement

Teacher feedback:

Student reflection:

Source for standard: College Board, 2018; National Coalition for Core Arts Standards, 2014.

Figure 4.1: Box and ball drawing assignment rubric.

The success criteria are the key aspects of the learning target to guide teachers' professional judgment and student reflection when determining how the evidence aligns to the proficiency level. The success criteria also represent essential background knowledge and concepts that teachers help students fully understand in order to meet course expectations. Figure 4.2 is another example of scaled learning targets addressing the skill of effective rehearsal practices.

Our visual arts teachers, in addition to referring to the National Coalition for Core Arts Standards (2014) artistic processes, also referred to the 2018 advanced placement studio art scoring guidelines, when creating their scales.

Standard: Content			
Skill: Effective rehearsal practices			
4—Refined Mastery	**3—Proficiency**	**2—Approaches Proficiency**	**1—Still Developing**
I present heightened artistic work that provokes empathy and connects with the audience through honesty and authenticity.	I present artistic work that provokes empathy and connects with the audience.	I present artistic work that resonates with the audience.	I present artistic work for an audience.
Success Criteria: • Collaboration • Judicious use of class time • Preparation • Feedback incorporation			
Teacher feedback:			
Student reflection:			

Source for standard: National Coalition for Core Arts Standards, 2014.

Figure 4.2: Effective rehearsal practices rubric.

Proficiency-Based Grading Is About Students' Growth in Fine Arts

Proficiency-based grading allows teachers to review all the evidence of student learning while taking into account student growth prior to teachers determining a final grade. Proficiency-based grading helps students understand their current performance level in order to improve as learners. This focus on improving student skill development (rather than assigning grades) was a major factor in helping my school's fine arts teams decide to implement proficiency-based grading.

When students understood their current state of performance and the pathway to improve their overall performance and skill development, we began seeing more self-reflective and self-motivated learners. To help students achieve this, teachers need to plan time for student reflection. This may be done by allowing time to write, by permitting students to talk to their peers, or through conferencing with the students. When students understand the class expectations from the learning target and accompanying success criteria, reflection time—especially when paired with specific teacher feedback—can help students recognize the growth they have made over time and consider strategies to improve, thus helping them recognize their abilities and provide motivation to reach higher levels of achievement in the arts.

Students often arrive to their fine arts classrooms with a range of experiences. Some students have had extensive training in the arts. Depending on the district, arts may or may not have been part of the students' early education. In other cases, students' interests and exposure to popular and visual culture may have led to enriching background and self-taught areas of study. Other students may have had extremely limited experiences with dance, media arts, music, theater, and visual arts. Proficiency-based grading allows teachers to focus on helping every student grow as a fine artist, regardless of his or her background and experiences.

Teachers use the proficiency scales to track and evaluate students on their growth on each learning target over time. Many of the fine arts learning targets extend beyond fine arts and are transferable in nature and further exemplify why the arts promote learning across the curriculum into other disciplines and skills: the ability to critique, nontextual comprehension, claim development using evidence, reflection, and establishing achievable goals. These are essential life skills.

Teachers are drawn to proficiency-based grading because they see immediate connections to how they teach and provide feedback to students in the classroom. Fine arts teachers continue to develop student skills around creating, performing, responding, and connecting to the arts. These teachers continue to provide feedback while honing students' ability to self-reflect on their learning, as well as their peers' learning. Teachers continue to provide direct and honest feedback regardless of experience while no longer hanging grades over the students' heads.

Removing grades from everyday conversations helps refocus students' attention on their actual learning and skill development in fine arts classrooms. Removing grades requires teachers to continue to create positive and safe classroom environments to help students feel comfortable in taking risks in the fine arts classroom. The goal is for students to engage fully in the arts without having to worry if they are good enough or doing it one right way. Risk taking may include experimenting with tools and mark making in the visual arts classroom, improvising new movements in dance, demonstrating vulnerability through character development in improvisational games, and performing music with emotion and expressiveness. In addition, ongoing dialogue with students about their strengths and ways to improve helps establish a class culture in which it is OK not to meet standards at the onset of the learning process. The goal of the proficiency-based grading classroom is to have continual dialogue with students about ways they can grow as artists. Teachers then can implement strategies to improve student skills over time.

Proficiency-Based Grading Puts Learning at the Center of Fine Arts Instruction

In proficiency-based grading classrooms, the learning targets and success criteria become the center of instruction and feedback and eventually help determine the students' grade at the end of term. Teachers must be clear about what students must know and be able to do, and also be able to explain and show the quality students must perform to achieve mastery. Creating well-developed scaled learning targets and success criteria that align with fine arts courses is essential. Teachers should consider using their state fine arts standards and the National Core Arts Standards during the first stages of this process. In the classroom, the scaled learning targets become the script teachers use to explain what students must be able to do. Scaled learning targets and success criteria reflect the major concepts and skills all students must learn and be able to demonstrate.

In this chapter's examples, you will see the success criteria listed as single words or phrases. The reader may notice the fine arts examples are different from the success criteria from other chapters that use complete sentences. The fine arts teachers who chose to differ in this area believed the single words or phrases play an important role in helping students better understand the vocabulary that is essential to our curricula. Then teachers and teams continue to frame course expectations, instruction, and feedback around these targets as students engage in and interact with the arts. The focus and clarity on this language improves the teachers' verbal and written feedback methods, while also eliciting more complex conversations with students.

Because scaled targets become the center of these discussions, teachers are able to clearly explain what they expect students to achieve at each level of proficiency that the student evidence reflects. At this stage, teachers should clearly write the scaled targets using student-friendly language. Fine arts teachers also need to make sure they provide plenty of examples that highlight the skills each learning target emphasizes and the quality of work that is expected. In the art courses, this includes displaying past student exemplars in the classroom. In the music classroom, students may listen to class recordings or model the quality of sound. In the dance studio, they can watch videos or demonstrate the choreographic phrase. In the acting class, students can watch videos or read scripts of student original monologues. When providing examples, teachers should review the learning target and how the exemplars achieve the success criteria.

By placing learning at the center of class instruction, teachers begin to implement engaging strategies for students to study their evidence, self-reflect, and discuss their observations with peers. Figure 4.3 is an example of the Frayer Model (Frayer, Frederick, & Klausmeier, 1969), which uses a graphic organizer to distinguish different focus areas. This graphic organizer example asks students to observe their peers' dance technique through the lens of multiple learning targets.

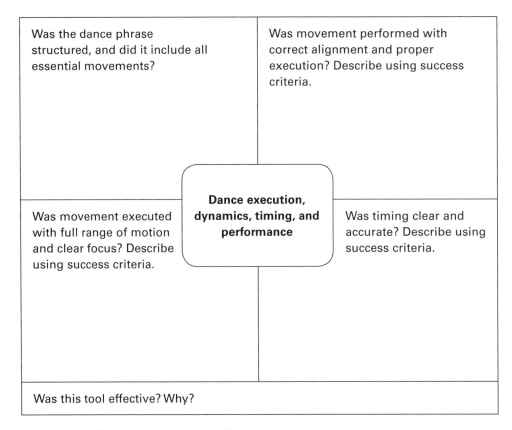

Source: Adapted from Frayer, Frederick, & Klausmeier, 1969.

Figure 4.3: Frayer Model graphic organizer for dance peer assessment example.

Figure 4.4 illustrates the scaled learning targets for a dance class, which include the categories of execution, dynamics, time, and performance under the standard of technique, as well as the success criteria.

4—Exceeding	3—Proficient	2—Developing	1—Beginning
Learning Target: Execution			
The student performs all movements (essential and previously learned) in a structured dance phrase.	The student performs essential movements in a structured dance phrase.	The student performs the essential movements in isolated segments of a structured dance phrase.	The student performs essential movements in isolation, separate of the structured phrase.
Success Criteria: • Alignment • Posture • Connectivity • Clarity of movement • Attention to correction and detail			
Learning Target: Dynamics			
The student performs all movements with given expressive qualities in a structured dance phrase.	The student performs essential movements with given expressive qualities in a structured dance phrase.	The student performs the essential movements with given expressive qualities in isolated segments of a structured dance phrase.	The student performs some movements with expressive quality, though they are given in isolation.
Success Criteria: • Flow • Accent • Movement qualities: swing or suspend, sustained, percussive, vibratory, collapsed			
Learning Target: Timing			
The student performs all movements with given rhythm, tempo, and musicality in a structured dance phrase.	The student performs essential movements with given rhythm and tempo in a structured dance phrase.	The student performs the essential movements with given rhythm and tempo in isolated segments of a structured dance phrase.	The student performs with given tempo or rhythm in isolation or with the teacher counting during the performance.
Success Criteria: • Tempo • Rhythm • Melody • Sound interpretation			

Figure 4.4: Dance technique rubric.

continued ➞

Learning Target: Performance			
The student engages the audience using full energy and full kinesphere (or range of motion) in a structured dance combination.	The student engages the audience using energy and kinesphere (or range of motion) in a structured dance combination.	The student engages the audience using energy and kinesphere (or range of motion) in isolated segments of a structured dance phrase.	The student engages the audience with some energy and some kinesphere (or range of motion) in isolation or with teacher prompting.

Success Criteria:
- Energy
- Risk
- Focus
- Kinesphere

Teacher feedback:

Student reflection:

Source for standard: National Coalition for Core Arts Standards, 2014.

When teachers use learning targets and rubrics regularly, students become familiar with the language and class expectations. Accompanying graphic organizers can further help students develop the ability to have complex conversations with their teacher and their peer. The goal as teachers is to always provide students with authentic, honest, and direct feedback that helps students improve their performance in a safe, nurturing environment. Removing the grade determination from the conversation helps create an environment of feedback and support for all students. The alignment of proficiency-based grading practices moves the fine arts teacher into the role of *facilitator of learning* rather than *sole evaluator*. Teachers in proficiency-based grading classrooms build environments that support this process and help students feel more comfortable with receiving and accepting feedback in a nonpunitive manner.

Proficiency-Based Grading Promotes Rubric-Based Fine Arts Assessments

Prior to proficiency-based grading, our fine arts teachers and teams continued to have problems using rubrics and trying to translate student-graded proficiency levels into a numeric grade required in the traditional grading systems of points and percentages. Previous rubrics identified levels of proficiency; however, teachers also connected a numeric value to each proficiency level used to calculate a score for the gradebook. In other cases, each proficiency level represented a grade. In these cases, *refined mastery* equated to an A, *proficient* equated to a B, *approaching proficiency* equated to a C, and *still developing* equated to a D. Often, if a student scored proficient or level 3 or 2 on a four-point scale, the student would earn a low letter grade once the teacher calculated all the points together. This caused the teacher to rethink the student's total assessment score. The teacher would then make adjustments to the rubric so he or she could report a higher letter grade to the student. While the intention was to accurately assess the student using the rubric, the rubric and grade adjustments prevented the teacher from providing accurate feedback.

While teachers use rubrics to assess products or processes that require them to observe students performing a skill in the moment, our teams also found rubrics to be valuable teaching tools when explaining the expected quality of learning and performance to students. In addition, teachers use rubrics to guide student self-reflection, peer assessments, and discussion.

Teachers use rubrics to provide feedback by identifying each student's current performance compared to the expectations for each class objective. In fine arts, the skills on a rubric might include the following.

- **Visual arts:** Use of media and tools, composition, artistic voice, criticism
- **Dance:** Execution, dynamics, time, performance, choreography
- **Music:** Performance, posture, tone, rhythm, dynamics, sight reading
- **Theater:** Preparation, delivery, blocking, collaboration, ensemble

The goal was to avoid rubrics that changed from one assignment to another and instead identify the essential skills that are assessed on a reoccurring basis over a class's duration. The transition to proficiency-based grading helped my school's teacher teams create a set of common learning targets to use across every dance, media arts, music, theater, and visual arts class. These learning targets also support our vertically aligned curricula as the learning targets and common language stayed the same as students progressed through our course sequences.

In the case of our visual arts classes, we kept the same learning targets, but as students experienced different media and art forms, including drawing, painting, ceramics, metals, photography, and animation, we changed the success criteria to match the course, while keeping the skill and scaled learning target identical across our department. This allowed our art teachers to collect evidence of student growth and learning from different art classes, yet have conversations comparing student performances regardless of the class, media, or project.

Proficiency-Based Grading Validates Fine Arts as Rigorous Academic Subjects

The fine arts include academic subjects essential for all students. Research finds the benefits the fine arts play in cognitive development, social-emotional growth, and well-being (College Board, 2012). No Child Left Behind (2001) identifies the fine arts as a core content area, and the Every Student Succeeds Act (2015) states that the arts and music are essential to all students' well-rounded education. Despite all this, people continue to view the arts as nonessential in most school districts.

Moving to proficiency-based grading, which outlines specific academic and social-emotional skills, helps re-establish the fine arts as academic and rigorous. Having clear learning targets with clearly defined success criteria helps make concepts concrete and more objective. When evidence of learning takes place in those classes, teachers can more easily demonstrate the importance of the fine arts.

Proficiency-based grading will further help with fine arts advocacy initiatives at the local, state, and national levels. School leaders and educators must place the arts on equal footing with core academic areas and require the same rigor and academic expectations across all content areas.

Preparation: The Commitments of Proficiency-Based Grading in Fine Arts

Teachers and teams make certain commitments to successfully implement this improved system of assessing and instructing. This can be difficult because teachers often have very personal and intense attachments to specific resources, literature, other curriculum, instruction, and assessment. When a team of teachers is preparing to do this work, there will be worries about losing autonomy and the challenge of adapting teaching and assessment in the near future. That is when making a series of commitments will allow teachers to support each other on the road to success.

The following commitments are discussed in subsequent sections: (1) align learning targets to unify curriculum across the fine arts, (2) use backward design and common assessments to document evidence of learning in the fine arts, (3) improve inter-rater reliability by removing grading subjectivity and bias in the fine arts, and (4) enable teacher autonomy.

Commitment 1: Align Learning Targets to Unify Curriculum Across the Fine Arts

Moving to proficiency-based grading helped unify a department of singletons in fine arts and improved how those teachers collaborate. The teachers create and use common rubrics across all courses and distinguish unique criteria for every art class. This model allows fine arts teachers to analyze assessment data around common learning targets and share effective teaching and assessment strategies with each other while continuing to recognize the uniqueness of individual classes.

Because proficiency-based grading demands that all team members collaborate, my school's fine arts teachers also benefitted from working with others to develop and use common curricular language while realigning assessment and grading practices. With a unified language, teachers can speak about their lessons, instructional strategies, and assignments using common learning targets. Teachers also gained the following benefits from using this common language.

- During observations, open houses, and informal conversations with students and faculty, this common language illustrates that the team is on the same page and articulates department learning outcomes clearly and easily.

- Throughout instruction, this common language became the script teachers use in the class and for feedback.

- Using this common language helps teachers stay on a path toward the essential outcomes for the course, semester, or school year.

To begin creating the collaborative learning targets, the fine arts team and teachers accepted a move away from using course-specific learning targets and toward common rubrics with common learning targets. This was a major shift since we had almost thirty different targets across all our different art classes. We recognized similarities existed and in many cases the skills or targets had the same intention. However, it was clear that our language did not align and needed to be cleaned up. The visual arts team determined what essential learning took place in our courses.

The team referenced the National Coalition for Core Arts Standards (2014) visual arts standards, including the specified four artistic processes of (1) creating, (2) presenting, (3) responding, and (4) connecting. Through discussion and debate, we reorganized our course outcomes according to the following standards and skills.

- **Standard 1: Technique**
  - Skill 1A: Use of media and tools
  - Skill 1B: Composition
- **Standard 2: Idea development**
  - Skill 2A: Planning
  - Skill 2B: Artistic voice

- ○ Skill 2C: Artistic intent
- ○ Skill 2D: Transformation and growth
- **Standard 3: Artistic process**
  - ○ Skill 3A: Time management
  - ○ Skill 3B: Art criticism
  - ○ Skill 3C: Content knowledge
  - ○ Skill 3D: Presentation

Commitment 2: Use Backward Design and Common Assessments to Document Evidence of Learning in the Fine Arts

Another positive result of moving to holistic learning targets was exemplified in Stevenson's visual arts department. Visual arts teachers unified their assessment and grading practices and collaboratively used backward design (Wiggins & McTighe, 1998). The visual arts teachers always valued student involvement and reflection as part of their instructional strategies, but the new common language allowed higher-level assessment practices among all team members, including common language across courses, and improved inter-rater reliability, student self-assessment abilities, and student exemplars.

The visual arts faculty then considered how they would use their common rubrics for different course projects and in their gradebooks. They listed specific success criteria near each learning target on the rubric that identifies the various elements associated with the target. The bulleted success criteria reflect the background knowledge and course vocabulary students need to understand. The list of key-words and observable traits continues to help both teachers and students understand the specific expectations for each fine arts project.

The team decided when they would enter scores into gradebooks for each class and then gather to review common student assessment data together. Together, they developed unit-by-unit plans for when to formally assess each learning target and enter the results into the gradebook. While the number of gradebook scores may vary per class and teachers, we agreed there should be a minimum of three scores per learning target over the course of the semester. The scores would reflect the initial assessment event, the midpoint assessment event, and the last assessment event at the end of the semester. Throughout the course, students continuously receive frequent feedback from the teacher, from their peers, and through self-reflection that teachers may or may not record in the gradebook.

Table 4.1 shows what the teachers determined is the best evidence to collect.

Table 4.1: Evidence Collected by Course

What Evidence to Collect	Why to Collect It
Dance Unit	
• Rehearsal etiquette • Performance and technique • Interpersonal: Collaboration • Creating: Spatial design • Responding and connecting: Criticism	• Students demonstrate proper rehearsal expectations, classroom procedures, and work ethic to reflect the dance studio environment. • Students demonstrate proper execution of movement, expressive qualities, timing, musicality, energy, and range of motion. • Students demonstrate collaborative behaviors with peers, assuming roles and following protocols in a productive, supportive manner. • Students use choreographic tools to create new movement phrases that express personal and collaborative visions, concepts, and ideas. • Students engage in peer, group, and self-reflection and assessment processes to identify strengths, growth areas, and steps to improve. This may be observable, written responses, or recorded using video or audio.
Music Unit	
• Technique and performance • Composition • Theory • Ensemble skills • Responding and connecting: Criticism	• Students perform with efficient and fluid coordination of mechanical elements, including properly executed articulations and correct performance positions. • Students demonstrate music notation and theory to write new, original music to be performed. • Students demonstrate an understanding of musical notations, symbols, terminology, and content knowledge. • Students work productively to support positive classroom culture, while also helping the ensemble grow musically. • Students engage in written and verbal peer and self-assessment, and formal analysis and critiques of student and professional performance.

continued ⟶

What Evidence to Collect	Why to Collect It
Theater Unit	
• Connecting: Text analysis • Interpersonal: Ensemble participation • Creating • Intrapersonal: Rehearsal habits • Performing • Responding and connecting: Critiquing	• Students analyze scripts, scenes, and characters through written responses, verbal responses, and performance. • Students actively participate and support the class ensemble work. • Students create new material through writing, rehearsal, and improvisation. • Students productively engage in the rehearsal process to develop new ideas and refine performance. • Students perform monologues, scenes, and devised work for audiences. • Students engage in formal written and verbal peer and self-assessments and critiques of class work and staged performances.
Visual Arts Unit	
• Creating: Use of media and tools • Creating: Idea development • Creating: Compositional design • Interpersonal: Time management • Presenting • Responding and connecting: Criticism	• Students play, experiment, and practice working appropriately with media and tools. • Students generate ideas, concepts, and artistic voice to be expressed through the visual arts, media arts, and artist statements. • Students design and plan the juxtaposition of visual elements in an artwork or series of work. • Students work productively, stay on task, and complete artistic work. • Students present artistic work through class displays, exhibitions, online galleries, contests, and portfolios. • Students engage in formal written and verbal peer and self-assessments and critiques of class work and professional exhibits.

The team's instructional plans included how and when to help students understand a learning target. At the beginning stages of a lesson, the *how* sometimes means providing exemplars to demonstrate the desired quality for mastery. These exemplars also help students develop their artistic judgment and ability to accurately self-reflect and reflect for their peers and teachers. The team allotted time for students to engage in activities for practice and to develop their skills together as a class, as well as time to work individually.

Proficiency-based grading also requires blocking out observation time for each student. During those times, students perform their skills and follow the teacher-made collaborative plans for helping students who need additional practice or support. The team also built in time for reperformance (see Core Belief 2: Reperformance Is Essential, page 117) for students not yet meeting expectations.

Commitment 3: Improve Inter-Rater Reliability by Removing Grading Subjectivity and Bias in the Fine Arts

Teams must work to continuously improve their *inter-rater reliability* so proficiency assessment scoring is consistent; it is essential to the grading system. Douglas Boughton (2016), professor of arts education, calls this process *moderation*. This process is an attempt to "reduce variations of interpretation among different examiners, and [it] serves to promote a climate of debate and discussion about the quality of student work" (Boughton, 2016, p. 15–16). As a result, team members can develop a collective understanding of quality as it relates to their success criteria and be consistent when assessing student performance and work.

During team meetings, members discussed course projects and specific qualities necessary for students to earn a 4, 3, 2, or 1 on each learning target. While the teachers initially used this as a time to share, they now score the artworks first, then discuss reasons why they assign specific scores. In other cases, following auditions in music and dance, teachers review recorded performances to determine students' proficiency levels. This process actively engages team members in collaborative activities that allow them to align scoring, benchmark student work at different proficiency levels, and address concerns if a learning target is not as clear as it should be. This may occur when teachers reflect on the curriculum, learning activities, and student evidence. Often, teachers recognize that the collected evidence does not align as closely to the specific learning targets and success criteria as first thought. An unclear learning target may result in assessments that vary greatly between two teachers.

Most impressively, toward the end of the first semester, the teachers used their gradebooks to determine how the initial pacing guide and assessment plans worked out. Together, they reflected on their grading practices and, when their plans diverged from one another, discussed ways to improve alignment. Teams may consider asking themselves the following questions at this point.

- "Were we able to teach and assess all of our learning targets as we had initially planned? If not, why?"

- "Did all learning targets receive equal attention? If not, why?"

- "Were teachers or students ever confused with the language in learning targets, proficiency scales, or success criteria? If so, explain."

Commitment 4: Enable Teacher Autonomy

Proficiency-based grading aligns course expectations and outcomes but provides flexibility for teachers to also use different methods and materials to help students achieve the same outcome. This model helps support teachers' creativity while maximizing their expertise in a given content area. For example, while planning to teach painting composition skills in an introductory art class, one teacher may choose to use northern European baroque artists, while another may choose to use Mexican mural artists. The goal is for students to understand key ideas and concepts, but then apply the new learning to their own artwork. Throughout this process, teachers continue to center the communication around the class learning targets, but how students get there may vary from teacher to teacher. This flexibility allows fine arts teachers to study different artworks, styles, or movements without veering away from all students learning the essential skills.

Incubation: The Unexpected Questions of Proficiency-Based Grading in Fine Arts

As teachers progress toward proficiency-based grading implementation, they will uncover some wonderful questions that drive inquiry and implementation. During this stage, several adopted practices may be working, but teachers may pay a lot of attention to the items that seem to threaten work or that have provided new challenges. With so much new information, it can be hard not to worry that some challenges will never be overcome.

Challenges at this stage will require teachers to take a fresh look at their fine arts curriculum through the lens of essential skills that reoccur throughout the courses. This challenges them to look beyond the content knowledge of fine arts vocabulary, tools, techniques, and processes, and instead strategically develop an assessment plan that includes student opportunities to practice the essential skills and then self-reflect, engage in peer assessment, and consider teacher feedback. The following questions are representative of the incubation stage challenges that require patience and persistence.

Unexpected Question 1: What Is Assessment's Role in the Fine Arts Classroom?

For a teacher or team to adopt proficiency-based grading, there needs to be a clear understanding of its purpose. Proficiency-based grading truly supports assessment *for* learning (Stiggins, 2008), thus making most assessment events formative feedback. It is important for teachers to place emphasis not on their judgment, but rather on providing feedback about the course expectations. By providing feedback to students, teachers focus their attention on student learning and where each student is relative to the course expectations. Feedback processes should require the entire class (through group- or peer-reflection processes) to identify strengths, areas of growth, and action steps to improve performance.

While students are going through the formative assessment process, teachers collect evidence but do not grade. Formative assessment evidence serves discussion points and focuses the teacher's attention on what the class or each individual student needs to continuously improve. The goal with assessment is for all students to improve and meet course expectations by the time they leave.

Unexpected Question 2: What Fine Arts Assessment Events Are the Most Important to Grade?

When teachers use proficiency-based grading, all assessment events become formative, since grades are not determined until the semester's end, and the gradebook represents evidence of student learning that directly correlates to the communicated proficiency level. The feedback students receive during these events aligns directly with the scaled learning targets and success criteria. The teacher chooses events that will give the best evidence of proficiency and that provide the most direct, honest feedback using the fine arts department's common proficiency language. This allows teachers to be honest when a student is, for instance, approaching proficiency in spatial design during the first dance choreography assessment; the feedback has no grade implications.

Proficiency-based grading means teachers no longer need to collect every assignment or grade every activity. Rather, these performances demonstrate evidence of exceeding, meeting, or not meeting course expectations. Take opportunities for students to reflect and discuss their progress toward the learning, but avoid grading every event. In the visual arts classroom, teachers often collect multiple evidence points to assess students. A student may share multiple technique studies, sketches, and artworks in progress. In a piano or guitar class, a student might have a list of songs he or she must perform accurately. However, teachers should only select a few songs to formally assess and enter in the gradebook. De-emphasizing grading every single item further supports the learning environment.

Proficiency-based grading teachers, and especially singleton teachers, should organize a collection of exemplars to illustrate student achievement for a given target at each proficiency level. They should then share these exemplars with students to help them develop an understanding of the proficiency levels and artistic quality expectations. Figure 4.5 (page 104) shows exemplars for levels 1, 2, and 3. (Not all assessments allow the opportunity to exceed expectations.)

Teachers can easily hyperlink these exemplars to the online scaled rubrics that house visual examples in cloud-based storage, like Google Drive. I often recommend using multiple examples for each proficiency level. The multiple examples provide a variety of options to demonstrate to students there is not a single approach to the lesson. This bank of examples helps students develop their understanding of what is expected, while also helping singleton teachers with their scoring consistency since each exemplar will represent the benchmark for each target. The bank is a valuable resource year after year also because teachers can regularly include new student work and determine whether to remove past examples.

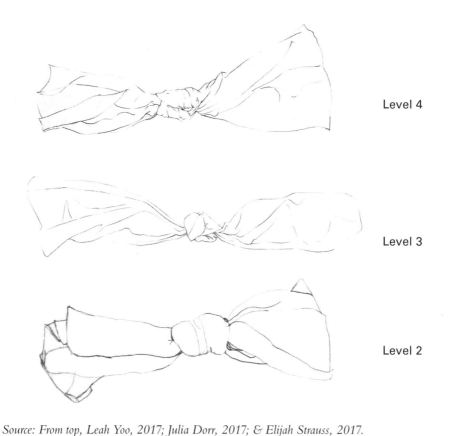

Level 4

Level 3

Level 2

Source: From top, Leah Yoo, 2017; Julia Dorr, 2017; & Elijah Strauss, 2017.

Figure 4.5: Student visual arts exemplars with proficiency levels.

Insight: The Essential Insights of Proficiency-Based Grading in Fine Arts

As teachers begin to move beyond the initial fears and roadblocks and gain insight, it is vitally important to take some time to look back on and appreciate how the team has passed some intimidating hurdles thus far. Teams should have a clear enough idea of how proficiency-based grading works, and they can play to its strengths as they teach and plan. They begin providing proficiency-based grading with more power instead of just trying to get their balance.

At this point, fine arts teachers might have the following insights: (1) proficiency-based grading can work effectively in large music ensemble classes, and (2) students must be involved in the assessment process.

Insight 1: Proficiency-Based Grading Can Work Effectively in Large Music Ensemble Classes

In traditional band, choir, or orchestra ensemble settings, class sizes can range well above fifty students. For the music teacher who has a full teaching load and multiple classes this size, it is challenging to collect evidence for each individual student. In addition, the primary outcome of a band, choir, or orchestra is to perform as a group, which may create added challenges for the ensemble music teacher.

This shift in practice will ensure teachers collect enough evidence to reflect each individual student's learning of the essential targets. At Stevenson, teachers were challenged to make proficiency-based grading work in the large ensemble classrooms, which led to evolving conversations around *how* and *when* to assess and grade students.

Prior to proficiency-based grading, teachers regularly gave students participation and attendance points. Students often received five points a day for a regular rehearsal. Since teachers viewed a concert as a summative assessment, they gave more points for just attending the concert. Students' grades never reflected their ability to perform a piece or play their instruments or demonstrate the skills or content from class. Rather, traditional grades in a music ensemble class are often based on participation—did the student attend class, follow directions, and engage throughout the class rehearsal? Using this model, the teachers recognized that students were either earning high grades that did not reflect their ability to perform musically, or receiving failing grades because of bad behavior or for not completing an assessment. The grade became a way to send an immediate message to students and families: they were failing. The failing grade then might impact a student's eligibility to participate in after-school co-curricular groups. I continue to see this problem in music ensemble classes that adhere to traditional grading.

This interesting dynamic forces music teachers to remain authentic to music instruction, feedback, and grading practices while they consider efficient strategies like the following.

- Provide sectional (small-group) instruction for students. Based on your school's current model, your ensemble program may occur weekly or require pulling students out of the ensemble based on their needs and related to the concert cycle. The goal is to provide direct, targeted individual *and* sectional feedback to these students based on their performance.

- Include social-emotional learning skills that directly relate to a musician's habits. These skills include the following.

    - *Self-awareness:* Realistic understanding and self-assessment of strengths and weaknesses of overall musicianship.

    - *Self-management:* Timely and dependable attendance at all required rehearsals and performances; responsible schedule management and timely conflict-resolution skills; decision-making skills; consistent practice and preparation; self-advocating and seeking help when needed; wearing proper attire to performances.

    - *Relationship skills:* Active, constructive participation in rehearsals and performances to encourage a positive, safe, collaborative, and productive ensemble culture; respect for self, peers, directors, instruments, and materials; advocacy, pride, and ownership of the music program; positive leadership traits and modeling; teaching reciprocally and learning with peers and teachers.

- Meet with each student at the beginning, middle, and end of the year. The goal is to personally connect with each student, establish individual music performance goals, and provide additional opportunities to assess and provide feedback around performance skills.

Use Small-Group Instruction

Changing to proficiency-based grading in the music ensemble classroom challenges conductor-centered teaching practices. Engaging students only from the podium and providing ensemble or large-group feedback are no longer acceptable practices in a proficiency-based grading classroom. Teachers must shift their focus to individual learning and collecting evidence of learning. Teacher Shaun Zimmerman says, "The biggest change I made this year was implementing a protocol for my guitar class playing tests. It's now a question of, Did you improve? rather than, How many notes did you miss?" (S. Zimmerman, personal communication, February 10, 2018).

Our team recognized that utilizing small-group instruction gave us moments to gather evidence of student performance around the essential learning targets. During sectional rehearsals, the teacher could document evidence while also establishing complex conversations with students or among students. These small-group instructional moments provided the teacher more time to give more individual feedback based on instrument groupings that was not always available during ensemble rehearsals due to considering the entire ensemble's performance goals. Skilled music teachers use verbal feedback to help students realize their current performance level, stepping students toward improvement per the scaled proficiency levels. Teachers can then use the rubric in figure 4.6 to evaluate students during individual playing assessments.

Changing to proficiency-based grading resulted in almost completely student-guided chamber rehearsals. The students know what the teacher expected. Students chose their music repertoire based on their group's instrumentation and performance ability. Students took the lead on running rehearsals, selecting the performance tempo, and developing moments to reflect on their performance and identify areas to improve. Teachers provided each group with a performance rubric at the beginning of the unit of study, plus an explanation of the expectations for work quality and for working together. Teachers even worked closely with students to model appropriate reflection questions to guide peer and self-assessment around the learning targets when working in small groups.

4—Refined Mastery	3—Proficiency	2—Approaches Proficiency	1—Still Developing
Learning Target: Tone Quality			
The student uses a characteristic tone and is consistent through the full range.	The student uses a characteristic tone and is controlled through most of the range.	The student only uses a characteristic tone in the middle range.	The student's fundamentals of using a characteristic tone production are in beginning stages.
Success Criteria: • Resonance • Control • Clarity • Focus • Consistency • Warmth			
Learning Target: Intonation			
The student achieves tuning in the full range with minimal noticeable problems in range extremes or with difficult intervals.	The student achieves tuning in the extended range with few noticeable problems in range extremes or with difficult intervals.	The student achieves tuning in the mid-range with more noticeable problems in range extremes or with difficult intervals.	The student has intonation errors throughout the range and with difficult intervals.
Success Criteria: • Realization of pitch accuracy • Adjustment according to pitch tendencies			

Figure 4.6: Band performance assessment target rubric example. continued ⟶

4—Refined Mastery	3—Proficiency	2—Approaches Proficiency	1—Still Developing
Learning Target: Rhythm			
The student performs accurate rhythm at the subdivided level when sight reading and playing prepared music at the notated tempo.	The student performs accurate rhythm at the subdivided level when playing prepared music at the notated tempo.	The student performs accurate rhythm at the subdivided level when playing prepared music at a reduced tempo.	The student performs accurate rhythm at the subdivided level when playing prepared music at a reduced tempo with intervention.

Success Criteria:

- Accuracy of note rest values, duration, pulse, steadiness
- Meter correctness

4—Refined Mastery	3—Proficiency	2—Approaches Proficiency	1—Still Developing
Learning Target: Note Accuracy			
The student performs accurate pitches when sight reading and playing prepared music at the notated tempo.	The student performs accurate pitches when playing prepared music at the notated tempo.	The student performs accurate pitches when playing prepared music at a reduced tempo.	The student performs accurate pitches when playing prepared music at a reduced tempo with intervention.

Success Criteria:

- Pitch
- Duration
- Notation

4—Refined Mastery	3—Proficiency	2—Approaches Proficiency	1—Still Developing
Learning Target: Articulation			
The student performs accurate articulations when sight reading and playing prepared music at the notated tempo.	The student performs accurate articulations when playing prepared music at the notated tempo.	The student performs accurate articulations when playing prepared music at a reduced tempo.	The student performs accurate articulations when playing prepared music at a reduced tempo with intervention.

Success Criteria:

- Attack and release

4—Refined Mastery	3—Proficiency	2—Approaches Proficiency	1—Still Developing
Learning Target: Technique			
The student demonstrates a controlled technique, and execution is consistent through the full range.	The student demonstrates a controlled technique, and execution is consistent through most of the range.	The student demonstrates a controlled technique, and execution is consistent through the middle range.	The student demonstrates the fundamentals of a controlled technique in beginning stages.

Success Criteria:

- Execution of instrument
- Performance elements

Learning Target: Musicianship

The student synthesizes musical elements in a performance when sight reading and in prepared music.	The student synthesizes musical elements in a performance in prepared music.	The student synthesizes musical elements in a performance in prepared music at a reduced tempo.	The student synthesizes musical elements in a performance in prepared music at a reduced tempo with intervention.

Success Criteria:

- Aural skills
- Artistic sensitivity

Teacher feedback:

Student reflection:

Source for standard: Illinois High School Association, n.d.

*Visit **go.SolutionTree.com/assessment** for a free reproducible version of this figure.*

Include SEL Skills

Proficiency-based grading separates academics from behaviors, but certain social-emotional learning (SEL) skills are necessary and teachable in the music classroom. These skills also transfer beyond the classroom, helping students prepare for life beyond school. Figure 4.7 (page 110) is an example of our orchestra's SEL rubric that scales each student's demonstration of self-awareness, self-management, and relationship skills. Find more SEL rubrics in this chapter's section called Core Belief 7: Behavior Can Be In or Out of the Grade (page 120).

Each of these broader SEL skills is in the context of the music classroom. For example, the teacher evaluates a student's self-awareness skills on his or her ability to self-assess the music performance accurately. That means the teacher must instruct students how to self-assess and to regularly practice this form of reflection. By establishing a culture of reflection that includes identifying strengths and growth areas, teachers allow music students to develop their ability to accurately assess themselves, their sections, and the ensemble. A student's self-management skills will reflect his or her ability to improve practice and the ensemble by setting goals. After reflecting, students write action plans to improve their musical performance or technique. Teachers then meet with students throughout the year to monitor their growth and progress toward their goals. Relationship skills are also important to a student's ability to engage, support, and collaborate with peers in the music classroom. These musician habits are why I believe these SEL targets become a factor in our fine arts students' overall proficiency, as well as in the students' final grade.

4—Refined Mastery	3—Proficiency	2—Approaches Proficiency	1—Still Developing
Learning Target: Self-Awareness			
I can identify strengths and areas for growth so much that it is a distinguishing trait.	I can identify strengths and areas for growth with relevant supporting evidence.	I can identify strengths and areas for growth with evidence.	I can attempt to identify strengths and areas for growth with prompting.
Success Criteria: • Self-perception • Areas of growth • Strengths			
Learning Target: Self-Management			
I can set and reach my musical goals so much that it is a distinguishing trait.	I can set and reach my musical goals.	I can take steps to set and reach my musical goals.	I can attempt to set and reach my musical goals with prompting.
Success Criteria: • Musical performance • Goals • Action steps • Perseverance • Revision			
Learning Target: Relationship Skills			
I can be an ensemble team member so much that it is a distinguishing trait.	I can be an ensemble team member who supports a collaborative, productive culture.	I can be an ensemble team member who sometimes independently collaborates and supports a productive culture.	I can attempt to be an ensemble team member with prompting.

Success Criteria:
• Engagement • Ensemble supportive, collaborative culture
Teacher feedback:
Student reflection:

Source for standard: National Coalition for Core Arts Standards, 2014.

Figure 4.7: Band social-emotional learning rubric example.

*Visit **go.SolutionTree.com/assessment** for a free reproducible version of this figure.*

Meet With Each Individual Student

Another strategy for making proficiency-based grading work in a large ensemble is focusing attention on the growth of individual students. Doing this caused our teachers to begin having individual meetings with students at the beginning of the year, midyear, and at the end of the year. While time-consuming for large classes, these brief three- to five-minute meetings require students to develop individual performance goals and allow teachers to do the following.

- Check in on every student.

- Individualize each student's focus based on that student's current performance.

- Build relationships with students.

- Gather evidence from one minute of the student performing, while reinforcing the proficiency-based grading assertion that all students grow.

- Establish the human connection that can get lost in the large ensemble class setting.

- Identify early on which students need the most help.

This approach can work with many large fine arts classes, including chorus and dance.

Insight 2: Students Must Be Involved in the Assessment Process

Proficiency-based grading identifies essential learning around cognitive and metacognitive skills that support students' ability to reflect, critique, and self-assess accurately. This can come in a number of methods: teacher led, self-reflection, or from peers. This preparation allows for very truthful feedback that students need to hear; however, proficiency-based grading does it in a way that does not punish students. In proficiency-based grading, it is OK for a student to not yet have mastered a skill. The attitude is that all students will have time to practice and improve their skills.

Helping students improve their ability to self-reflect or assess their work is crucial to a proficiency-based classroom. In the fine arts, this improvement also helps develop students' aesthetics and artistic eye. In proficiency-based grading, it all begins with the teacher helping students understand and use the learning targets when they write and talk about the arts. In addition, following each assessment event, proficiency-based grading teachers can ask students to self-assess, as in the example in figure 4.8.

Standard: Technique			
Skill: Use of media or tools			
4—Refined Mastery	**3—Proficiency**	**2—Approaches Proficiency**	**1—Still Developing**
I show controlled and advanced media and tools use through the inclusion of subtle changes or intricate details.	I show controlled and appropriate media and tools use.	I show controlled use of media and tools.	I show media and tools use.
Technique for this assessment event: Paint application			
How is your painting application exceeding, meeting, approaching, or not meeting expectations? What steps did you need to take so that your painting demonstrates your ability to meet or exceed standards?			

Source for standard: College Board, 2018; National Coalition for Core Arts Standards, 2014.

Figure 4.8: Painting class self-reflection example.

Visit go.SolutionTree.com/assessment for a free reproducible version of this figure.

In the fine arts proficiency-based grading classroom, I have observed many successful reflection activities focused on one target that teachers can implement quickly, or more structured, extensive activities that address a multitude of targets and use entire class periods. Reflection time can help break the ice at the beginning of the lesson, enable the student to take a moment in the middle of a rehearsal, consolidate the learning for the day's lesson, or follow an extensive performance assessment.

At the same time, the teacher should be assessing the students. This provides an opportunity for teachers to examine the evidence of the students' self-assessment score with their score. When the teacher and student meet to discuss the assessment event, they discuss where their assessments align and differ, allowing for complex conversations around not only the areas where the students are meeting or exceeding standards but also areas of improvement. The conversations allow students to identify the steps they must take to improve their skills, while also helping them improve their ability to assess themselves and others accurately compared to the expectations of the class and teacher. As students develop their ability to reflect and assess their work, their peers' work, or that of professionals, the goal is also for their artistic eyes or ears to grow and develop artistically.

As students become more familiar with the learning targets, providing exemplars and having them work together to identify what proficiency score the piece would receive is helpful to improve the students' ability to score accurately. Exemplars demonstrating the proficiency levels help students analyze and discuss the work with teachers and each other.

Evaluation: The Key Questions of Proficiency-Based Grading in Fine Arts

Implementation's beginning stages bring a perspective of evaluation. While professional growth never takes one path, reaching this point allows teams to set a goal of reaching regular practice and to confidently look into ways that the system impacts feedback and grading.

Evaluation can lead fine arts teachers to ask the following key questions: (1) "How do teams ensure inter-rater reliability?" (2) "How do fine arts teachers change the way they talk to students about grades?" (3) "Is fine arts teacher feedback helping students grow?" and (4) "How do fine arts teachers have meaningful conversations around learning?"

Key Question 1: How Do Teams Ensure Inter-Rater Reliability?

When preparing to use proficiency-based grading at this stage, teams of teachers must commit to planning and using assessments in a like manner. Commitment 3 (page 101) specific to fine arts teachers specifies that teachers must have a common language and clear understanding for each scaled target and success criteria before beginning instruction. Teacher teams must plan to assess students at similar times throughout the course and ensure their assessment practices are reliable. When assessment timing and reliability are not thoughtfully planned, problems often will arise from students and parents recognizing grading concerns and inequities from one teacher to another.

Teachers at this stage should make it a goal to work together to score evidence accurately and consistently. Calibrate scoring and improve inter-rater reliability during collaborative team meetings, through peer observations, or during designated professional development time. Teachers who engage in peer observation commit to observing their colleagues as they teach and assess students. This may occur by visiting a class during the teacher's planning time or with support from the school administration to support release time from teaching by hiring a substitute. During peer observation, the observer should have access to the scaled learning targets or rubric, and pay particular attention to the teacher's language and feedback. Teachers meet afterward and reflect on these observations, determining whether their language, feedback, and scoring evaluations align to each other's. It is essential for teams to build in time to ensure that teachers score similarly.

When calibrating team scoring, do the following.

1.   Review the scaled learning targets and success criteria.

2.   Determine the assessment events that will provide evidence.

3.   Discuss which specific learning targets to evaluate.

Assessment will look different depending on the evidence of learning. In the visual arts, teachers may review a portfolio of artwork or individual artwork together. In the performing arts (such as dance, theater, and music), teachers may review video performances, observe individual performances, or assess concerts or recitals together.

These activities ensure aligned scoring among all teachers. For example, if one teacher scores a learning target as 2 (approaching expectations), colleagues must score the learning target the same way. Teachers need to check their vocabulary to ensure they use accurate success criteria and alignment in their feedback. On occasions when teachers see different qualities in the work or bring in personal biases, it is crucial for the team to address them together. When teachers score the learning target differently, the team must dialogue to explain the nature of the decisions. These discussions can help clarify expectations and remove personal biases when teachers grade.

In my school, there have been numerous times when calibrated scoring has helped in difficult situations with students, parents, and teachers. When students disagree with feedback and evaluation of an assessment event, teachers can take the student's performance evidence and review it with a colleague, who will evaluate it again and share his or her professional judgment with the school administrators, students, or parents. We had an experience when the teacher happened to be sick during final performance assessments. Luckily, we were able to have colleagues substitute for this sick teacher and complete all of the class performance assessments during finals. We video-recorded all performances to double-check the colleagues' scores, but it was immediately clear that all scores were aligned; the scores were identical. If scores are not aligned—if students score different proficiency levels on the same assessment—teachers discuss their perspectives on why they chose to score the work as they did. The conversations allow teachers to understand the nuances of the proficiency scales and correct misconceptions about their scoring practices. The end result is inter-score reliability, benefitting students, and strengthened collaboration among team members.

Key Question 2: How Do Fine Arts Teachers Change the Way They Talk to Students About Grades?

Change is hard for most people, and it is human nature to resort to past practices. When we changed from century-old grading practices to proficiency-based grading, we found this to be true. Teachers were resorting to past terminology consistent with traditional grading as they transitioned into proficiency-based grading. For example, teachers would often accidentally describe proficiency scores as *grades*. This caused some initial confusion for students, who would then want to associate the numbers representing levels of proficiencies with letter grades. This misconception, for example, was that a 4 equates to an A letter grade, a 3 equates to a B letter grade, and a 2 equates to a C letter grade. However, in proficiency-based grading, the assessment scores of 4, 3, 2, and 1 do not equate or align to letter grades. Rather, the numbers represent the descriptive performance level represented by the student evidence.

It is natural for students to want to take the conversation toward grades, but teachers had to try to break this grades culture. Rather than associating a grade with each assessment event, teachers had to commit to using the words aligned with each proficiency level. For example, when a student performance of sight reading in choir earned a score of 2, the vocal teacher clarified that the student's performance was *approaching the standard* and that this one performance demonstrated the student was not proficient yet. The teacher reviewed the scaled learning target and pointed out that the student performed a few notes inaccurately and the tempo was too fast at times. The teacher then offered suggestions to improve, such as continuing practicing scales and studying the notes, rhythms, and dynamic changes. The teacher also asked the student to reflect on his or her performance and identify strategies to continue improving performance and sight reading ability. At this point, the teacher sometimes documented the 2 in the gradebook as evidence, or used this event as practice for sight reading and let the student reperform later.

Teachers need to be careful that scores (numbers) do not become the focus of feedback. The goal is to help students understand that collected evidence around a learning target results in the number, which is not a grade but, rather, a numeric representation of the evidence associated with a written description (usually presented as a rubric). The script for feedback must also include the score descriptor language of *exceeding*, *meeting*, *approaching*, or *not meeting* standards.

Key Question 3: Is Fine Arts Teacher Feedback Helping Students Grow?

Ideally, students will begin using standards and learning target language once proficiency-based grading is established. Rarely should students ask how they can get a few more points to earn an A. Rather, a student might ask, "Can I come in before school so we can talk about how I can improve my composition?" Since grades are undetermined until the end of the semester, teachers also recognize when students take more artistic risks, which helps create stronger artistic products.

Receiving feedback—via a scored rubric, written notes, or verbal feedback—and additional time to reperform instills a culture of continuous improvement, which gives students the opportunity to take the feedback and continue practicing the skill. By applying the feedback, students take ownership to improve their craft and grow in the fine arts.

Key Question 4: How Do Fine Arts Teachers Have Meaningful Conversations Around Learning?

Grades seem to always be the primary focus for students and parents in the traditional grading environment. Regardless of how they perform, there always seems to be a handful of students who want to know how they could accumulate a few additional points to improve their grade. Rarely are students approaching the teacher to discuss improving their learning and performance of the art form.

When my school moved to proficiency-based grading, students changed their focus to the learning outcomes. Most students no longer talked about grades, points, or extra credit; the conversations shifted to students wanting to improve their performance. For example, when the teacher evaluates a dance student as *approaching standards* in execution, the student and teacher can discuss the corresponding success criteria that address alignment, posture, connectivity, clarity of movement, and attention to correction and detail. Using proficiency-based grading, teachers and students reflect that the end of grading periods are not as stressful anymore and make for a more relaxed learning environment. Teachers and students focus on conversations about how to improve, and the classroom environment is one of support and growth.

Elaboration: The Core Beliefs of Proficiency-Based Grading in Fine Arts

Teachers at the elaboration phase of implementation have reached a mature and clear perspective of using a proficiency-based grading system. They have discovered that the system does not push them out of valued projects, simulations, or other assessments and activities they know help students learn; instead, they see there is depth to be gained from such work, with an underlying and clear focus on skills. With their comfort in this system, teachers are resources for their colleagues and on the cutting edge for new ways to provide more support for and collaboration with their students.

Teachers who successfully implement proficiency-based grading adhere to all seven of the core beliefs explained in chapter 1 (page 9): (1) growth is a central concept, (2) reperformance is essential, (3) building students' reflection abilities is essential, (4) homework has a role, (5) communication with parents and the community is key, (6) culminating experiences like final exams have a different purpose, and (7) behavior can be in or out of the grade. The following sections, which reflect the core beliefs' original numbering, explore the core beliefs that fine arts teachers in particular should never lose sight of.

Core Belief 2: Reperformance Is Essential

Reperformance is essential to learning in the fine arts. As students engage in the artistic processes, they learn that everyone can continue to improve his or her artistic skills through deliberate practice and reflection. Structured or unstructured activities allow students to set goals to improve their performance and achieve their goals over time by continuing to practice and reperform. The process of practice and multiple performances is authentic to how fine artists work in the professional industry, and must continue to be reflected in fine arts classrooms.

In a proficiency-based grading system, fine arts teachers must embrace the essential mindset that it is their job to ensure all students learn and it is their responsibility to collect evidence of student learning. All students must have opportunities for reperformance. Reperformance allows students to improve their performance and potentially their scores in the gradebook. In the art classroom, teachers structure class critiques when art projects are due. Following the critiques, students take teacher and peer feedback and resubmit their artwork after a set time. In music ensemble classes, students reperform after an individual test. In dance classes, students reperform choreography after receiving assessment scores.

You can schedule time for reperformance during the regular schedule or establish before- or after-school hours. Keep in mind each student's individual needs for extended time when considering reperformance. In the performing arts, students may get a few more days to rehearse and refine their technique. In the visual arts, students may need even more time and access to tools and equipment to enhance unfinished aspects of the artwork following critique activities.

When teachers offer fine arts students opportunities to retake or reperform, the extension is not open-ended. In other words, students cannot reperform their assessment whenever they choose at whatever time of the year they feel ready. Rather, teachers establish clear time lines when the reassessments can take place or the window to reperform closes. Teachers do not lower assessment scores when a student is late or needs additional time. If the reassessment score improves, teachers enter the new evidence. If the student chooses not to take the opportunity to reperform, then the initial assessment evidence stays in place. For example, teachers may allow students to rework their artworks after the final critique. Teachers may also allow students who are below standard in technique to perform their final acting scene prior to the end of the grading term. By allowing struggling learners an additional assessment opportunity, teachers meet students where they are and then provide additional support and time as needed for them to be successful.

Teachers embrace reperformance because they know that not all students learn at the same rate. Teachers embrace reperformance because they know students improve their learning after receiving direct and honest feedback that focuses on the essential learning targets. While teachers should offer reperformance to all students, our teachers found that students who accept the option tend to be the ones not meeting expectations. The added reperformance supports response to intervention Tier 1 strategies, including implementing team assessment and ensuring access to grade-level curriculum (Buffum, Mattos, & Malone, 2018). Further, reperformance supports efforts to ensure all students can learn and be successful in the arts.

Core Belief 4: Homework Has a Role

Students are expected to complete classwork outside the fine arts proficiency-based grading classroom. The difference is, rather than every assignment being worth a set number of points and traditionally graded, homework in a proficiency-based grading system is viewed as an essential component to the artistic process, and teachers may or may not collect evidence for evaluation. Students who do not do the outside classwork often struggle to achieve the assessment. As a result, students begin to recognize the value of doing the outside work, so they have higher levels of achievement in the classroom.

In some cases, fine arts homework is a way for teachers to make sure students are rehearsing their choreography, monologues, or music. It might include students continuing to work on their art projects, if they need additional time to stay on pace with the class. In that case, if students do not rehearse or practice, their learning evidence often is below expectations. When teachers meet with these students to discuss their strengths and areas of growth, they often identify outside class rehearsal or practice as an area of growth and improvement.

In other cases, fine arts homework is an essential component in the artistic process, and evidence of this homework aligns closely to the class learning targets. For example, in an art classroom, the teacher may require students to complete outside research, plans, and sketches for artwork. If students do not complete these learning activities, it is difficult for them to move forward in the class. These components are reflected in the time-management learning target—*I engage in the artistic process and manage my time as an artist*—that aligns to artists' habits.

Core Belief 5: Communication With Parents and the Community Is Key

Interestingly enough, I found that parent phone calls regarding concerns about grades have significantly decreased since teachers moved to proficiency-based grading. In the past, a parent might contact me because it was summer break or he or she was displeased with the initial communications with the teacher. In these situations, I talked to the teacher to make sure I understood the student and his or her assessment performance. Then, I had a follow-up conversation that sometimes led to a meeting with the student, parents, and teacher. The teacher and I would clarify the assessment task and criteria, explain our observations and the student's performance evidence, and then explain how it translated to some sort of point value and a grade. Often these conversations were difficult, and parents perceived the grading as subjective or, worse case, as biased against their child.

Since moving to proficiency-based grading, teachers can open up the gradebook, and the alignment of evidence to the learning targets is clear; this was always difficult to describe to parents when opening a traditional point system gradebook. The narrative in the proficiency-based gradebook for the individual student is clearly laid out and to the teacher can clarify what the student is succeeding in, where the student is struggling, and what the student needs to do to meet expectations. In proficiency-based grading, the focus on learning becomes central to instruction and feedback, and in the gradebook, it is just as crystal clear. The evidence there helps parents better understand their child's performance and, when needed, helps school support staff to address questions about the student!

To illustrate the importance of communication, the following is an email exchange I had with a parent one summer.

> Dear Mr. Grice,
>
> I was hoping to speak to you about my daughter's grade for acting. According to your school's grading system, she received almost all 3s during the semester and so it's not clear why she received a B for the class. I don't want to wait until the fall to get this resolved.
>
> Thank you, Mr. Smith

> Hello Mr. Smith.
>
> In my quick analysis of your daughter's final grade . . . I see she earned a proficient (3) on the standards of writing and ensemble skills. She earned an approaching standard (2) in the standard of performance. This equates to a final score of 3–3–2 in the academic standards of acting 1 and earns a B for the semester. A brief proficiency-based grading reference follows.
>
> > A: Score of 3 or 4 in all the academic standards
> >
> > B: Score of 2 in any one of the academic standards
> >
> > C: Score of 2 in more than one academic standard
> >
> > D: Score of 1 in any one of the academic standards
> >
> > F: Score of 1 in more than one academic standard
>
> I have contacted your daughter's teacher and hope to hear from her soon. She will be able to offer any additional evidence to support this grade. Feel free to reach out to me if you have any questions or would like to discuss this further. I will follow up once I hear back from the teacher.
>
> Sincerely, Mr. Grice

The proficiency-based gradebook becomes a collection of evidence that reflects patterns of student learning over time. The gradebook clearly identifies the skills students meet or exceed standards on or those they are approaching or not meeting. This gradebook clarity allows teachers, parents, school administrators, and interventionists to have evidence access to support learners.

Core Belief 7: Behavior Can Be In or Out of the Grade

While some argue that SEL and Collaborative for Academic, Social, and Emotional Learning (CASEL; 2017) behaviors should be excluded from students' grades, I believe these essential life skills align with the habits of artists and fine arts learning. These behaviors can include self-awareness, decision making, and social awareness as it relates to the context of fine artists' habits. This includes working effectively with others in the ensemble, accepting constructive criticism, and empathizing with others through character and script analysis. As a result, fine arts teachers should take extensive steps to better understand SEL skills and explicit strategies to embed SEL in their curriculum, instruction, and assessment.

At Stevenson, teachers have spent years developing a deeper understanding of SEL and how to explicitly teach these skills in the classroom. They have observed SEL behaviors to see what skill development should look and sound like. The fine arts faculty took one additional step—to discuss what these skills look and sound like in fine arts classes. Not surprisingly, this process made it very easy to identify aspects of SEL that relate to classroom curricula and instruction. SEL closely aligns to what they teach and is crucial to building positive learning environments.

Stevenson curricular teams developed learning targets based on the CASEL (2009) SEL competencies. These learning targets included success criteria to help ensure the community of the teams' understanding and expectation of aligned targets. Figure 4.9 is an example of the SEL target *I exchange accurate and constructive art criticism* (Illinois State Board of Education, n.d., & CASEL, 2017).

Learning Target: Criticism			
4—Refined Mastery	**3—Proficiency**	**2—Approaches Proficiency**	**1—Still Developing**
I can expertly engage in the exchange of accurate and constructive criticism.	I can engage in the exchange of accurate and constructive criticism.	I can engage in the exchange of constructive criticism.	I can engage in the exchange of criticism.
Success Criteria: • Delivering and receiving • Description, analysis, interpretation, and evaluation • Claim and evidence			

Source for standard: Illinois State Board of Education, n.d., & Collaborative for Academic, Social, and Emotional Learning, 2017.

Figure 4.9: Fine arts SEL target.

Figure 4.10 is a rubric for SEL in dance classes.

	Interpersonal Skill: Social Awareness and Relationships	Intrapersonal Skills: Self-Management	Responsible Decision Making
4	I demonstrate respect for all individuals and movement diversity, and encourage others to do so as well.	I implement specific action steps to achieve my personal and academic goals.	I make responsible decisions and influence others to do the same.
3	I demonstrate respect for all individuals and movement diversity.	I demonstrate skills related to achieving personal and academic goals.	I make responsible decisions.
2	I demonstrate respect for most people regardless of their differences.	I demonstrate skills related to achieving personal and academic goals with guidance.	I make responsible decisions with guidance.
1	I demonstrate respect only for people like me.	I need help identifying personal and academic goals.	I can articulate the steps necessary to make a decision.
Success Criteria			
	• I respectfully interact in class. • I respectfully discuss and pose questions to all class members. • I am open to and always invite and welcome feedback from the teacher and others. • I easily transition from small- to large-group activities. • I adapt to different friend groups. • I use language appropriate for addressing the person or group (adults versus students).	• I am completely prepared and have obviously rehearsed for class or a performance. • I consistently demonstrate hard work and diligence. • I make changes into appropriate dance attire every day, as outlined in the course description. • I exemplify initiative.	• I contribute effort. • I support the efforts of others in the class or group. • I exhibit a positive attitude about class, tasks, and others. • I actively look for and suggest solutions to problems.

Source for standard: Illinois State Board of Education, n.d., & Collaborative for Academic, Social, and Emotional Learning, 2017.

Figure 4.10: Dance SEL rubric example.

*Visit **go.SolutionTree.com/assessment** for a free reproducible version of this figure.*

In the fine arts classrooms, Stevenson teachers have embraced proficiency-based grading. They recognize the positive impact it has on students, instruction, and the division, but also acknowledge the collaborative work it takes to alter fixed mindsets and long-established grading practices.

Key Points

To ensure full understanding, review the following key points from this chapter.

- The language of learning targets become a central component of the class when using proficiency-based grading effectively. Teachers clearly identify the skills and quality of performance students are expected to learn and achieve. The learning targets become part of the day-to-day instruction, as teachers frame lessons, engage students in activities, and reflect on learning. Students begin to immediately use the class's learning target language to seek feedback and reflect on their performance too.

- A proficiency-based grading classroom exemplifies a culture of feedback to improve learning. Teachers and students are constantly reflecting on their current state of performance in relation to expectations of the class. Teacher, peer, and self-assessments are embedded in almost all facets of the classroom, which places an emphasis on identifying areas of strengths and growth. Teachers facilitate discussions that allow students to establish action plans to improve their learning in any area necessary. The process of learning and opportunities for reperformance support teachers' efforts for all students to learn and achieve the essential course outcomes. Individual student growth and learning take precedent over teachers assigning grades.

- The proficiency-based gradebook focuses on the essential learning of the class and communicates student progress toward learning targets. The gradebook informs students, parents, and support staff how each student is progressing and growing over time. Proficiency-based grading improves the traditional grading system, which lacks clarity and penalizes students.

Darshan M. Jain is director of mathematics and computer science at Adlai E. Stevenson High School in Lincolnshire, Illinois. Darshan began his professional career as a mechanical engineer in the manufacturing and machine design industries where he helped support design, develop process, and manage change.

Darshan's passion and commitment to students' learning of mathematics was inspired through work with the University of Illinois at Chicago's Hispanic Mathematics, Science and Engineering Initiative. Supporting students' learning in mathematics through a constructivist, co-learning, and collaborative approach led to a defining career change.

As a mathematics teacher, Darshan has worked with students through an array of courses and has also served as a curriculum team leader and mathematics team coach. Darshan has been honored with the 2010 Golden Apple Award for Excellence in Teaching, 2011 National Board for Professional Teaching Standards recognition, and a 2013 Presidential Award for Excellence in Mathematics and Science Teaching.

In his current role, Darshan works to transition curricular teams in adopting state standards and articulating curriculum centered on effective and high-leverage pedagogy and assessment. Darshan has extensive experience in developing and leading adult professional learning and speaks at various local, state, and national professional organizations including the Illinois Council of Teachers of Mathematics, National Council of Teachers of Mathematics, and National Council of Supervisors of Mathematics. He has served on NCTM's Research Agenda Committee as well as served as committee chair for Student Exploration in Mathematics. Darshan has been featured on pbslearningmedia.org for his leadership in supporting problem solving and student perseverance in learning mathematics.

Darshan earned a bachelor's of science degree in mechanical engineering and master of science in teaching secondary mathematics education from the University of Illinois at Chicago. He earned a master of arts in educational leadership and is currently pursuing a doctorate in education policy, organization, and leadership. Darshan can be reached at djain@d125.org and djainm7712@gmail.com.

To learn more about Darshan's work, follow @djain2718 on Twitter.

To book Darshan M. Jain for professional development, contact pd@SolutionTree .com.

Chapter 5

Implementing Proficiency-Based Grading in Mathematics

Darshan M. Jain

> An excellent mathematics program ensures that assessment
> is an integral part of instruction.
>   —*National Council of Teachers of Mathematics*

Mathematics education leaders should expect and invite questions and concerns around how shifting to proficiency-based grading may impact teaching practices or what the value of descriptive feedback in a hard science like mathematics may be. For teachers, proficiency-based grading provides professional growth for articulating, monitoring, and supporting the mathematics learning. For students, proficiency-based grading provides avenues for growth as reflective, self-directed mathematics learners.

As teachers develop a deeper rationale for the benefits of proficiency-based grading, they will address thoughtful concerns and develop expertise, and innovation will surface. For example, teacher Eva Lange says:

> Teaching mathematics with proficiency-based grading has allowed me
> to make better connections in and outside the classroom. Not only can
> my students readily self-reflect, identify areas for growth, and imple-
> ment strategies for improvement; I too am better able to identify these

in individual students. This has allowed me to help students continually
grow as learners in and out of the classroom. As a teacher I have grown.
(E. Lange, personal communication, May 30, 2018)

This chapter explains the reasons to implement proficiency-based grading in
mathematics courses through five phases: (1) preparation, (2) incubation, (3) insight,
(4) evaluation, and (5) elaboration (Csikszentmihalyi, 1990).

Reasons to Implement Proficiency-Based Grading in Mathematics

When considering proficiency-based grading in a mathematics classroom, teachers often worry about changes that would undercut values they hold around teaching. A common concern is how aligning class work, homework, or assessments
to learning targets may reduce students' independence in creatively approaching
mathematics problems. A related concern is balancing the desire to clearly communicate specific growth areas at the cost of oversimplifying mathematics problems.
It is common for teachers to wonder how their curriculum rigor changes or how
to provide specific feedback when students can approach problems in so many
different ways. Concerns around how this may affect mathematics instruction,
content, and grading workload are common and something teachers can address. As
teachers learn about this grading and feedback method (which sounds valuable, but
so unfamiliar), they begin to understand the deeper rationale—the *why*—behind
proficiency-based grading, and their concerns diminish.

The following sections address how proficiency-based grading supports the process of learning and doing mathematics, helps teachers communicate learning targets and proficiency expectations in mathematics, helps students understand these
mathematics learning targets, helps interventionists support mathematical skill
transferal, supports growth mindset and resilience while learning mathematics,
and supports social-emotional competency integration into mathematics planning
and teaching.

Proficiency-Based Grading Supports the Process of Learning and Doing Mathematics

Mathematics teachers have long bemoaned the mile-wide and inch-deep curricular demands of many school programs. CCSS and subsequent state standards
brought the opportunity for addressing these decades-long laments. These standards clarify essential learning around number and quantity, algebra, functions,
modeling, geometry, and statistics and probability—the *what* of mathematics
(NGA & CCSSO, 2010b). In addition, the CCSS distill the essential transferable

skills of learning and doing mathematics—the *how*—into the eight Standards for Mathematical Practice (NGA & CCSSO, 2010b).

1. Make sense of problems and persevere in solving them.

2. Reason abstractly and quantitatively.

3. Construct viable arguments and critique the reasoning of others.

4. Model with mathematics.

5. Use appropriate tools strategically.

6. Attend to precision.

7. Look for and make use of structure.

8. Look for and express regularity in repeated reasoning.

When teachers organize course expectation and course standards around *how to learn* mathematics, there is greater clarity and focus on communicating what areas need further growth and what areas continue to be strong (and ready for extension). In addition, since transferable skills transcend coursework, students develop *ways of learning* (in addition to the content or the *what* of learning). This is essential in developing an efficacious mindset in students. The purpose of teaching mathematics is to help students develop the overarching (or transferable) skills of learning and performing mathematics, just as the goals of science, communication arts, and the languages are to develop ways to learn and act as scientists, writers, and linguists.

Students must experience mathematics as a cohesive multiyear narrative, and they can develop tools to deepen their learning in a sequence of courses across a mathematics program. However, teachers must purposefully plan and explicitly teach students' experiences with overarching practices. These Mathematical Practices—or transferable skills—bring cohesion to multiyear coursework. It is the Mathematical Practices that bring familiarity in the processes of mathematics to unfamiliar contexts.

For instance, consider a student who has already experienced transformations applied to quadratics. In this, you can view transformations through recognizing structure (Mathematics Practice 7). When learning focuses on applying transformations (through the use of structure) as the transferable skill, then students are more prepared for a change in context to transformations applied to higher-order polynomials. Here, despite the significant complexity of a quintic function, the transferable skill applied in exploring quadratic transformations still applies. As the student moves to advanced coursework, transformations of transcendental functions require the same essential transferable skill. In this, the primary focus shifts from a study of specific functions (polynomials, exponentials, trigonometric, and so on) to a study of general transformations and structure. The context change offers opportunities to apply the transferable skills in increasingly complex explorations.

Proficiency-based grading shifts students' perspectives on the purpose of learning from one of acquiring daily granular knowledge to also acquiring the discipline's broad transferable skills. When grading communicates students' proficiencies around *what* and *how* to learn, teachers support students' acumen in transferring those skills to unfamiliar contexts.

Proficiency-Based Grading Helps Teachers Communicate Learning Targets and Proficiency Expectations in Mathematics

Most mathematics teachers organize gradebooks around measures of learning (events) rather than directly reporting on the learning itself (outcomes). For example, events such as homework, quizzes, and tests are commonly reported in gradebooks (and there may be other fields that report participation, extra credit, or projects). Consider a score of 75 (of 100) on any of these types of events. At most, parents can surmise that their child received 75 of 100 available points on a specific event; they cannot ascertain their child's strengths or areas for further growth. Furthermore, a 75 of 100 does not indicate performance against a standard. That is, was the expectation that the student earn the full 100 available points, or would 85 of the 100 also have indicated mastery? Is it possible that, even if a student earned 90 points, the 10 remaining were of such consequence that they would signal a need for remediation?

This is akin to a mechanic sharing that the overall courtesy check on your vehicle resulted in 75 of 100. You would rightfully wonder if the 25 uncredited points were due to a broken headlight or degraded brakes. This report would lead most people to believe the car expert was not communicating fully or—more detrimentally—not an expert at all. This should never be the case about students' learning. Teachers are the learning experts who are best positioned to communicate students' progress toward proficiency. Their reporting should reflect their expertise, which is grounded in knowledge of each student's learning and appropriate next steps. For example, just as a customer must prioritize degraded brakes over headlights, parents can, with a teacher's help, appropriately guide and prioritize their child's effort toward the graphical effects of vertical scaling versus procedures computing and plotting the y-intercept. This is not to say that they ignore the second outcome; they simply reprioritize it.

When viewing a semester's worth of entries, typical gradebooks report on how well students perform on *types of assessments* rather than on *proficiencies of learning*. The following poignant experience comes to mind. A parent observing her child's struggle in English and mathematics asks both teachers, "Why is Chloe struggling in class?"

After reviewing the gradebook, the mathematics teacher responds this way.

> I see that Chloe has been struggling on tests; she has turned in homework and her quizzes show proficiency. She needs to do better on tests in order to improve her grade.

The English teacher responds this way.

> In terms of her listening and speaking work in class, Chloe has grown in all areas. Occasionally she has a dip in her response skills, summarizing what previous speakers have said, or connecting her ideas to previous ideas. She tends to begin her contributions with "Also . . ." or "I agree or disagree and . . . ." We try to get students to focus on less superficial ways to show they have been listening to each other by quickly summarizing what they heard from another person: "I heard you say . . . . This is different from how I thought the narrator foreshadowed the climax. What you said reminded me of how John explained . . . ."
>
> In all, to really master all her targets for this semester (which would equate to an A), Chloe will need to focus on demonstrating consistency with her response skills in the upcoming weeks. She can also work on articulating a theme in reading and supporting it through close analysis of the text.

From both a student's and parents' perspective, the first reply, while accurate, does not provide specific action or focus. That is, how is Chloe to improve performance on tests (assessment events) relative to her performance on quizzes? What learning must she improve *in order to* improve her test score? This reporting focuses attention toward the instrument that measures learning (assessments) rather than the evidence of learning (specific target outcomes).

The English teacher's response is descriptive and action oriented. This is well within the mathematics teachers' and program acumen. Consider the actions that Chloe (or her mother) might take if the response were presented as follows.

> In terms of her work around mathematical representations, Chloe is progressing well, except she struggles when writing equations given a graph. Specifically, she needs to focus on the key features of the graph. She often interchanges vertical and horizontal translations. We are currently practicing these with polynomial functions, but we will continue to use this all year and in years to come. She can practice this on homework assignment three and also on class notes from days three and four. After Chloe practices, she can see me and I will provide feedback with a few problems I create for her.

For students to develop as efficacious learners, they must receive and understand feedback around the specific outcomes they are striving to meet. The specificity of mathematics is predisposed to this type of clarity in learning outcomes! Proficiency-based grading draws teachers to communicate progress around proficiencies rather than assessment types.

Proficiency-Based Grading Helps Students Understand Mathematics Learning Targets

In mathematics, the term *learning target* often specifies the planned, taught academic content. In addition, it is common to describe development of procedural or algorithmic processes as *mathematical skills*. *Success criteria* describes the granular academic content that is developed in class. In addition, *skills* describes enduring learning through the development of transferable skills. In this context, *transferable skills* are the eight Standards for Mathematical Practice. As an example, consider an introductory lesson focused on quadrilaterals. The success criteria would be the specific properties or definition that each quadrilateral holds. A possible learning target may be *Apply geometric relationships algebraically.*

Finally, the transferable skills that students are developing may be creating mathematical representations. Taken as a whole, fluency with the success criteria supports students' access to the intended learning target. Finally, the act of connecting algebraic and geometric relationships helps students develop the transferable skill of creating mathematical representations working fluidly between contextualized and decontextualized presentations. As the assessment and grading fields have matured, a *learning target* has become understood as a broader skill or transferable learning. At Stevenson, our teacher teams have adopted the same understanding, though generally, mathematics teachers equate learning targets with what we call *success criteria* at Stevenson. You may notice that distinction in this chapter.

Proficiency-based grading can help students identify the specific mathematics learning intended in class. Students can develop this skill when their teachers explicitly identify the day's work and how it relates to the unit's or course's broader goals. In addition, when teachers use the language of proficiency-based grading, students begin to understand the relationship between success criteria, learning targets, and skills and their function in developing proficiency. Consider the difference between "Today, we will work with quadrilaterals" and the following.

> Today, we will explore relationships between the sides and diagonals of quadrilaterals and their internal angles. Our purpose is to create a list of properties that each quadrilateral holds; these are your success criteria. You will use this regularly to set up problems to solve algebraically. Our focus

> will be on writing geometric relationships using algebra. As you work, be aware of the problem statements. What information do you need? What is extraneous? When will you need to redraw figures? We are continuing to strengthen your skills in building mathematical representations. Notice today how we work on concrete problems and then generalize them.

While both statements convey the day's focus, the latter positions the student as an active learner rather than as a passive recipient of teaching. With proficiency-based grading, teachers increasingly develop, communicate, and incorporate success criteria, learning targets, and skills into instructional planning and classroom practices. With clear learning outcomes, students are more capable of identifying a day's work and naming specific areas of struggle. The teacher may verbally state outcomes in class (as shared earlier), share them visually on the board, write them on students' daily work, or ask students to identify the outcomes when the lessons are explorative or discovery based.

Proficiency-based grading's clarity about the specific, planned learning helps students monitor and track the work they are responsible for. This is most observable as students seek help from teachers or from paraprofessional staff. In my experience, it is rare to hear students say, "I don't understand anything today." Rather, more often, students say, "I don't understand this target" or "I don't understand when to redraw figures or find corresponding side relationships."

At the heart of proficiency-based grading is its potential to develop efficacious learners. For students to develop as independent learners, they must identify what they seek to improve on, further explore, or strengthen. Making the planned learning outcomes explicit helps students know what they know and do not know, and then grow their learning.

Proficiency-Based Grading Helps Interventionists Support Mathematical Skill Transferal

When students work with interventionists, it is important for the remediation to be timely and targeted (Buffum, Mattos, & Weber, 2009). Further, intervention works best when "focused on the *cause* of a student's struggles rather than on a symptom" (Buffum, Mattos, & Weber, 2010, p. 15). A symptom-based intervention may focus on helping a student only check for extraneous solutions algebraically. It is natural for a student to seek this specificity, as it may support strengthening his or her fluency with success criteria in a particular unit. In fact, the student may not be able to move forward without mastering this success criteria. Symptom-based support has the added benefit of *immediate gratification* for students as they master algebraic double checking. Yet, what made them struggle initially is not addressed.

Here, it is possible that the student may return for intervention when he or she is unable to correctly identify extraneous solutions in a different context.

Often, interventions solely focus on remediating procedural skills (success criteria). It is important that the teacher specifies to the interventionist which *transferable skills* he or she must also attend to. Here, it may be appropriate—and necessary—to do so using the specific symptom as an exemplar. In short, the interventionist, with the teacher's direction, must focus on the reason for the student's struggle using the success criteria as a relevant and timely context. Consider the case of an interventionist helping a student identify extraneous solutions. It is reasonable to presume that the interventionist (given specific details about the student's struggle) can support the necessary relearning over specific examples. One can imagine a student exiting intervention feeling a sense of mastery. However, it is also possible given the scope (of identifying extraneous solutions) that the interventionist's support produced limited long-term growth. If the intervention only focuses on relearning specific examples, the root cause of the learning gap is unresolved—although the student has a sense of mastery.

In this example, the intervention did not help the student *transfer* essential skills across various changing contexts. Thus, only addressing remediation through specific contexts narrows the depth of learning desired. When teachers report to interventionists the supporting content *and* the overarching or transferable skills that need attention, there is greater value for relearning and greater transference of those relearned skills.

Proficiency-based grading can help expand the work of interventionists and enrich learning by providing access to skill *transfer*. For instance, consider how the work of the interventionist changes if the support is prescribed as the following.

> The student is struggling with identifying extraneous solutions. Help him observe the structure of equations and what features suggest the possibility of extraneous solutions. Using structure and connecting this to graphical significance of roots is a major overarching idea. When the student is able to apply these concepts across various contexts—radical, logarithmic, exponential, and so on—he will understand the process and procedures for solving and the significance of these roots.

While the original statement, *identify extraneous solutions*, yields focused results, the revised plan supports the transfer of overarching skills across many units of study in a mathematics course. While both foci can be helpful, proficiency-based grading supports communicating the latter. In my experience, when interventionists address and communicate the transferable skills that transcend multiple courses (algebra 1, geometry, algebra 2, and so on), students' belief in their ability to grow their learning improves. Here, students' impressions shift from "I need help on this [radicals], and this [logarithms], and this [rationals]" to "If I can improve on this big skill [nature of solutions and structure of equations], then I can also get better at all these [solving radical, logarithmic, and rational equations]." The shift in perspective allows students to engage knowing their efforts will have broader impact. This effective effort is *transferable* and promotes students' efficacy. This perspective shift not only supports deeper student engagement in remediation but has the potential to eliminate the need for out-of-class intervention.

Proficiency-Based Grading Supports a Growth Mindset and Resilience While Learning Mathematics

Resilience, according to psychology professor and motivation researcher Carol S. Dweck (n.d.), "is essential for great accomplishment." That is, the expanse of time available for students to learn, relearn, and demonstrate mastery without the penalizing effects of early struggles supports resilience and the development of a growth mindset. Students are more apt to persist in learning (and remediation) because teachers reward their efforts with opportunities to demonstrate improved learning.

Most educators have experienced students' frustrations when students *perceive* their learning gaps to be insurmountable. To develop resilience and promote efficacy, students must not only exert effort toward developing proficiency but also view the pathway to proficiency as achievable. In mathematics, proficiency-based grading's cohesive alignment with overarching standards and focus on growth over time provide repeated opportunities for students to perform and reperform.

Consider a typical mathematics course where learning and feedback are primarily organized around success criteria. Here, teachers, though well meaning, inadvertently convey that learning mathematics is the sum of its innumerable component parts. That is, students will erroneously believe that proficiency in mathematics is the mastery of a myriad of daily topics such as factoring by sum and product, by grouping, by difference of squares, by completing the square, and by inspection and revision. While the example speaks to familiar factoring methods, another unit can present a number of ways to solve a system of linear equations, including substitution, elimination, linear combination, and inspection and revision. From a student's perspective, just these two units have nine distinct topics to master.

For a student in those cases, doing mathematics has become the daily acquisition of topics; for a struggling student doing mathematics, this has become insurmountable as the topics are presented in increasing variances. The student cannot develop proficiency. The pathway for growth is daunting. Figure 5.1 (page 134) further illustrates this with an example from an algebra 2 course.

Polynomial Functions

1. Factor polynomials using various factor techniques and division.
2. Solve polynomial equations using zero-product property, quadratic formula, and square root method.
3. Interpret key features of polynomial functions including zeros and end behavior.
4. Graph polynomial functions, identifying zeros when suitable factorizations are available, and showing end behavior.
5. Write equations of polynomial functions.
6. Divide polynomials.
7. Use technology to analyze key features of polynomial functions.
8. Perform the operations of addition, subtraction, and multiplication on complex numbers.

Rational Functions

1. Add, subtract, multiply, and divide rational expressions.
2. Identify key features of rational functions, including zeros, asymptotes, domain, and range.
3. Graph transformations of the function $f(x) = \frac{1}{x}$ using vertical stretches and shifts and horizontal shifts.
4. Graph rational functions in quotient form, identifying zeros and asymptotes when suitable factorizations are available, and showing end behavior.
5. Rewrite rational expressions in different forms.

Figure 5.1: Traditional learning targets; proficiency-based grading success criteria.

Consider a full-year course with twelve units with five to eight topics in each unit. The student must try to gain sixty to ninety-six granular academic knowledge skills. A path to mastery through dozens of success criteria can feel daunting and be discouraging. However, by understanding the relationship between success criteria and learning targets, students can manage and negotiate their learning. Proficiency-based grading provides access to this.

Refocusing on *why* students are doing all of this allows them to manage between four and seven standards practiced *through the use* of five and eight academic knowledge skills in each unit *over the span of the year.*

Since the proficiency measure remains consistent across the course, addressing how well they are doing is more manageable for students and for teachers. Students' perspective on effective effort is centered not on mastering between sixty and ninety-six criteria, but rather on developing proficiency between four and seven recurring core ideas.

Proficiency-Based Grading Supports Social-Emotional Competency Integration Into Mathematics Planning and Teaching

The Standards for Mathematical Practice provide access to students regarding *how* to do mathematics (NGA & CCSSO, 2010b). Central to doing mathematics are the interpersonal and social-emotional skills that students engage in (Charles A. Dana Center & CASEL, 2016). The Mathematical Practices emphasize "that learning is a social process, implicitly calling for teaching practices that leverage the power of group work and collaborative learning" (Charles A. Dana Center & CASEL, 2016, p. 1). As such, teachers must develop students' interpersonal and intrapersonal skills so that group work and collaborative learning yield positive outcomes. CASEL (2017) identifies these competencies as self-awareness, self-management, responsible decision making, relationship skills, and social awareness.

Mathematics teachers may wonder how they can help students develop soft skills in a hard science like mathematics. What role does social awareness or relationship skills have in learning mathematics? Here, teachers can attest that schools are spaces where students' hallway or lunch conversations do not immediately cease upon entering a classroom. Silent compliance does not guarantee that students are not preoccupied with the elations or dejections of social interactions they have experienced before class or *within* their current class. Social settings require cognitive and emotional energy to navigate, and "because social and emotional factors play such an important role, schools must attend to this aspect of the educational process for the benefit of all students" (Schonert-Reichl & Hymel, 2007). Furthermore, social and emotional factors are not limited to nonacademic interactions; when learning is a collaborative public endeavor, the same factors affect academic interactions.

Consider Mathematical Practice 3, "construct viable arguments and critique the reasoning of others" (NGA & CCSSO, 2010b). This practice standard is active in classrooms where learning is grounded in reasoning and sense making. What are the skills necessary to offer or receive critique? What skills does a student need in order to construct a rebuttal argument to a peer—perhaps to a peer with whom the student has a strained relationship? Can learning progress as intended if collaboration is not productive? Mathematical Practice 3 calls students to "listen or read the arguments of others, decide whether they make sense, and ask useful questions to clarify or improve the arguments" (NGA & CCSSO, 2010b). Here, competency in social awareness helps students to understand others' perspectives. This is worthwhile learning on its own merit. However, in the context of mathematics, we "understand others' perspectives *to effectively interpret their arguments*" (Charles A. Dana Center & CASEL, 2016, emphasis added). A careful read of the Standards for Mathematical

Practice invites teachers to address social-emotional competencies in order to advance the skills of doing mathematics by teaching specific prosocial strategies.

Evidence-based grading is not *necessary* to promote students' growth in social-emotional learning (SEL). However, evidence-based grading *is* best positioned to focus mathematics learning around the Standards for Mathematical Practice that *rely* on students' growth in social-emotional competencies. Sustained engagement in learning mathematics is supported not only by developing academic competencies but also by developing social-emotional competencies.

Preparation: The Commitments of Proficiency-Based Grading in Mathematics

Teachers and teams make certain commitments to successfully implement this improved system of assessing and instructing. This can be difficult because teachers often have very personal preferences for specific supporting resources, curriculum, instructional approach, learning tools, and assessment. When a team of teachers is preparing to do this work, there will be worries about losing autonomy and the challenge of adapting their teaching and assessment in the near future. Making a series of commitments will allow teachers to support each other on the road to success.

The following commitments are discussed in subsequent sections: (1) focus on the right mathematical skills, (2) use a four-level scale for mathematics, (3) use the four-level scale as an instructional or formative tool for learning mathematics, and (4) apply a consistent proficiency scale for mathematics.

Commitment 1: Focus on the Right Mathematical Skills

Historically, in mathematics (and to a certain degree in computer science), the day-to-day learning focuses on acquiring content. That is, there is roughly a new topic of study every one to one-and-a-half days. The National Council of Teachers of Mathematics' (NCTM; 2014a) *Principles to Actions*, CCSS (NGA & CCSSO, 2010b), and other state and provincial standards help articulate the importance of building curriculum so there is topic interconnectedness and so students experience learning through sense making and reasoning.

Yet, the majority of mathematics curricula continue marching students forward, day by day and from topic to topic, where each topic has roughly the same weight in importance and impact. As mentioned, this leads students to experience mathematics as the mastery of nearly sixty to ninety-six granular topics over a year—between roughly 240 and 384 topics over four years. No wonder struggling students believe they can never catch up; there is just too much to address in mathematics. Mathematics teachers must ask themselves if students understand the cohesive narrative written about mathematics over several years of study, or if students are *simply* excelling at completing given work efficiently and effectively.

For the majority of teachers, the daily topics represent mathematics skills. Typically, these skills represent procedural or algorithmic skills used to develop students' procedural fluency. The National Research Council (NRC; 2001) defines *procedural fluency* as "skill in carrying out procedures flexibly, accurately, efficiently, and appropriately" (p. 16). It is vital to support students' procedural fluency as it serves to deepen their exploration of mathematical ideas and relationships and support flexible thinking (NCTM, 2014b). When teachers and teams begin working toward proficiency-based grading, they must redefine the term *skill*. Here, mathematics teachers must adopt the perspective of colleagues in English, science, and the fine arts. The skills teachers seek to develop (and report on) with students must be those transferable *thinking* and *doing* skills that represent the overarching value of the discipline. In mathematics, these transferable skills of the discipline are the Standards for Mathematical Practice.

Teachers and teams must commit to identifying transferable skills. The skills represent the expectations of the course *and* program (the latter is with emphasis). Doing so allows students to transfer experience and expectations across a sequence of courses, between four and six years, that form a program of study. Thus, as students develop transferable skills, they grow to have tangible access to unfamiliar content across courses. Mastery of dozens of topics does not provide access. Rather, it is the manner in which the daily topics support and strengthen the transferable course skills that provides access and depth in understanding and *doing* mathematics. Transferable skills traverse a multiyear program of study.

This perspective shift calls for greater attention for teachers to make the Standards for Mathematical Practice explicit in lesson design, instruction, and feedback. Due to the importance of these transferable skills, it is natural to adopt the eight practices verbatim as the course standards. However, research offers that ideal reporting of learning organizes around four to six domains or overarching skills or standards (Guskey & Bailey, 2010). All eight standards may make it difficult for students to manage the corresponding scales, rubrics, and success criteria for each standard. In addition, based on the current focus or priority in the mathematics program, a given mathematical practice may not yet be well integrated into the curricula, instruction, or feedback tools. If not, it should not be a learning expectation that students are assessed against. This is not to imply that a particular standard should not be valued or developed; it is that students should not be held to performance expectations until the teaching and learning around the standard is well developed.

For instance, consider Mathematics Practice 5 (use appropriate tools strategically; NGA & CCSSO, 2010b). Here, a tool can be a protractor, compass, or template. However, it can also be concrete models, manipulatives, dynamic software, digital resources, or internet access. For various reasons, perhaps the use of *tools* is not presently attended to in a mathematics program. This may be due to lack of funding, lack of professional development, or lack of integration. Though it is a critical transferable skill, it is not yet appropriate to mark as a standard. Use caution when identifying the overarching skills that become the course standards.

As teachers delve deeper into the Standards for Mathematical Practice, they will observe key student actions that highlight the *doing* in mathematics; often verbs, these words make it clear what students need to be able to do (NGA & CCSSO, 2010b). Figure 5.2 shows how algebra 1, geometry, algebra 2, and precalculus teams adopted a subset of the practice. In turn, the course standards represent some of the transferable skills these teams valued over the three- to four-year program. Students can identify these succinct skills as they work in class.

Standards for Mathematical Practice	Course Standards
2. Reason abstractly and quantitatively.	**Standard 1:** Create mathematical representations.
7. Look for and make use of structure.	**Standard 2:** Simplify, solve, and evaluate.
3. Construct viable arguments and critique the reasoning of others.	**Standard 3:** Analyze and interpret.
4. Model with mathematics.	
6. Attend to precision.	**Standard 4:** Attend to precision.

Source for standard: NGA & CCSSO, 2010b; source: Adapted from Adlai E. Stevenson High School, 2017.

Figure 5.2: Standards for Mathematical Practice as course standards.

In these examples, the use and promotion of Mathematical Practice 1 ("make sense of problems and persevere in solving them") and 5 ("use appropriate tools strategically") were not adopted as course standards (NGA & CCSSO, 2010b). The teams view these practices as continually present and employed through instruction in all contexts. In a sense, they help form the ethos of *doing* mathematics in this program.

Though teams did not explicitly incorporate Mathematical Practice 8, "look for and express regularity in repeated reasoning," as a course or program standard, a viable argument could be made to incorporate it as such (NGA & CCSSO, 2010b). Mathematics education experts Grace Kelemanik, Amy Lucenta, and Susan Janssen Creighton (2016) share that Mathematical Practices 2, 7, and 8 support "three different avenues of mathematical thinking that provide entry into and through all kinds of math problems" (p. 4). Based on a mathematics program focus and curricular outline, teachers may be able to organize course standards around Mathematical Practices 2, 7, and 8, with the balance of the practices serving supporting roles.

Once a team commits to the overarching transferable skills or standards, team members can then establish the specific course targets. The following shows how teams developed the same two transferable skills differently through varied emphasis on learning targets across two different courses.

- **Algebra 1 course standards:**
  - Create mathematical representations.
  - Analyze and interpret.
- **Algebra 1 learning targets:**
  - I can create graphical representations.
  - I can create symbolic representations.
  - I can interpret key features.
  - I can make arguments and decisions.
- **Geometry course standards:**
  - Create mathematical representations.
  - Analyze and interpret.
- **Geometry learning targets:**
  - I can apply geometric relationships numerically.
  - I can apply geometric relationships algebraically.
  - I can apply coordinate geometry.
  - I can justify geometric relationships.
  - I can reason and make decisions.

These standards and learning targets represent how teams can value and distill the Standards for Mathematical Practice succinctly as their course or program's transferable skills. Here, each team maintained the program focus but adapted the learning target into the context of the course (algebraic focus versus geometric focus). A multiyear program of study maintains global, program-level continuity in standards, but local, course-level adaptation to serve specific context.

Commitment 2: Use a Four-Level Scale for Mathematics

Feedback on mathematics learning has typically comprised awarding points for work completed at full mastery. This system communicates that full points awarded to errorless completion of work represents the expectation of the course. (That is, "getting math" is equated to "getting math without errors.") Deductions in points represent a lack of full proficiency. However, in practice, with the range the teacher or school establishes, students may still be deemed proficient with minimal deductions. For instance, in some schools, 88 of 100 available points represent proficiency while other programs require 90 or even 94 points for validating proficiency.

Considering this, teams must commit to articulating a proficiency scale as the feedback mechanism. For instance, consider a class where earning 88, or 90, or 94 points out of 100 is considered proficient. As some deductions were made, there is a shortfall toward so-called perfect work. There are some errors. A point score doesn't give the student feedback that describes *how proficient* he or she is toward achieving mastery. Further, can a student transfer the learning that yielded an increase of one point to another unit of study, if again the student needed to grow from 88 to 89? Is the learning to move from 88 to 89 the same learning needed to move from 89 to 90? Feedback must communicate where students are on the continuum of learning but also make transparent how students can impact their learning along the continuum. This supports their efficacy as agents of their learning.

In addition, feedback must communicate attention toward remediation or extension. How many deductions from 100 would signal immediate intervention? Do four two-point deductions communicate proficiency differently than a singular eight-point deduction? Is it possible that the nature of four two-point deductions still communicates valued learning but poor computational accuracy, whereas a singular eight-point deduction represents a more egregious level of misunderstanding? A student doesn't know.

Assessment, feedback, and reporting are complex acts. Undoubtedly, mathematics teachers have worked with systems and developed ways to allow points to communicate a deeper understanding and expressions of students' work. With effort, and in some cases with much manipulation, teachers can *make* points have meaning. Yet, even in this, point assignment does not communicate how well students demonstrate proficiency toward an expectation. That is, teachers do not communicate to students the relative impact on learning through deductions.

When transitioning to proficiency-based grading, teachers must commit to a four-level scale—like that in table 5.1— that describes the proficiencies students *can* demonstrate toward mastery. Here, teams must commit to a common understanding of what each level represents.

Table 5.1: Communicating Proficiency Using a Four-Level Scale

When a student . . .	When a student . . .	When a student . . .	When a student . . .
accurately demonstrates proficiencies in new and unfamiliar contexts . . .	accurately demonstrates proficiencies in the current contexts . . .	demonstrates emerging proficiencies in the current contexts . . .	focuses on prerequisite knowledge acquisition . . .
then learning . . .	**then learning . . .**	**then learning . . .**	**then learning . . .**
shows refined mastery.	shows proficiency.	approaches proficiency.	is still developing.

For mathematics teachers, the four-level scale will feel unfamiliar and may appear inadequate.

As teachers begin their work in proficiency-based grading, there may be a temptation to add an additional level. Teachers may initially experience that a given level is too broad. This may result in added increments (4, 3.5, 3, 2.5, and so on). In learning mathematics, teachers' communication of students' states of learning must remain broad (in four levels). While there may be some reduced precision in identifying where within each level learning is trending, students more accurately know what actions they can take to grow from a given level to another. Students can more readily manage their learning with a few levels versus learning requirements for numerous (ever-widening) levels. Having fewer levels invites deeper teacher-to-teacher and teacher-to-student conversations around expectations and paths to proficiency. Doing so provides models of thinking and expectations of behaviors for students that build ownership in learning and promote self-efficacy.

Commitment 3: Use the Four-Level Scale as an Instructional or Formative Tool for Learning Mathematics

Teachers and teams must commit to using the proficiency levels in instruction. This is a shift, since in prior grading and feedback systems, the instrument of assessment was only available *after* the learning; with a proficiency-based grading system, teachers use assessment in the stream of learning. It is common to hear teachers point out that mathematics is sequential. This aspect encourages students to use the scale as a formative tool. As students engage in tasks, identifying their state of learning provides a path for advancing their work. Consider the problem presented here.

> Point A is positioned between points B and D. Point B is located between points A and C. AB = $5x - 4$, BC = $2x^2 - 6$, BD = $6x + 3$, and CD = 33. Justify whether points A, B, C, and D serve as bisection or trisection points in the relationship.

Once students establish the geometric and algebraic relationships, they observe that the points are colinear and sequenced as D, A, B, and C (relative to each other). The segment lengths of DA, AB, and BC are 10, 11, and 12, respectively. As such, A and B neither bisect nor trisect CD. A written explanation accessing definitions and algebraic work justifying evaluation of segment lengths would follow.

This exercise can be used formatively within instruction and provide opportunities for students to interact with the proficiency scale (or scaled learning targets). Figure 5.3 has two learning targets from the geometry example. The learning targets are scaled to form a gradation that represents the continuum of learning within that target.

Here, the teacher can guide students in self-assessment of their work. Through practice, feedback, and refinement, students can begin to locate their levels of learning on the scale. When used regularly in instruction, students begin to view scales not as instruments of judgment but as familiar tools that support and guide learning. If students are to reflect and grow their efficacy, then they must have experiences in class that teach them to identify their current proficiency level and build supportive pathways to close any gap to mastery.

Commitment 4: Apply a Consistent Proficiency Scale for Mathematics

Teachers must commit to maintaining a consistent proficiency scale throughout the learning. This consistency supports students' work, reflection, and actions. Doing so establishes the scale as the same feedback instrument used regardless of changing contexts. If the proficiency gradation (the feedback instrument) changes from topic to topic or unit to unit, then students must learn not only new academic content but also a new assessment instrument.

4—Refined Mastery	3—Proficiency	2—Approaches Proficiency	1—Still Developing
Standard: Mathematical relationships and representations			
Learning Target: I can apply geometric relationships algebraically.			
I can accurately interpret geometric relationships to set up a symbolic representation and determine an unknown quantity in an unfamiliar setting.	I can accurately interpret geometric relationships to set up a symbolic representation and determine an unknown quantity.	I can interpret geometric relationships to set up a symbolic representation and determine an unknown quantity.	I can attempt to interpret geometric relationships to set up a symbolic representation and determine an unknown quantity.
Standard: Analyze and interpret			
Learning Target: I can apply logical reasoning and make decisions.			
I can use logical reasoning to make a valid decision in any geometric context in an unfamiliar setting.	I can use logical reasoning to make a valid decision in any geometric context.	I can use logical reasoning to make a decision in any geometric context.	I can attempt to use logical reasoning to make a decision in any geometric context.

Figure 5.3: Scaled geometry learning targets.

Figure 5.4 (page 144) is an example of a scaled target that, when used across multiple units of study in algebra 1, geometry, algebra 2, and precalculus, maintains expectations and communication of those expectations consistent across a program of study. Students moving from topic to topic within the course become familiar with the scale through repeated exposure. In addition, as students move from course to course, their efficacy in applying past knowledge and transferable skills in new contexts grows.

Standard: Create mathematical representations			
Learning Target: I can create graphical representations.			
4—Refined Mastery	3—Proficiency	2—Approaches Proficiency	1—Still Developing
I can create an accurate graphical representation in any given context in unfamiliar situations.	I can create an accurate graphical representation in any given context using key features.	I can create an appropriate graphical representation in any given context.	I can create a graphical representation in any given context.

Source for standard: Adlai E. Stevenson High School, 2017.

Figure 5.4: Example of a scaled learning target that works across programs of study.

Incubation: The Unexpected Questions of Proficiency-Based Grading in Mathematics

As teachers progress toward using proficiency-based grading, they will uncover some wonderful questions that drive inquiry and implementation. During this second stage, several adopted practices may be working, but teachers may pay a lot of attention to the items that seem to threaten work or that have provided new challenges. One such past practice questions the adherence to daily pacing guides. Often, teachers hold fast to pacing guides as they represent a prescription for delivering curriculum within a fixed period of time. Deviation of a few days here or there (for remediation, exploration, extension, team building, unexpected mandatory testing, or state testing, for example) can invite consternation.

However, when daily lessons focus on advancing transferable mathematics skills, teachers experience liberty in organizing learning more flexibly, knowing there will be multiple opportunities to revisit topics throughout the course. With so much new information, it can be hard to not worry that some challenges will never be overcome. The following questions are representative of the incubation stage challenges that require patience and persistence.

Unexpected Question 1: What Are Mathematical Proficiency and Calibration?

One area to discuss and plan for is how teachers and teams ensure all students receive equitable feedback on their work. That is, how can teams make sure different teachers view a student's work and yield the same assessment of proficiency? Calibration is key. Early in implementation, teams must dedicate time to specify what type of work exemplifies categories of refined mastery, proficiency, approaching proficiency, and still developing. In doing so, the team can also build exemplars to share with students to support their understanding of what they need to do to meet expectations. It is key for teachers to model the course expectations during instruction, rather than as postassessment revelations. When students have artifacts to compare their work against, as well as have opportunities to engage in dialogue about their work, they can build accurate perceptions of their learning.

Just as reporting feedback using a scale is new for teachers, it is also new for students. Both teachers and students need practice in calibrating their understanding of expected outcomes. As teachers and teams develop exemplars, there will be moments when team members have different perspectives on quality work. It is important to remember that these differences do not imply a faulty proficiency-based grading system, but rather require teacher communication and collaboration. When there are differing perspectives on proficiency, the team must address them so teachers can clearly explain the learning targets and success criteria to all students. Once they do, all students have an opportunity to grow toward the same expectations, regardless of their teacher.

Conversations around proficiency expectations will also surface when teams begin to provide formal feedback through assessments. Frustration can emanate from a sense of loss of clarity as teachers review students' work (as opposed to teacher-generated exemplars). It may feel as if prior calibration conversations were ineffective as they *should have* normalized the team's understanding. True calibration and understanding of proficiency comes when interacting with actual student work. When reviewing student work, calibration conversations may need to be revisited. When juggling professional and personal schedules—all the while ensuring timely feedback—the need to re-examine the team's understanding of proficiency can feel like lost time or lost effort. Teachers might question the benefits of proficiency-based grading. These are natural conversations and questions that will arise as teachers increasingly focus on students' artifacts and on how best to provide feedback to guide mathematics learning. Teachers who work to calibrate and recalibrate will experience tremendous growth as educators as well as increased confidence in their team and colleagues. With commitment and practice, initial calibration conversations begin to bear fruit, and recalibrations are necessary less often.

To support conversations and professional learning, teams should calibrate using a structured protocol. One such protocol helps teams calibrate through *blind selection*; that is, randomly assign several student papers to teachers on the team. Teachers then individually score each student's work and offer feedback. Next, as a team, teachers share their scoring, and *every* deviation is discussed until it is resolved. The discussion not only supports the team's learning and inter-rater reliability, but builds team confidence that students will receive the same quality feedback and be held to the same proficiency expectation, regardless of teacher. When differences in scoring arise, a structured conversation can help identify the gap between team members. In doing this, the proficiency scale, along with student work, should be at the center of the conversation. The following questions are helpful.

- What in the student's work justifies the score?

- Has the student demonstrated proficiency elsewhere or in different ways?

- What is the source of the error? Is the teacher or team assessing that skill (and thus deserving feedback)?

- In what ways does an error impact the wider proficiency development on transferable skills?

- How does a team understand or value the action verbs *analyze, solve, interpret,* and *explain*?

Teams should document their conversations so there is transparent understanding of the team's decisions. Adding notes to proficiency exemplars can help teachers remember why they made decisions and how they formed their understanding. Initially, these conversations can be long and even frustrating. Teachers may feel traditional grading practices do not warrant such *intense* conversations or negotiations or strain long relationships. When teams welcome inquiry in safe environments and commit to resolutions, professional learning advances. As trust develops and calibration practices persist, members ensure equitable learning experiences, as well as accurate, verifiable grading for all students.

Unexpected Question 2: What Is Truly Different With Proficiency-Based Grading While Learning Mathematics?

During the planning and initial implementation stages of proficiency-based grading, some teachers or teams may struggle to differentiate their current practices from what is called for in their proficiency-based grading practice. In these cases, it is important to acknowledge that many effective, conscientious teachers may have already begun to adopt a proficiency-based mindset. For these teachers, it may seem they already practice proficiency-based grading, and this may indeed be true. Celebrate this. So what is different? Proficiency-based grading offers a cohesive systemwide approach replete with individual or team innovation to scale what individual teachers may have done in isolation to the benefit of all students across all disciplines. The proficiency-based grading system is coherent, cogent, and cohesive in rationale, beliefs, and implementation. A proficiency-based grading system codifies and scales the individual innovations and adjustments teachers have long practiced as exceptions. Proficiency-based grading celebrates the moral judgments teachers have exercised and makes the intense focus on students' work, personalized feedback, and flexibility in the assessment of growth the norm for all students.

For example, one team began reporting learning around specific outcomes rather than as aggregated assessment results. The team did this for two or three years before formally adopting proficiency-based grading. Consider the innovation of another team that eliminated scoring homework and worked to build a culture of practice and feedback that increasingly helped more students complete independent practice, value feedback, and respond with action two years before implementing proficiency-based grading. This second team valued all the work students produced and built a culture to make out-of-class independent practice meaningful—even appealing—based on the focused feedback team members gave students.

Another team developed a reassessment cycle three to four years before exploring proficiency-based grading. This team acknowledged that students' learning is not always linear; some students need additional time to demonstrate mastery. Still another team investigated the way students retained skills over time and instituted cyclic trimester assessments. This team valued students' experience with increasingly complex and integrated problems as the course progressed, and the trimester assessment allowed students to revisit and integrate prior concepts in new contexts. These examples suggest that effective, conscientious teachers find a way to respond to new challenges and responsibly advocate for students.

Some teachers and teams may find refining their current practices cogent within the new proficiency-based grading framework. Celebrate this, too. Well-meaning teachers have customized, or *hacked*, existing gradebook structures, grading, learning cycles, and time lines to offer the best for their students. These teachers are innovators. However, teachers *should not have to hack* ineffective structures in an effort to achieve the good they seek. The system must change. Proficiency-based grading supports the flexibility, responsiveness, and equitable professional decision making only possible by ineffectively and inconsistently system hacking.

It is important for teachers to know how proficiency-based grading challenges some practices and beliefs; however, it is also important for teachers to know that some of their past practices and innovations laid the foundations for the proficiency-based grading framework. Proficiency-based grading need not be a wholly new idea; to some teachers, proficiency-based grading will be their isolated good practice formalized.

Unexpected Question 3: What Happens to Multiple Choice Questions in Proficiency-Based Mathematics?

The role of multiple choice in assessments is an additional consideration for teachers. In my experience, early on, teams choose to assess students using only performance tasks—mathematics problems that require students to fully demonstrate their work or give written justification for a response. When they have access to students' work and thinking, teachers have a wide base to assess proficiency and offer appropriate feedback. More importantly, students have their full work to reflect on and compare to the scaled target and proficiency expectations.

The depth of knowledge that performance tasks reveal to both teachers and students about student understanding is significant. However, the teachers' timely scoring and feedback can also be an unexpected concern for consideration. The question is not whether students should demonstrate their learning only through multiple choice tests, performance tasks, or portfolios. The questions are, What value do these modes (in addition to others) offer students in demonstrating their learning? and How can teachers access student learning to ascertain proficiency levels and provide actionable feedback?

The efficiency of multiple choice in scoring is unparalleled, but this mode is also detrimental because it provides *toggle feedback*—a student response is either correct or incorrect. In such cases, multiple choice is very limiting, and teachers should avoid it. However, teachers often cite the need for students to practice multiple choice–style questions in preparation for college entrance exams or advanced placement exams. There is some credence to this assertion. However, teachers should not build learning experiences around assessments but, rather, structure school and learning to support students' success in an ever-changing assessment landscape.

Yet, students *do need exposure and practice* on varied assessment types, including multiple choice. Teachers can address this need through classroom learning experiences. The diversity of assessment modes in class can include complex instruction tasks, true/false, multiple choice, sort and select, choose all that apply, choose and justify, develop an alternative, and more. The key is for students to not only engage in these types of assessment styles but also have opportunities in class to discuss their responses, receive feedback on the demonstrated (or the lack of) knowledge, and improve their strategic approach to different modes. Well-crafted question formats offer variety in instruction and also provide rich opportunities for classroom discourse.

Unexpected Question 4: How Can Assessments Be More Effective in Proficiency-Based Mathematics?

This question may arise as teams wrestle with assessment construction and scoring. The source of the question is in observing unexpected student performance results. That is, a student may perform exceptionally well on a formalized assessment, and a teacher may wonder if there is validity in that result. Similarly, a student may demonstrate proficiencies at a lower level than expected, and the teacher may question the fairness of a singular performance event. As teams implement proficiency-based grading, they should expect both scenarios to occur. Assessments are effective when administered in the stream of learning where teachers have enough time to adjust instruction and students have enough time to respond to feedback. Numerous informal assessments can support adjustments and response. Variances will gradually diminish as the feedback loop continues.

Another area of dissonance that may surface is in assessment construction. Here, teams and teachers must ensure their expectation of students on assessments matches the expectation they had of students in the stream of learning. That is, students should have opportunities to practice work that represents full proficiency (and receive feedback) prior to teachers formally evaluating them on the same. Often, teachers and teams take pride in creating assessment problems that do not resemble work done in class or through practice. While this may be acceptable, there must also be assurance that the proficiency expectations from classwork, assessment, and feedback are the same.

In addition, as many mathematics curricula successively build on prior learning, students' first experience to the integration of multiple targets typically occurs on an assessment. Often, I hear that students are expected to put it all together on the test. This is a mismatch to students' learning experiences and their understanding of expected proficiency. To avoid this, students must have practice with and feedback around expectations prior to the formal assessment. Expecting students to put ideas together is not an objectionable expectation! However, if this is the expectation, then the teacher must teach the transferable skills needed to achieve this expectation. If teachers expect students to put it all together, then they must teach students how to use feedback along the way on how well they are progressing toward this proficiency.

Finally, teams can innovate the methods they use to score performance tasks. Feedback need not only be around when work is correct. Rather, a teacher can try the following approaches.

- Indicate the first occurrence of a mistake in a problem and ask students to revise their work from that point.

- Highlight the problem that *contains* a mistake and ask students to review and resubmit.

- Conference with students about their work and jointly co-construct the proficiency assessment.

Conferences allow students to view formalized assessments not as pronouncements of status, but as additional opportunities to calibrate their understanding of proficiency alongside their teacher. Regardless of the methodology teams and teachers take, it is the power of continued student engagement from assessments that brings value rather than efficiency in assessment scoring.

Unexpected Question 5: How Much Evidence Is Enough to Show Proficiency in Mathematics?

This question may also arise in an attempt to understand an unexpected performance result. Perhaps the results were expectedly weak or inconsistent. This question suggests that the only valid source for student learning evidence is from formal assessment events. Did this test really have all the valued types of questions? Can a test really capture all the learning? What if the student had a bad day? These are valid concerns and suggest a conscientious teacher striving for fair, valid, and reliable judgment of student work.

A perspective shift addresses these concerns. If a formal assessment is the only acceptable indicator of student performance, then these questions will remain. That is, the formal assessment's purpose is *not to uncover* proficiency but rather to *validate expected proficiency*. Simply put, if students have had frequent and commensurate practice demonstrating proficiency, then there is reliability in the expected results. The formal assessment validates what the teacher has already observed and the student has already self-assessed during reflection. Typically, a minimum of three performance opportunities are needed to establish a trend and establish reliability. These need not be formal events, but they do need to align with learning targets and proficiencies. Teachers can glean proficiency from in-class work, board presentations, student performance videos, portfolios, teacher–student conferences, and more.

That being said, teachers may not be able to resolve outlier scenarios with just three performance opportunities. It is vital for the team to adopt flexibility for reassessment on a case-by-case basis if the formal assessment appears to challenge the breadth of evidence from teachers' observation and knowledge of the learner. If a teacher and student jointly expect result A based on a trend in demonstrated work, but witness result B, then a conversation and retake as appropriate should also follow.

Insight: The Essential Insights of Proficiency-Based Grading in Mathematics

As teachers begin to move beyond the initial fears and roadblocks and gain insight, it is vitally important to take some time to look back on and appreciate how the team has passed some intimidating hurdles thus far. Teams should have a clear enough idea of how proficiency-based grading works, and they can play to its strengths as they plan and teach. They begin providing proficiency-based grading with more impactful power once they have internalized the vision and purpose, and gained flexibility and familiarity.

At this point, mathematics teachers might have the following insights: (1) the difference between standards and learning target language in mathematics is vital, (2) proficiency scales are at the center of mathematics instruction and learning, (3) instruction and assessment blend in proficiency-based mathematics, (4) mathematics teachers must be creative with reassessment or reperformance, and (5) teams and teachers incorporate differentiated instruction in mathematics.

Insight 1: The Difference Between Standards and Learning Target Language in Mathematics Is Vital

As teams embark on the journey to develop standards and learning targets, leaders must give them patience, resources, and time to engage in dialogue. It is during sustained collaborative conversations about what values teachers hold that the focus of instructional planning, learning, and assessment is defined. It is also important that a sequence adopt consistent standards, as this helps articulate learning outcomes over a program of study. Figure 5.2 (page 138) is one example of articulated outcomes over a multiyear mathematics program.

As teams begin to write learning targets based on standards, leaders should ensure all teachers understand what they are defining and what the learning targets call for. This supports the adoption of a guaranteed and viable curriculum (Marzano, 2003). Consider, for instance, a proposed learning target, *Create symbolic representations.*

Teachers with in-depth pedagogical and content knowledge can engage passionately over the scope of various terms. For instance, what constitutes *symbolic*? Are diagrams and figures symbolic? If so, does the target encompass geometric representations? Are student-generated symbols valid representations? Or, what does it mean *to create*? Do students *create* or *replicate* a known technique? Is *representing* the same as *showing* or *demonstrating*?

All of these are thoughtful questions that emanate from the teachers' and teams' desire for clarity in communication with students. However, it is important not to belabor nuanced meanings. What is vital is that the team establishes scope through artifacts and exemplars. The team should also be open to refining the learning target as members gain proficiency and expertise in interacting with students about the target. In my experience, this understanding often involves the following.

1. Editing initial learning target language for precision and clarity, making it more verbose.

2. Further refining the second iteration to avoid qualifiers that have limited the usability of the target in varied contexts.

3. The team adopting student-accessible phrasing (but broad in a teacher-knowledge perspective).

This correlates with teachers developing proficiencies; they use the target language first as a descriptor, second as an assessment tool, and finally as an instructional tool.

Insight 2: Proficiency Scales Are at the Center of Mathematics Instruction and Learning

The proficiency scale should take center stage when teachers interact with students. That is, just as teachers plan explicitly for developing students' content learning and social-emotional competencies, teachers must explicitly plan for instruction for when students interact with the proficiency scale. Doing so allows the development of students' efficacy in identifying their learning against an established standard. Students ought to be able to identify how well they need to know something, how well they are doing, and what they will be able to do if they are proficient (Gobble et al., 2016).

An objection to using scales in classroom instruction and learning is that it focuses too much on assessment and that the emphasis is on grading. This, of course, can be true. However, the practitioner has some control over how students view the scale. If he or she uses it only as a measure of learning, then it can overemphasize status. If, however, it introduces learning, invites peer critique, facilitates metacognition, or develops pathways for remediation or extension, then the scale serves as a tool for growth in learning.

Insight 3: Instruction and Assessment Blend in Proficiency-Based Mathematics

As teachers begin to integrate the roles of the proficiency scale and target language in planning and learning, the lines between instruction and assessment blend. Consider a typical classroom sequence: teachers deliver planned lessons, and students engage in planned learning; and later, students demonstrate their proficiency, and teachers deliver planned lessons. Though dramatically oversimplified, this sequence asks students to interrupt learning to demonstrate their understanding at a point in time. Using proficiency-based grading with fidelity requires a shift in assessment mindset. Teachers move away from assessment *of* learning (summative assessments) and even away from assessment *for* learning (formative assessments; Stiggins, 2008), and toward assessment *as part of* learning or assessment *as* learning.

This shift will take time. However, teams will gain familiarity with seamlessly using the proficiency graduation as part of instruction, and gain confidence in the validity of informal assessment of learning. This shift will require explicit teaching and modeling by teachers with their students. This shift allows for increased flexibility in what constitutes reliable evidence of learning and provides opportunities to meet the varying needs of students at the time of need, rather than at the end of an assessment cycle.

Insight 4: Mathematics Teachers Must Be Creative With Reassessment or Reperformance

As teams develop comfort with blending assessment and instruction, greater opportunities for creative reassessment or reperformance events emerge. That is, as teachers work with struggling students, teachers need not wait for formal assessment events to validate this growth. In fact, a student's consistent and accurate demonstration of proficiency through teacher–student exchanges (out-of-class help sessions, in-class whole-group contributions, board work, and the like) is more reliable and valid than a singular formal assessment. This shift will take time. It must be preceded by confidence in classroom work modeling full proficiency expectations and facility in designing assessment events as learning moments.

Most importantly, it is vital for teams to recognize that when helping every student succeed, not every student will demonstrate expectations at the same pace. Thus, flexibility and confidence in validating learning outside of expected pacing is equitable, though not equal. This does not make the implementation and management of time any less difficult. This insight will begin to challenge teams as they continue gaining proficiency and confidence in their work with students and observe that they have not yet reached all students. The realization that, for example, "a student could not show me then, but *can* show me now and has learned it well" draws teachers to consider why demonstration of learning ought to be arbitrarily time-bound. To accept this shift, teams must work closely to calibrate their beliefs and establish guidelines for team practice. This insight will begin driving teams toward the next innovation of their proficiency-based grading model.

Insight 5: Teams and Teachers Incorporate Differentiated Instruction in Mathematics

With an articulated understanding of standards and transparent proficiency levels, teachers must be more prepared to address the varying needs of learners in their classrooms. Since students learn at different paces and bring to bear varying background knowledge, skills, and interests, teachers can develop varying access points to learning knowing there are multiple ways to meet the same course standards. This is not to imply that an individualized learning plan for every student or ability grouping constitutes differentiation. An example of mathematics differentiation is varied instructional planning to address content (what students learn), process (how students make sense of new learning), and product (how students demonstrate their learning; Tomlinson, 2017). Having clarity around course standards, clear exemplars of proficiency, an articulated and actionable proficiency scale, and flexible assessment methods makes teachers more ready to consider how they may still provide the same exceptional learning experience while being mindful of students' readiness, interests, and learning profiles.

Evaluation: The Key Questions of Proficiency-Based Grading in Mathematics

Implementation's beginning stages bring a perspective of evaluation. While professional growth never takes one path, reaching this point allows teams to set a goal of reaching regular practice and to confidently look into ways that the system impacts feedback and grading.

Evaluation can lead mathematics teachers to ask the following key questions: (1) "How can mathematics teachers help students take next steps in their learning?" and (2) "What is the role of co-constructed feedback in mathematics?"

Key Question 1: How Can Mathematics Teachers Help Students Take Next Steps in Their Learning?

At the core of adopting proficiency-based grading, teachers must strive to build student self-efficacy. In order for students to develop their own learning, they must have a clear pathway for continued learning. Teachers must help students identify their current state of learning in relation to the course expectation, and also coach students to identify (and sometimes develop) a pathway to engage in remediation or further extension. With traditional grading and scoring, the onus on what to do after an assessment is predominantly on the teacher. After all, it is the teacher who holds the criteria for correctness and wields the pen of evaluation; thus, the teacher knows the most appropriate next steps for learning.

However, as teachers develop students' competency in their ability to manage and extend their learning, the pathways for continued learning become a shared effort, with gradual release to the student. In helping students identify next steps, it is important for teachers and students to talk about adjustments to students' learning while they are still in the stream of learning, rather than at the end of an assessment cycle. When done in the midst of learning, customizing ways of learning allows students to receive immediate feedback; if a teacher waits for formal assessment to be completed, then the weight may overwhelm students. Teachers must keep action and feedback closely linked for students to correlate the two and adopt reflective practices.

One way to help students adopt these practices in the midst of learning is for teachers to break from the traditional lesson-lesson-lesson-quiz-lesson-lesson cycle. When teachers adopt a lesson-reflect-lesson-reflect-lesson-reflect-assess-reflect-activate-lesson-reflect cycle, they support students by giving them timely informal feedback strung together like incremental story lines for learning actions and learning progress. Interjecting moments for students to activate or take action on these developing story lines helps students have control over their learning and choice in how to make corrections. Teachers must teach these shifts, however, through support and validation. In time, teachers can make a gradual release to students, knowing there is consistency in the manner students identify their trend lines, and identify and take appropriate action.

Key Question 2: What Is the Role of Co-Constructed Feedback in Mathematics?

If teachers want students to value feedback, they must invite varied feedback from multiple sources. Teachers must invite students to co-construct feedback through teacher-to-student, student-to-student, group-to-group, and, most importantly, student-to-self interactions. To support students taking action in their learning, the feedback must be timely, accurate, and actionable. This again brings the proficiency scale to the center of instructional planning and classroom reflection.

As students gain facility in understanding the relationship between categorical (level) and classification (success criteria) feedback, they will develop understanding of the necessary look-fors in their lessons that support learning and performance toward proficiency. Instructionally, the identification of look-fors need not be an external act but, rather, should be integral to the planned lesson and sound like this: "In order to develop proficiency with target A, we will work with problems and context like _____. What should we attend to when we work with these problems? What do you think good work would include?" When this dialogue includes the student, it can help build efficacy. With consistent exposure, practice, and metacognition, students can develop exemplars that serve as anchors when assessing proficiency.

Elaboration: The Core Beliefs of Proficiency-Based Grading in Mathematics

Teachers at the elaboration phase of implementation have reached a mature and clear perspective of using a proficiency-based grading system. They have discovered that the system does not push them out of valued projects, simulations, or other assessments and activities they know help students learn; instead, they see there is depth to be gained from such work, with an underlying and clear focus on skills. With their comfort in this system, teachers are resources for their colleagues and on the cutting edge for new ways to provide more support for and collaboration with their students.

Teachers who successfully implement proficiency-based grading adhere to all seven of the core beliefs explained in chapter 1 (page 9): (1) growth is a central concept, (2) reperformance is essential, (3) building students' reflection abilities is essential, (4) homework has a role, (5) communication with parents and the community is key, (6) culminating experiences like final exams have a different purpose, and (7) behavior can be in or out of the grade. The following sections, which reflect the core beliefs' original numbering, explore the core beliefs that mathematics teachers in particular should never lose sight of.

Core Belief 1: Growth Is a Central Concept

Mathematics may be the most sequentially dependent discipline students experience in high school. All too often I have heard students exasperate, "I can never catch up; every day is new, and it builds!" Not all students achieve proficiency daily, for a variety of reasons, including learning gaps they bring to the class. Another reason is gaps as a result of absences due to medical matters. Some students disengage due to lack of interest, and others simply make poor choices. Regardless of *why* or *how* students experience a proficiency gap, it is the teacher's responsibility to support their learning.

It is important for teachers not to penalize learning when students *do* begin to show proficiency. That is, early student struggles should not be weighed against ultimate mastery. While some learning targets do have meaningful windows of opportunity to demonstrate learning, most others have wider windows in which to demonstrate learning. For instance, consider the study of simple one-step linear equations that represents much of the first semester in many curricula. If a student begins showing improved mastery on the subsequent multistep linear equations, there is no need to revisit the former. The window on practicing single-step linear equations has closed, and proficiency is confirmed.

Core Belief 7: Behavior Can Be In or Out of the Grade

In productive learning environments, students are developing academically as well as social-emotionally. Behavior matures as students develop their SEL competencies (CASEL, 2017). When assessing a student's learning, teachers should not confound observed academic growth with behavioral shortcomings. While these aspects of adolescent development are interconnected, teachers must separate student progress reports and grades to avoid diluting academic growth or misrepresenting behavioral deficits. That being said, there is value in communicating behavioral growth to parents, students, and school support personnel; it impacts academic readiness, progress, and achievement. However, teachers should do this separately from academic progress reporting.

In some contexts, teachers can make a case for incorporating behavior as part of academic growth (and allow it to impact the course grade). Consider when a curricular team values the students' collaborative efforts in class. If the team elects to incorporate collaboration as part of the academic grade, then this team must also commit to explicitly teach students how to collaborate and provide feedback on how to grow toward proficiency on this behavioral standard. By doing so, the team recognizes that collaboration is vital to the course and will develop specific SEL competencies to advance students' growth. Attention toward this must not be passive. Purposeful instructional and assessment planning, in addition to feedback, supports students' growth in this area.

Key Points

To ensure full understanding, review the following key points from this chapter.

- In developing proficiency-based grading in mathematics, the focus must remain on advancing transferable skills and building targets, scales, and instructional opportunities for students to grow in their use of transferable skills in varied contexts.

- During the assessment development process, teachers can calibrate what type of evidence students produce to answer each question. Teachers using proficiency-based grading can analyze each question more in depth, ensuring what they are asking students to do will ultimately produce the right evidence to determine mathematical proficiency.

- With an articulated understanding of standards and transparent proficiencies that represent competency toward the standards, teachers must be more prepared to address the varying needs of learners in their classrooms.

Eric Ramos, MEd, is the director of physical welfare at Adlai E. Stevenson High School in Lincolnshire, Illinois. He taught physical education and health at Maine West High School in Maine Township, where he led one curricular team and was an active member on several others. He started his teaching career in driver education at York High School in Elmhurst, Illinois.

Eric is an active member of the state physical education and health organizations and, at the national level, Society of Health and Physical Educators (SHAPE) America. Eric has worked with health and physical education teams with the focus of creating curricula that are both personalized and relevant. He is committed to teacher development that leads educators to focus on the behaviors and thought processes that lead to positive, healthy behavior change, both now and well into students' futures.

Eric received a bachelor's degree in biology from Illinois College and a master's degree in educational leadership from American College of Education.

To book Eric Ramos for professional development, contact pd@SolutionTree .com.

Chapter 6

Implementing Proficiency-Based Grading in Physical Education and Health

Eric Ramos

> When health is absent, wisdom cannot reveal itself, art cannot manifest, strength cannot fight, wealth becomes useless, and intelligence cannot be applied.
>
> —*Herophilus*

Physical education (PE) teachers oversee the original lab class; few other subjects allow students the opportunity to practice what they learn in their everyday life: Teach the squat, pick up something heavy off the ground. Teach balanced nutrition, go decide what you will have for your next meal. There is no one right way, and as society's understanding of wellness improves (diet, exercise, mindfulness, self-efficacy, and grit), the health care industry is moving toward producing guiding principles. Proficiency-based grading focuses on identifying skills and focusing PE courses on key competencies. Shifting from learning specific facts about health and wellness (content knowledge) and toward broader skills provides the platform to teach students to use the world as one large experiment, and for them to try things and find an individualized combination right for them.

Proficiency-based grading encourages PE teachers to identify the guiding principles of their classes, provide the guiding principles to students in the form of learning targets and success criteria, and let them explore. *Learning targets* focus students around each lesson and assessment; *success criteria* guide students toward understanding what learning evidence will look like. I know this is the right shift, but all educators know that theory does not mirror practice. There is plenty of evidence that shows what PE teachers have been doing has not been working. The Centers for Disease Control and Prevention (CDC; 2017) documents the rise in childhood obesity. A lack of confidence and time, and the fear of being injured, is in a list of the top ten barriers to exercise.

Our goal should always be creating students who understand what it means to be well into adulthood, and all the decisions and barriers to achieving that. PE teachers are teaching the wrong skills to students, and the need to change is now. The standards created by SHAPE America (2013) are a good place to start developing these changes. Those targets, coupled with the implementation of proficiency-based grading, would create the framework necessary for personalized instruction around topics that will lead to long-term positive change.

This chapter explains the reasons to implement proficiency-based grading in PE and health courses through five phases: (1) preparation, (2) incubation, (3) insight, (4) evaluation, and (5) elaboration (Csikszentmihalyi, 1990).

Reasons to Implement Proficiency-Based Grading in PE and Health

When considering proficiency-based grading in PE and health classrooms, teachers often worry changes will undercut their teaching values. PE and health teachers tend to talk more about relationships, and these changes force teachers to focus on the learning targets. This will only last as long as it takes for the teacher to become comfortable with the targets, but it may still prove difficult for some. Concerns around how this may affect PE and health instruction, content, and grading workload are common. Questions such as, How are students going to learn the important content that they will only get in our classes? and Because we spend so much time talking, when are students going to be able to get to the activity that they need? As teachers learn about the proficiency-based grading method (which sounds valuable, but is unfamiliar), they begin to understand the deeper rationale—the *why*—behind proficiency-based grading, and their concerns diminish.

The following sections address how proficiency-based grading can directly improve wellness by gathering evidence and providing feedback on physical and health literacy; gets students active for tomorrow, not just for today; promotes real conversations with students around their physical and social-emotional growth; and supports the evolving understanding of physical fitness and nutrition.

Proficiency-Based Grading Can Directly Improve Wellness by Gathering Evidence and Providing Feedback on Physical and Health Literacy

SHAPE America (n.d.) defines *physical literacy* as the "ability, confidence and desire to be physically active for life" and *health literacy* as a person's "capacity to access information, resources and services necessary to maintaining and promoting health." *Wellness* includes physical, social, mental, emotional, and spiritual aspects of a person's life.

The first and primary thing PE and health teachers must remember is that they teach two of the most important things students learn. Former U.S. president Harry S. Truman understood that importance. When he proposed a national health program, Truman (1945) said, "We should resolve now that the health of this Nation is a national concern; that financial barriers in the way of attaining health shall be removed; that the health of all its citizens deserves the help of all the Nation."

In life, no one can promise longevity, but gathering evidence and providing feedback on physical and health literacy can directly improve quality of life. Many people can attest to the fact that, without your health, you will never reach your full potential. It is not only about teaching the positives of exercise; it is also about teaching the barriers such as time, energy, and motivation, and creating a plan to deal with these barriers before they arise. It is not about the right regimen or food; it is about the right thing for each individual and adapting to the changes in his or her life. Educators need to stay focused on teaching the bigger picture of fitness, such as the ability to meaningfully reflect. This requires teachers to focus on guiding students toward performance self-assessment, identifying strengths and weaknesses, and addressing specific reasons for these strengths and weaknesses (such as motivation or personal experiences). Evaluating students' understanding of that bigger picture and providing timely feedback will help them learn to anticipate and respond to what they cannot possibly know.

Life is full of the unexpected; it's not about knowing the future. Teachers must provide an environment where students can learn about themselves in terms of health and wellness, and what it means to be health literate. Focusing feedback to help students do the following will provide them with the tools they need to navigate whatever life sends their way.

- **Understand themselves:** Identify things that are common to their development and things that are unique to them.

- **Know what questions to ask:** Am I an early riser or a night owl? Will this event pass, or is this the new normal that I need to adjust for?

- **Know where to find credible information:** Is this advice from a body-building website or Harvard Health?

Proficiency-Based Grading Gets Students Active for Tomorrow, Not Just for Today

All stakeholders need to see wellness as a lifelong process, rather than an isolated event teachers report in a gradebook. PE and health classes are no longer just about physical activity, time in the zone, or gains in the weight room. Researchers Rachel Cooper, Gita D. Mishra, and Diana Kuh (2011) cite very real and positive effects of physical activity over the course of a person's life.

Physical education and health teachers should shift their focus from getting students moving today to getting them moving today *and* keeping them moving for the rest of their lives. These skills and habits are transferable. This shift requires teachers to start teaching with their eyes on a different target. Proficiency-based grading demands that a teacher team determine the most important parts of the curriculum and focus everything on teaching and assessing those things. Teachers need to ask themselves, "What is the ultimate judge of our success and failure in our subject matter? If we are not building student understanding of *why* they are doing what we ask them to do and *where* it fits in their lives once they leave us, what are we doing that is more important?"

Proficiency-based grading helps teams answer these questions by getting specific about three PE and health responses in table 6.1.

Table 6.1: Physical Education and Health Responses to Proficiency-Based Grading Specifics

Required Proficiency-Based Grading Specific	PE and Health Response
What do we want students to know, understand, and do?	We want them to know the various barriers that may arise, understand how the barriers to becoming and remaining healthy will impact them personally, and begin making decisions with these barriers in mind.

How do we clearly state our performance expectations?	We provide clear learning targets, success criteria, proficiency scaled targets, and timely feedback around those targets.
Why must we gather visible evidence of student learning to address proficiency gaps and extend mastery?	We want students to understand the importance of overall wellness in an individualized way. We must determine how we are helping them identify gaps in their knowledge, and what we are doing to improve on that thinking.

Proficiency-Based Grading Promotes Real Conversations With Students Around Their Physical and Social-Emotional Growth

Teachers must remember throughout their careers that many are at their best when working directly with students. Teachers must not let conversations with students about their progress move from the center of instruction. Their job is about building understanding. Teachers should ask themselves, "How do we build this understanding?" The answer is to do what they do best: have real conversations with students around their growth.

When preparing to transition from traditional grading to proficiency-based grading, teachers should clearly articulate learning targets and, in turn, what they *are* and *are not* looking for when assessing student proficiency. This clarity is especially useful when a student approaches a teacher and wants to know how to get a specific grade on an assessment or in the class. The teachers can redirect the student back to the scaled learning target and focus the conversation around the success criteria associated with the result the student is looking for. Proficiency-based grading ensures that teacher–student conversations provide the opportunity for both to clarify specific areas of growth. In PE and health, students often think they know the information and are blind to the significant gaps in their knowledge. Research verifies what many of us have known: that adolescents are still developing as decision makers. Now we have concrete evidence that this is a developmentally appropriate barrier that interferes with students' ability to internalize how PE and health topics apply to them personally (Hartley & Somerville, 2015).

Clarifying conversations with their teachers about scaled learning targets, success criteria, and actionable feedback can directly address any gaps in students' knowledge, putting them on the right path while providing the teacher the opportunity to strengthen the overall relationship and build trust. Teachers need students to talk differently about their own learning.

Additionally, PE and health learning environments are uniquely positioned to gather evidence and provide feedback on social-emotional skills. For example, a health classroom is full of discussions around mental health, diet, exercise, and *social health* (including life cycles, relationships, and sexual health). This is an opportunity to help students identify and name their feelings, and therefore work on their intrapersonal skills such as self-awareness and self-regulation. Figure 6.1 is a rubric for the skill of self-awareness.

Standard: Intrapersonal skills—self-awareness and self-management	
Objective: I manage my emotions.	
Score	**Proficiency Scale**
4—Refined Mastery	I am able to identify the reasons for my feelings and make adjustments.
3—Proficiency	I am able to identify the reasons for my feelings.
2—Approaches Proficiency	With support, I am able to identify the reasons for my feelings.
1—Still Developing	With support, I am unable to identify the reasons for my feelings.

Source for standard: Collaborative for Academic, Social, and Emotional Learning, 2017.

Figure 6.1: Self-awareness rubric.

Someone who has mastered or exceeded mastery in this skill might have internal dialogues that the teacher is unaware of, but show good decision-making skills, initiative, and self-control. Someone who is approaching mastery might tell a teacher "I'm angry" and, when the teacher asks whether she is angry because of her poor class performance, respond with "Yeah, that class has been frustrating me." That student doesn't yet know what is truly causing her feelings. A student who is at proficiency level 1 and still developing these skills might say "No, that isn't it" in response to that same question when, in fact, that is the problem.

Another example is how the PE setting lends itself to assessing and providing feedback on students' ability to work collaboratively with others—teamwork. Whether on the basketball court or in the weight room, it is essential for students who are working in collaborative groups to successfully run a class or attend to safety like those that come up in our unique environments. Figure 6.2 is a rubric for teamwork.

Standard: Interpersonal skills—social awareness and relationship skills	
Objective: I work collaboratively with others.	
Score	**Proficiency Scale**
4—Refined Mastery	I improve the informal processes by which work gets done in the team or organization.
3—Proficiency	I navigate the informal processes by which work gets done in the team or organization.
2—Approaches Proficiency	I recognize the informal processes by which work gets done in the team or organization.
1—Still Developing	I identify informal processes by which work gets done in the team or organization.

Source for standard: Collaborative for Academic, Social, and Emotional Learning, 2017.

Figure 6.2: Teamwork (collaboration) rubric.

Success criteria for collaboration might include equitably distributing tasks and completing a task with minimal guidance.

Although this is not traditionally where PE and health teachers have spent their time and energy, you can see how it benefits both the teacher and the student to explicitly teach to and provide timely feedback on social-emotional learning in our classrooms.

Proficiency-Based Grading Supports the Evolving Understanding of Physical Fitness and Nutrition

Remember to not get caught up in the specifics of current best practices throughout this process. Our understanding of physical fitness, nutrition, and overall wellness has evolved tremendously and will continue to do so. Do remember that proficiency-based grading is about teaching transferable skills and habits. Don't get caught up in the specifics of having students memorize what you believe to be true today. By teaching students habits and skills to make healthy decisions and find information, teachers ensure students will continue to grow along with the science.

In 2015, the fitness industry reported revenues over $25 billion, and the fitness industry grew more than 5 percent in 2012 and again between 2013 and 2015 (Steverman, 2017). There is no shortage of new fitness trends (the vast majority of which are garbage), some leading to real breakthroughs in our understanding of what it means to be well. As always, circle back on relevant and reliable sources.

Be ready to evolve your understanding of what it means to be well, and teach your students how to determine by themselves how reliable a source is.

Before individuals in PE or health embark on the journey toward proficiency-based grading, they must understand the roadblocks unique to this subject matter and commit to attacking these barriers. For teachers to say they focus on students' lifelong health and wellness, they must shift toward identifying and teaching a curriculum that focuses on identifying and providing feedback on the skills necessary to ensure lifelong health and wellness. Proficiency-based grading requires teachers to think differently about what they are trying to accomplish.

For example, the obesity epidemic has thrust PE into the spotlight, and many people say, "Good" and "Finally." With this spotlight came a dramatic change in what the field of education expects from teachers and students. Research shows a temporary cognitive boost associated with physical activity, and heart rate monitors have become how teachers measure students' so-called learning (Ratey & Hagerman, 2013).

This is problematic for several reasons. First, according to researchers Frances O'Callaghan, Michael O'Callaghan, Gail Williams, William Bor, and Jake Najman (2012), the cognitive boost is short lived and does not actually make someone any smarter; what it does do is prime the brain for learning. Second, according to authors John M. Jakicic et al. (2016), heart rate monitors have no long-lasting effect on weight loss, which seems to speak to student desire to work out or develop an understanding of where wellness fits into their lives outside of PE and health class.

If PE and health teachers truly focus on creating lifelong wellness in students (which relates to the epidemics of obesity, depression, and anxiety), they must think differently about their instructional practices.

Preparation: The Commitments of Proficiency-Based Grading in PE and Health

Teachers and teams make certain commitments to successfully implement this improved system of assessing and instructing. This can be difficult because teachers often have very personal and intense attachments to specific resources, literature, other curriculum, instruction, and assessment. When a team of teachers is preparing to do this work, there will be worries about losing autonomy and the challenge of adapting teaching and assessment in the near future. That is when making a series of commitments will allow teachers to support each other on the road to success.

The following commitments are discussed in subsequent sections: (1) physical wellness proficiency can be different than traditional expectations, (2) learning targets are based on overall wellness proficiency, (3) learning targets truly reflect physical education and health concepts, (4) wellness success criteria align to the learning targets, (5) don't rely on content knowledge to change student thinking around long-term health and wellness, and (6) physical education and health expectations are created collaboratively.

Commitment 1: Allow Physical Wellness Proficiency to Be Different Than Traditional Expectations

Traditional expectations in physical wellness may have centered on dressing out in the required uniform, fully participating, and memorizing content. Proficiency-based grading calls for all teaching to focus on what teachers truly want students to know—a team's agreed-on learning targets. Proficiency-based grading helps teachers identify and students learn what exploring their options and educated choices look like. Proficiency-based grading also helps teachers and students measure these skills. Talking to high school students about how to make healthy decisions knowing these same students are at a stage in their lives when they feel invincible is no small task!

With traditional grading, students do the required work to accumulate the points for an A, while proficiency-based grading requires students to understand proficiency, self-reflect, and work toward demonstrating the skills at the center of the course. The required demonstration forces students to think deeply about a topic that in the past was much less challenging. The focused approach toward demonstrating skill mastery in various situations is a key component of proficiency-based grading. PE and health teachers don't all work out the same way—in fact, some don't work out at all—but they all understand the importance of exercise. Every day, these teachers use professional judgment about how they spend their time.

Nobody starts with an understanding of the barriers to becoming and staying well throughout life because nobody could possibly anticipate all of the things yet to come. As students grow in their understanding of what life will bring, teachers can help them build the mental models they will need for addressing the unexpected parts. It is important to provide students with long-lasting experiences, so when they are faced with a barrier, it will not be the first time they have considered it. With experience, students can make the right decisions for themselves and weigh future decisions against each other. They will begin to understand that life is not a single event, but a series of events all strung together that make each life unique. Educators need to commit to the same shift in thinking as they teach students skills to help them in multiple instances and across their lives.

Commitment 2: When Creating Learning Targets, Calibration Takes Priority Over Autonomy

When using proficiency-based grading, it is imperative to create learning targets strongly tied to team expectations. It is common for everyone on the team to have the same idea of what it means to be proficient in a skill based on general conversations. These conversations typically offer ideas in a take-it-or-leave-it fashion, and sound something like this: Teacher A—"Hey, I have been giving this project to my students that I really like." Teacher B—"Oh, do you mind sharing it with me?" Teacher A—"No problem!"

In this interaction, Teacher A has a certain idea of what captures student learning and offers it to Teacher B via an assignment. But, without explicitly talking through how this assignment captures evidence of proficiency, they never have to agree. Because Teacher B positively receives Teacher A's assignment, the assumption is made that they are on the same page. In reality, Teacher B oftentimes takes the assignment and modifies it, or does not use it at all. There is often no follow-up and no calibration. This way, teacher autonomy stays intact, as does the illusion of authentic proficiency-based grading practices. This is an example of the barrier associated with maintaining teaching autonomy when transitioning from traditional grading to proficiency-based grading.

Proficiency-based grading challenges these assumptions and resulting illusions. It is when the team begins to identify and scale learning targets, an essential part of the transition from traditional grading to proficiency-based grading, that show these types of interactions fall short. The question driving this discussion and challenging thinking is, Are the targets based on proficiency? On the surface, this appears to be a question about learning targets, but in reality, it is a question about individual definitions—in this case, proficiency with learning targets.

Calibrating what qualifies as *proficiency*, or any grade, is a challenge to teacher autonomy and can become a significant obstacle to progress, and it is tempting to take the easy way out. At this point, it is important to define both proficiency and professional judgment, as having a working knowledge of these things will keep the team members on track as they try to answer these types of questions. *Proficiency* (as used in this chapter) is target-specific and team-developed, and occurs when a student displays competency in the identified learning target. *Professional judgment* is a team-developed definition of what it means to be proficient. There is no professional judgment in the absence of the team.

Commitment 3: Learning Targets Truly Reflect PE and Health Concepts

Agreeing on the concepts students should learn could lead to a course correction. In the world of PE and health, teachers spend much of their time focusing on what they want students to *do*. In proficiency-based grading, learning targets reflect what teachers truly want students to *learn*. In health class, I personally remember teaching and assessing my students on definitions of various drugs, expecting them to know about the uses and effects of each one. Finally, a coworker asked me, "Why are we teaching our students to become better drug users?" I was initially shocked, then I was a little embarrassed because of how obvious this suddenly was, and then I committed to change. I took a critical look at everything I was teaching in health and realized I was asking my students to memorize a series of facts and figures with the misguided notion that this would scare my students into behavior change.

There are many resources available online that cite the most recent research regarding the effectiveness of scare tactics, which the Massachusetts Technical Assistance Partnership for Prevention debunks. (See "The Facts About Scare Tactics" at https://bit.ly/2r4uGEr.) This may have motivated a few students in the moment, but I was not providing them with the *skills* they need to make a good decision when the time comes. Because of that, I felt the learning target I was teaching toward did not reflect what I truly wanted students to learn. What good is knowledge if you are not willing or able to act on it when you need to the most?

I was asking students to work hard in my presence without a thought toward what that meant for their future. In my heart, I wanted them to love exercise and see its value by experiencing it firsthand. Again, I was misguided. The vast majority of the time, this does not lead to long-term positive behavior change. The students may have worked hard for me, but I did not change their overall view of physical activity or understanding of how it fits differently in everyone's life.

Commitment 4: Wellness Success Criteria Align to the Learning Targets

This commitment goes back to the constant cycle of growth associated with the transition to proficiency-based grading. Once the team agrees on and articulates learning targets, success criteria, and assessments, it is time to put all this work into action. Both my school's PE and health teams' instruction and assessments have changed to more fully capture student evidence of proficiency as the teachers' understanding of proficiency-based grading evolves.

As instruction and assessment evolve, teachers should review the learning targets and success criteria to ensure they still align with the evidence teachers want to see.

In our school's courses, the learning targets and success criteria needed adjusting to more clearly coincide with instruction and assessment updates—an example of theory versus practice. As teams in other schools write their new targets, they may be too specific in their language. Once they begin teaching and receiving student evidence, they find that they can assess understanding a multitude of ways. Making those learning target and success criteria adjustments usually spurs new assessment ideas, and the cycle continues.

Commitment 5: Content Knowledge Doesn't Change Student Thinking Around Long-Term Health and Wellness

The health education setting has its own unique barriers. This often is the only place students receive information about mental health, drug use and abuse, social health, and cardiopulmonary resuscitation (CPR), so the content is often at the center of teaching. Content knowledge is foundational, but content knowledge alone does not lead to long-term behavior changes. Students can find all of this content online, and probably have already.

When asking students to build their ability to reflect, it is important to be specific. Personalizing discussions with barriers specific to students' experiences is an essential first step. For example, you could have students reflect on their transition between grade levels (from eighth grade to ninth, for instance) by posing a question that relates specifically to that time in their lives while encouraging them to look back on how they navigated that situation. You may create a learning target around reflection (*I can meaningfully reflect*) with accompanying success criteria and give them feedback on their ability to reflect with depth and breadth. This can lead to a very personalized form of reflection that results in transferable skills.

Commitment 6: PE and Health Expectations Are Created Collaboratively

A unique aspect is there are often many curricula under the single umbrella of PE and health. For example, the strength and conditioning teacher does not often interact with the aerobics teacher, who does not interact with the health teacher. Although these teachers all want the same thing for students, they treat their roles like they are unique.

To get students to effectively reflect on their behavior and the current and future barriers to wellness, teachers must commit to establishing common proficiency expectations for all courses. Proficiency-based grading provides a support for moving teachers out of silos and encouraging them to highlight their commonality and work together. If teachers create proficiency expectations unique to their courses—for example, weight training—and students can no longer weight train, the teachers have unknowingly built a barrier to lifelong wellness. If teachers work together to create a common message around the skills students need to build to develop lifelong health and wellness habits right for them, then teachers have knowingly worked to break down barriers to a healthier lifestyle.

Singleton teachers are often paired with other singletons. Teachers should identify the common skills—such as decision making—on which they will assess their students. This skill is not subject specific and would allow teachers to create common learning target language when scaling the target and common success criteria.

Incubation: The Unexpected Questions of Proficiency-Based Grading in PE and Health

As teachers progress toward using proficiency-based grading, they will uncover some wonderful questions that drive inquiry and implementation. During this second stage, several adopted practices may be working, but teachers may pay a lot of attention to the items that seem to threaten work or that have provided new challenges. This usually centers on work that is valued by one teacher, but does not align to the newly formed targets. The challenge lies in seeing the value in an assignment, but being unsure how it fits with the updated curriculum. With so much new information, it can be hard to not worry that some challenges will never be overcome. The following questions are representative of the incubation stage challenges that require patience and persistence.

Unexpected Question 1: Does the Proficiency Scale Reflect Lifelong Health and Wellness Goals?

As things progress through this early stage of implementation, assessments push back against teaching and the targets. A variation of one question seems to emerge at this time: Does our proficiency scale reflect what we are trying to accomplish? The answer to this question is rooted in what teachers think is important. For many years in physical education and health—and education in general—there was the belief that a teacher's job is to present information and the student's job to learn it. Teachers have since shifted their thinking, and the expectation for the student to learn has become the adults' responsibility. For many years in PE and health, it was about what was happening in class today, right now: learn these health terms, then take a quiz on them or back squat at the beginning of the term, test at the end, and measure strength gains.

Reflection has become the foundational piece linking what students learn in class to what they will do long after they have left school. Objective, deep personal reflection is a skill teachers can build with hard work and practice, so the team identified it as a learning target and built reflective opportunities in all team members' lessons. Figure 6.3 is a rubric for that learning target.

Learning Target: I can meaningfully reflect.		
Score	**Proficiency Scale**	**Success Criteria**
4—Refined Mastery	I reflect with additional insight.	• There is a future action, solution, or option for change. • Additional resources were cited. • Emotional, personal, or social impact was included.
3—Proficiency	I meaningfully reflect.	• The reflection addresses wellness. • The reflection has the potential to lead to success. • The reflection includes reasons for the success or failure. • The reflection cites personal experience. • The reflection provides details and examples. • The reflection acknowledges potential barriers. • The reflection specifies both intrinsic and extrinsic motivators.
2—Approaches Proficiency	I reflect.	• The reflection lacks depth or specific detail.
1—Still Developing	I reflect with prompting.	• The reflection lacks content knowledge. • The reflection does not link back to the question.

Source: Adlai E. Stevenson High School, 2018.

Figure 6.3: PE self-reflection learning target example.

*Visit **go.SolutionTree.com/assessment** for a free reproducible version of this figure.*

Figure 6.4 is from a health curriculum. The horizontal formatting is intentional. It makes the most sense for how the target is displayed in classrooms.

4—Refined Mastery	3—Proficiency	2—Approaches Proficiency	1—Still Developing
I advocate for myself or others in a way that will have a sustained health impact.	I advocate for myself or others in a way that will have a healthy impact.	I advocate for myself or others in a way that is unclear or inconsistent.	I recognize the need to advocate for myself or others.

Success Criteria:

- The message is clear.
- The verbal or nonverbal communication is consistent.
- The student is proactive, resulting in a timely response.
- The student seeks advice from a trusted adult or professional.
- The student displays refusal skills.

Source for standard: Collaborative for Academic, Social, and Emotional Learning, 2017.

Figure 6.4: Health communication rubric.

It is important to note that all of these targets are taught across multiple units. The skill is the target, and the unit is the vehicle through which that skill is assessed. For example, teachers can assess a student's ability to communicate and advocate in a CPR unit based on his or her ability to communicate effectively in an emergency situation and advocate for widespread training on this life-saving technique. The same can be said when teaching a mental health unit; students can advocate for the importance of mental health education while being able to communicate if they or a friend needs mental health support. Our targets are the common thread that tie our units of study, and thus our entire curriculum, together.

At Stevenson, students receive general feedback on their ability to reflect as they work through topics such as cooperation, teamwork, communication, and leadership. We teach these topics in minilesson format (fewer than ten minutes per lesson) using a series of questions that prompt thinking. We then ask students to discuss the question with a peer or in small groups; then the teacher drives the discussion back to the main point. In a communication lesson, for example, we may ask students to identify the three main types of communication as determined by Arkansas State University (2016): (1) verbal, (2) nonverbal, and (3) visual. Then the teacher might highlight how humans exchange information primarily in these three ways and ask students to be aware of those methods as they participate in class that day. Students would then participate in the activity and, at the end of class, reflect with the class on their experiences.

The lessons build throughout the week until students (typically at the end of the week) receive and reflect on prompts like the following.

- Describe a time you had a communication breakdown. What happened? How could it have been avoided?

- In what ways do you use communication in PE, or outside of school? Is it effective communication? Explain each example.

- In what ways can talking to someone face-to-face be more beneficial than texting him or her?

The target is posted at the top of the assessment, and students are provided feedback on their reflection. Teachers gather evidence and follow up with students periodically, but do not measure student success on whether they achieve a goal. Successful completion of the assignment requires students to reflect on the process itself and build on what they learned for the future.

Unexpected Question 2: Do the Learning Targets Unintentionally Fit the Traditional PE and Health Assessment Methods?

Along the path to embracing evidence of skill mastery, our teams desired assessments that measured cognitive skill development and application. When the teachers thought about what it means to develop a new mental skill, they looked at what they wanted students to leave these classes with. That didn't mean getting rid of everything and starting over from scratch, but they did need to look at everything through a new lens, repeatedly asking themselves the question, "What is the new cognitive skill that we want our students to develop?" With this, the teams took a hard look at the skills they measure in both PE and health, and realized rote memorization—especially information readily available on the internet—does not develop into a new skill. Although students may need to learn new information so they can perform the skill teachers will measure, teachers (or students) should not focus their attention on the memorization of vocabulary terms or general rules of the games they play. However, this information is foundational, transferable, and essential for the deeper learning that we are asking our students to do.

For example, if teachers ask students to use their understanding of a game to reflect on how they work with a team on a given day, they need to have an understanding of how the game is played, strategies, and the rules (foundational content knowledge) to answer effectively. So, teachers need to provide this knowledge to students, but they do not need to make it a formal assessment event to be able to assess it, as it will come out in the students' reflections.

Similarly, in health, a teacher would not need to directly assess a student's memorization of the vocabulary words in the drug education unit in order to assess it. The teacher could ask students to use unit-specific vocabulary when describing a party, complete with what choice they would make, how, and why. This is not as much about the target as it is about how the team structures the assessments and introduces them to the class. If a teacher instructs the students around a particular unit of study—mental health, for example—then when he or she evaluates the students' evidence for decision making in a mental health unit skill, they should be talking about mental health topics and using terminology that was discussed in class. If either of these are missing, it becomes difficult to assess the student's ability to show proficiency in the target. There are ample opportunities for students to answer questions about decision making while showing an understanding of their drug education. Assessments beyond content knowledge focus on two things: (1) putting students in a position to show what they know and (2) putting students in a position to show how they can use this knowledge.

That is not to say teachers should replace physical skill acquisition; rather, that physical activity becomes the vehicle through which teachers measure cognitive skill acquisition. The same holds true for content knowledge: creating assessments that require students to understand the physical or content aspects of the activity in order to complete the assessment is the key. For example, having students talk about how to identify signs of depression using content-specific language allows the teacher to gauge their understanding of the unit's general content as well as the learning target's larger skill. In a PE setting, having students reflect on how the dead lift improves everyday human functionality using proper terminology will allow them to display their understanding of the general terminology and apply this information outside the classroom.

It is just impossible to give appropriate feedback in the gradebook using traditional grading. Can you imagine telling a student he or she is a 74 percent decision maker? Or that his or her teamwork and cooperation is 85 percent? To focus curriculum on skills and success criteria, it is essential for teachers to determine what it means to be proficient in that skill and articulate those behaviors for students. I am not sure what it means to be a B-level PE student, but I am sure what it means to be proficient in teamwork. These three things must occur: (1) the teacher must explicitly teach the criteria for that skill, (2) the student reflects on where he or she is in relation to that criteria, and (3) the teacher gives the student specific, actionable feedback on his or her self-reflection.

Unexpected Question 3: Are the Cognitive and Physical Assessments Flexible Enough to Allow Students to Show All Levels of Learning?

Lastly, something that often surfaces once teachers begin instruction and give and collect assessment data is that these do not align with learning target scaling. After giving each assessment the first time, it would be wise for teachers to ensure the assessment is flexible enough to allow students to truly show all the levels of learning (1–4) using the learning targets scaling. Some assessments are too easy, others might make a 4 impossible, or some might not align with the target as well in practice as they did in theory. These pitfalls become evident once students have the success criteria. If it is too easy, it will become obvious when students become proficient very quickly, without being challenged. If it is impossible to meet or exceed mastery, a student will bring it to your attention, or you will see it in the evidence once you begin grading the assessment.

It is essential for the team to continue to objectively align each assessment with the scaled learning targets. In my experience, it was often the assessment our teachers needed to adjust. Over time, our teachers also needed to adjust the learning targets and the success criteria affixed to those targets. These were difficult conversations, but all of the adjustments came from objective team discussions about student work and continual reflection on the overall course objectives.

Insight: The Essential Insights of Proficiency-Based Grading in PE and Health

As teachers begin to move beyond the initial fears and roadblocks and gain insight, it is vitally important to take some time to look back on and appreciate how the team has passed some intimidating hurdles thus far. Teams should have a clear enough idea of how proficiency-based grading works, and they can play to its strengths as they teach and plan. They begin providing proficiency-based grading with more power instead of just trying to get their balance.

At this point, physical education and health teachers might have the following insights: (1) PE teachers must change how they teach health and wellness, not just how they grade, (2) assessment opportunities are everywhere, and (3) there is time in the day for instruction and physical activity in PE class.

Insight 1: PE Teachers Must Change How They Teach Health and Wellness, Not Just How They Grade

Another assumption some teachers make is that proficiency-based grading is just a change in the gradebook. A teacher can give the same assessments, teach the same way, and base each assessment on a four-point scale. What my team experienced is that students quickly become confused by this because traditional grading does not require a detailed explanation of what it means to be proficient. Teachers quickly realize that if they are going to ask a student to present mastery of a skill, they must clearly define mastery when they give the assignment (at the very minimum). In fact, clarity on what students are working toward (the learning target) throughout instruction of the topic, as well as when assessment events occur, produces better outcomes on the assessment. Better outcomes on the assessments create student confidence and minimize reperformances, thus decreasing teacher workload. It truly is a win-win situation.

Insight 2: Assessment Opportunities Are Everywhere

With proficiency-based grading, teachers must move past the traditional mindset structure that includes teachers making assessments during specific times (typically at the end of the unit), and completing those assessments in written form. At Stevenson, with so much collaboration going on between students in our classrooms, evidence is now everywhere.

As students participate in class, teachers are walking around and hearing their thinking as it happens and as it evolves over time. With the understanding that evidence is everywhere, how can teachers structure lessons and deliver instruction with the intent on capturing and reporting on evidence as it happens during the class? As students struggle through a problem or articulate their thinking and how it has grown or changed, they are displaying evidence of growth and understanding. It seems only logical for teachers to want to capture these moments and provide students with feedback. Students and teachers can capture the moments, both formally and informally. The key component is the presence of accurate and timely feedback.

Insight 3: There Is Time in the Day for Instruction and Physical Activity in PE Class

In the PE setting, it is common for teachers to struggle to find time to impart the lesson of seeing the big picture, but if they continue to do what they have always done (focus exclusively on getting students moving today), they will continue to get what they have always got (another crop of students who cannot transfer what they are learning to the future, when they will need it most).

There is no question that physical activity needs to remain the primary focus in PE classrooms. For many students, this is the only activity they get all day, and we cannot rob them of that. With that said, there is room in the day for teachers to provide students with the knowledge it will take to transform their thinking around PE and help them engage with barriers in a meaningful way. The three minutes a teacher takes at beginning of class, coupled with the two minutes that he or she takes at the end, can and should frame the activity in terms of something bigger than the activity itself. Every day, teachers should work to answer these questions: What will students leave with today? and How does this fit in students' lives? Once this is clear to the teacher, it is his or her job to work to ensure students can answer these questions as well.

Evaluation: The Key Questions of Proficiency-Based Grading in PE and Health

Implementation's beginning stages bring a perspective of evaluation. While professional growth never takes one path, reaching this point allows teams to set a goal of reaching regular practice and to confidently look into ways that the system impacts feedback and grading.

Evaluation can lead physical education and health teachers to ask the following key questions: (1) "What types of conversations are teachers having with students?" (2) "Can a teacher give a student any grade he or she wants?" and (3) "How can teachers continually improve their professional judgment about what constitutes evidence in PE and health?"

Key Question 1: What Types of Conversations Are Teachers Having With Students?

One of the biggest changes when shifting to proficiency-based grading is how conversations between teachers and students immediately center on the learning, not the points. Health homework is often the last to get done, and often students do the minimum required to get the desired grade. In my experience, there were countless times students would approach me, often toward the end of the course, and ask, "What do I need to do to get an (fill in letter grade here)?" I talked to them about how the content was the important part, and that I wanted them to learn, but we both knew it would come down to points. They were going to do what it took to get the grade they wanted. This required no learning, just doing.

In proficiency-based grading, the conversation might start with the same question: What do I need to do to get an (fill in letter grade here)? Now, however, the teacher says, "You need to show me evidence that you are proficient in this skill."

Usually the question, How do I do that? emerges, and the conversation can really begin. At this point, the teacher refers the student back to the feedback he or she gave on the assessment, where all teachers include the learning target and scaled rubrics (to aid students as they complete the work and help facilitate these kinds of conversations). The teacher clarifies any misunderstandings or misconceptions around the content and the expectations. Once the student understands, he or she gets the opportunity to show additional evidence. It comes through a reperformance of that assessment or a future opportunity on another assessment. It is refreshing to have conversations center on *showing* learning rather than just *doing*.

In the PE setting, it is slightly different. PE teachers focus on the *doing*, as it is a large part of the curriculum. Think of a lab class in science. The science teacher is very interested in the completion of the lab as well as the way students act in the laboratory and interact with each other throughout the process. A PE class would operate much the same way. The teacher would be interested in, and provide feedback for, the cognitive skills that students are being asked to build (reflection), as well as how they are interacting with the activity and with the other students. PE teachers will continue instructing around this, and continue giving students feedback on this, but it cannot stop there.

National PE Standards 3 and 5 focus on achieving and maintaining a health-enhancing level of physical activity and fitness *as well as* recognizing the value of physical activity (n.d.). There is no question that a focus on these standards causes educators to shift their mindset toward instilling the importance of lifelong activity in students. The *doing* of the activity becomes the vehicle through which teachers instruct, not the focus. Students need to come to classes prepared to participate safely in a set activity so teachers can get to teaching students where physical activity will fit in their lives, while also explicitly teaching and giving feedback on the social-emotional skills so critical to this discipline. Each student is different, so teachers need to tailor feedback, but keep it broad enough so each student can apply it no matter what lies ahead.

Key Question 2: Can a Teacher Give a Student Any Grade He or She Wants?

With proficiency-based grading, learning targets become the focus early in the implementation process, and this is where many past assumptions begin to surface. Everyone brings his or her own understanding of proficiency to the discussion, and when the team is asked to work to define proficiency for a given target, disagreements on practice begin to arise. In health and PE, many teachers rely on their subjective judgment to assess students. Although it is true that proficiency-based grading is built on the idea that educators can and should use their judgment to assess students and give feedback, it does not support teachers giving a student any grade he or she wants under the guise of professional judgment. As stated earlier in this chapter, there is no professional judgment in the absence of team calibration. It is important to remember that it is each teacher's responsibility to use best-known practices with his or her team. When the team has decided on the same learning target, teachers should find it easier to collaborate and calibrate around grading.

Key Question 3: How Can Teachers Continually Improve Their Professional Judgment About What Constitutes Evidence in PE and Health?

Professional conversations about specific examples of student work are the cornerstones to calibration and continual improvement. One way to accomplish calibration is to have students create a product and then have the team collectively grade that product. This is a common task when transitioning from traditional grading, but proficiency-based grading allows teachers to be creative in how they capture evidence. Lesson studies, filming lessons, or simply inviting other teachers into your classroom are practical ways to capture evidence to share with other teachers. Exploring the collective understanding of common resources—the standards, learning targets, assessment adaptations, and teacher postassessment reflection—are all ways to ensure refined professional judgment in line with the group. It is not uncommon for a teacher to hold a postassessment reflection with the team and then, based on that discussion, change the assessment, instruction, or grading with the team.

Elaboration: The Core Beliefs of Proficiency-Based Grading in PE and Health

Teachers at the elaboration phase of implementation have reached a mature and clear perspective of using a proficiency-based grading system. They have discovered that the system does not push them out of valued projects, simulations, or other assessments and activities they know help students learn; instead, they see there is depth to be gained from such work, with an underlying and clear focus on skills. With their comfort in this system, teachers are resources for their colleagues and on the cutting edge for new ways to provide more support for and collaboration with their students.

Teachers who successfully implement proficiency-based grading adhere to all seven of the core beliefs explained in chapter 1 (page 9): (1) growth is a central concept, (2) reperformance is essential, (3) building students' reflection abilities is essential, (4) homework has a role, (5) communication with parents and the community is key, (6) culminating experiences like final exams have a different purpose, and (7) behavior can be in or out of the grade. The following sections, which reflect the core beliefs' original numbering, explore the core beliefs that PE and health teachers in particular should never lose sight of.

Core Belief 1: Growth Is a Central Concept

Lack of knowledge is one of the top barriers to starting and sticking with a fitness program, and it is pervasive. Students are entering high school with a very basic understanding of what it means to be well, but teachers cannot expect to reshape their habits overnight. Health and wellness is not achieved in a short amount of time, and maintenance is a lifelong endeavor that requires consistency and determination. Putting growth at the center of learning frees PE and health teachers to focus on the most important part of their work: lifelong behavior change. Teachers continually work with and grow students based on incremental behavior changes. Instead of testing a physical skill or the ability to memorize something and then moving on, teachers focus on the deeper work of building student understanding of how it is possible to work slowly and create healthy habits that lead to lasting change.

Core Belief 2: Reperformance Is Essential

Accountability is prevalent in physical education and health. Although true of all of disciplines to some degree, it seems to be especially prevalent in these courses. Many of Stevenson's PE and health teachers are current or former coaches and athletic trainers, so holding students accountable is ingrained in them; further, this accountability is an important and difficult hurdle to overcome when shifting teachers' mindset to proficiency-based grading. Initially, teachers believed students would simply not turn in the work, instead relying on reperformance opportunities to eventually get all of their work done. This can become a significant barrier to a team wanting to make the change from traditional grading to proficiency-based grading, even if members believe proficiency-based grading is better for students.

In my experience, the concerns about reperformance being abused are largely unfounded. The vast majority of students do the work if teachers create assessments *required* for student learning. Part of this means teachers must realize that there cannot be any busy work or pet projects not directly related to the learning target. Asking a teacher to let go of a favorite assignment or nightly homework that he or she has always given is difficult, but if teachers really focus on developing skills, then that is where they should devote all of their time and energy.

Key Points

To ensure full understanding, review the following key points from this chapter.

- PE and health teachers should not lose sight of a need to shift their focus from getting students moving today to getting them moving today and keeping them moving for the rest of their lives. Teachers must focus on building student understanding of *why* they are doing what they are doing, and where it can fit in their lives once they leave high school.

- In the PE world, teachers spend much of their time focused on what they want students to *do*, but their targets need to reflect what teachers want students to *learn*.

- Grades in a gradebook need to reflect learning, not behavior. In a PE class, teachers watching students actively participating should ask themselves, "What are students' actions showing about their learning?" In a health classroom, that means teachers should not give penalties (and embed those penalties) for late or missing work in students' grades.

 **Steven M. Wood, PhD,** is director of science at Adlai E. Stevenson High School in Lincolnshire, Illinois. In his role, he provides support and leadership for science learning, including the science faculty's professional development. Steve began his career in the health care industry, but soon realized that his passion was in helping students become better science learners. In addition to his science teaching and leadership roles, Steve has coached many athletic teams and led several international science travel courses. He is a member of many professional organizations.

Steve earned a bachelor's degree in biology education from Taylor University, a master's degree in biology from Northeastern Illinois University, and a doctorate in educational leadership and policy studies from Loyola University Chicago.

To book Steven M. Wood for professional development, contact pd@SolutionTree.com.

Chapter 7

Implementing Proficiency- Based Grading in Science

Steven M. Wood

Science is as much a way of knowing as it is a body of knowledge.
—*Adlai E. Stevenson High School Coursebook*

onsider this: many teachers approached the transition to the Next Generation Science Standards (NGSS) as an *evolution*, either tweaking or redoing lessons only to rebuild the course with the original materials. However, the change to proficiency-based grading is a *revolution* in thinking, requiring new construction materials and new tools. To make this change requires time and deep thought. Changing too quickly from a traditional grading model to proficiency-based grading will not work. To use a physics analogy, it's not the velocity that will kill you; it's the acceleration!

This chapter applies to the full range of science courses in high school, including biology, chemistry, physics, and Earth science, along with the more specialized electives that fall within these domains. In addition, the focus will link directly to the performance expectations in the NGSS. This includes the Disciplinary Core Ideas (DCIs, or key science concepts), the Science and Engineering Practices (SEPs, or skills; the *doing* of science), and the Crosscutting Concepts (CCCs, or themes that span across all science coursework; NGSS, 2013a, 2013b, 2013c). While proficiency-based grading and the NGSS do not depend on one another, this chapter will weave the two together as there is to be a common theme of developing skills—SEPs—over the span of a students' science education, just as the development of discipline-specific skills are explained in other content areas in other chapters in this book.

This chapter explains the reasons to implement proficiency-based grading in science courses through five phases: (1) preparation, (2) incubation, (3) insight, (4) evaluation, and (5) elaboration (Csikszentmihalyi, 1990).

Reasons to Implement Proficiency-Based Grading in Science

When considering proficiency-based grading in science classrooms, teachers often worry changes will undercut their teaching values. Concerns around how this may affect science instruction, content, and grading workload are common. For example, teachers wonder: "How can I provide instruction and assessment that focuses on both the science content and the science practices? How will I assess and provide feedback on science-specific skills in a meaningful, efficient way?" As teachers learn about the proficiency-based grading method (which sounds valuable, but so unfamiliar), they begin to understand the deeper rationale—the *why*—and their concerns diminish.

The following sections address how proficiency-based grading supports the doing of science, supports alignment with the NGSS, supports clarity in the science gradebook, focuses conversations around learning science, supports the belief that all students can learn science, and supports the removal of averaging points in science courses.

Proficiency-Based Grading Supports the Doing of Science

Throughout my entire career, science teachers have said that science is *a process* and *a way of thinking*. Teachers believe this to be true, and it is what they most hope for students. However, when taking a look at our curriculum, instruction, and assessment, I see there is still work to do if teachers want to align this belief with their practice. Proficiency-based grading supports the perspective that what makes great science education is the *doing*. These insights are coming at the same time that science education is shifting to support the learning that the NGSS calls for.

Science classes are about more than students' accumulating facts and then teachers measuring the percentage of facts students are able to recognize or recall. Rather, there must be an intentional focus on developing, teaching, and assessing science process skills such as analyzing and interpreting data or developing and using models over time. This expands the practice of teaching science beyond delivering content, allowing practice, giving quizzes, and then administering tests, to developing proficiency on transferable skills that scientists regularly use. We certainly see the direct transfer of these skills to other courses, such as mathematics and English, but also to every career path a student could possibly take.

In proficiency-based grading, students demonstrate proficiency in science skills while demonstrating an understanding of DCI (NGSS, 2013c). The DCIs include concepts that are familiar to science teachers, including Newton's third law, that "for any pair of interacting objects, the force exerted by the first object on the second object is equal in strength to the force that the second object exerts on the first, but in the opposite direction" (MS-PS2-1; NGSS, 2013c). Similarly, in high school biology, "Systems of specialized cells within organisms help them perform the essential functions of life" (HS-LS1-1; NGSS, 2013c).

Proficiency-Based Grading Supports Alignment With NGSS

Since the introduction of these standards in 2013, science educators have been busy wrestling with how to implement the NGSS's vision of learning. Most notable is the intentional move toward so-called *three-dimensional learning* (NGSS, n.d.). This 3-D vision of science instruction calls on teachers to explicitly teach the following three components.

1. The SEPs articulate what students will do to demonstrate proficiency, such as develop and use models, construct explanations, and design solutions. In this chapter and approach, the SEPs will form the scaled proficiency target.

2. The DCIs represent the science ideas (what many teachers refer to as *content*) all students should learn. This includes concepts such as plate tectonics and large-scale system interactions or the structure and properties of matter. In this chapter, DCIs are treated as success criteria for demonstrating proficiency in the SEPs. Since the learning targets in proficiency-based grading are recursive and span the duration of study, the DCIs support the development of proficiency in the SEPs over time.

3. The CCCs are themes in all science disciplines, including patterns, cause and effect, and energy and matter. These apply throughout the science course and the assessments used in class.

In Stevenson's vision of the best implementation of the NGSS, students and teachers focus on developing proficiency in the SEPs. Students demonstrate proficiency by meeting established success criteria, including demonstrating understanding of the DCIs and making connections through the CCCs. By moving to proficiency-based standards that focus on science practices, teachers' gradebooks better align with the vision for learning science. In addition, this focus on science practices allows more common vocabulary with mathematics and English colleagues, as those teachers have been implementing the same state or provincial standards.

This is not *evolution*, but a *revolution* in instruction, assessment, and feedback. Yes, science teachers have always asked students to engage in the SEPs. However, these practices have not typically been the focus of instruction; most teachers have not developed guiding structures to explicitly teach students how to carry out the practices. Traditionally, their science practices supported learning the DCIs. Since this shift, the science practices have taken the lead, and the DCIs are interchangeable pieces that change throughout the skill-building process.

Proficiency-Based Grading Supports Clarity in the Science Gradebook

Typically, science gradebooks are a list of tasks (homework, labs, quizzes, tests), with points or percentages reflecting the ratio of correct to incorrect answers. However, teachers have been lulled into an illusion of precision and reliability, with complex calculations and formulas that calculate percentages to the tenth of a percentage point. In proficiency-based grading, the gradebook clearly communicates student mastery (or a need for more practice) of science knowledge and skills. This provides clarity for students, parents, and teachers about where the students need to focus. Providing this feedback on evidence collected from students requires the professional judgment of thoughtful educators using scaled learning targets, not points and percentages.

Proficiency-Based Grading Focuses Conversations Around Learning Science

One of the greatest benefits of shifting from points to proficiency is that it changes the conversations with students and among teachers. I'm sure teachers have all heard many students (or parents) saying that they need "just one more point on the lab report" to get the grade they want. Shifting the conversation to proficiency moves the focus to how the student demonstrates proficiency. Here's a challenge: the next time you hear teachers talking about grading in a traditional, points-based system, consider how often you hear them talk about *learning* compared with how often they talk about the *accumulation of points* (that is, How many points will the teacher assign each section of that lab report?). Unfortunately, the latter is too often the case in office and classroom conversations.

Proficiency-Based Grading Supports the Belief That All Students Can Learn Science

The transition to proficiency-based grading in science requires and presumes several core beliefs. Teachers must firmly understand and believe all students can, will, and must learn—a belief clearly outlined by the National Research Council (2012) in *A Framework for K–12 Science Education*. This learning might not occur during the first exposure to an idea, nor will it happen at the same time or in the same way for all students. Teachers and students alike will need to embody a growth mindset, seeing how mastery of the SEP takes time to develop and then express in multiple contexts.

Proficiency-Based Grading Supports the Removal of Averaging Points for Science Courses

Grading approaches that focus on the accumulation of points and averaging don't make sense. Thought leaders guiding the transition to proficiency-based grading will need to be patient—and ever so persistent—in helping most parents, students, and teachers at the high school level see this reality. Although this new system might not have extensive *experimental* data to support the goal of improved learning, the traditional grading system of collecting points and reporting on events (assignments, tests, quizzes, labs, and homework) just doesn't make sense. Grades should be based on the science skills a student is capable of performing, not a punishment or reward for behavior choices like not doing homework or being really organized and on time. Likewise, with this new system, teachers will call on students to do more than understand and communicate knowledge of science core ideas; students must truly be able to carry out the three dimensions of learning in the NGSS.

Preparation: The Commitments of Proficiency-Based Grading in Science

Teachers and teams make certain commitments to successfully implement this improved system of assessing and instructing. This can be difficult because teachers often have very personal and intense attachments to specific resources, literature, other curriculum, instruction, and assessment. When a team of teachers is preparing to do this work, there will be worries about losing autonomy and the challenge of adapting teaching and assessment in the near future. That is when making a series of commitments will allow teachers to support each other on the road to success.

The following commitments are discussed in subsequent sections: (1) develop learning targets that focus on more than disciplinary core ideas, (2) outline mastery levels on scaled, proficiency-based science practices, (3) focus on all three dimensions of science as called for in the NGSS, (4) focus on transferable science skills that provide lasting value to students, and (5) continue weaving mastery into other NGSS dimensions.

Commitment 1: Develop Learning Targets That Focus on More Than Disciplinary Core Ideas

To begin this process, teachers must commit to developing proficiency-based, scaled learning targets that focus on science practices or skills. Students will demonstrate mastery and growth in science practices in the context of the DCIs. The wording of these targets is important; teachers should determine exactly what they expect students to do and how well students must do it. Underlying this commitment is the belief that while traditional, content-based learning targets might be good, proficiency-based targets will be better.

This change also presumes that the first attempts at proficiency-based teaching won't be perfect, and there will be an ongoing process of improvement. Our teams found that simpler theories and approaches often turn out to be the best. However, I can't underscore enough the value of wrestling through complex thinking as teachers arrive at the final, workable (and often relatively simple) solution. This will require teacher expertise and, in the best-case scenario, collaboration.

Many schools choose to focus their targets on the SEPs from the NGSS, which is what we did in our school. As Stevenson teams made this transition, they chose approximately three to five learning targets that they value and use regularly in their classes. Teams standardized these learning targets across all courses (see figure 7.1). Then, these teams chose the *essential components* (or success criteria) that students must use to demonstrate proficiency. The following pattern recurs in the science learning targets.

- 4—Student uses all essential components in unfamiliar contexts or making connections to related science concepts.
- 3—Student uses all essential components in familiar contexts.
- 2—Student uses some essential components in familiar contexts.
- 1—Student performs the SEPs in familiar contexts with support.

Figure 7.1 is an example of two science practices.

In creating, communicating, and using proficiency-based targets, teachers come to realize the words they use in a target matter a great deal. While it can be counterproductive to belabor or overanalyze, it has become clear that teachers need to determine if they are asking students, for example, to analyze data or to create data representations. Determining if you truly want students to analyze or interpret and what that means can take a great deal of time, but it is critically important to have a working understanding and agreement on these semantics.

4—Exceeds Proficiency	3—Demonstrates Proficiency	2—Approaching Proficiency	1—Developing Foundational Skills
Learning Target: Analyzing and interpreting data			
I can analyze and interpret data using all essential components in unfamiliar contexts or make connections to related science concepts.	I can analyze and interpret data using all essential components in familiar contexts.	I can analyze and interpret data using some essential components in familiar contexts.	I can analyze and interpret data in familiar contexts with support.
Learning Target: Constructing scientific explanations			
I can construct an explanation for a scientific phenomenon using all essential components in unfamiliar contexts or make connections to related science concepts.	I can construct an explanation for a scientific phenomenon using all essential components in familiar contexts.	I can construct an explanation for a scientific phenomenon using some essential components in familiar contexts.	I can construct an explanation for a scientific phenomenon in familiar contexts with support.

Figure 7.1: Two proficiency scales.

*Visit **go.SolutionTree.com/assessment** for a free reproducible version of this figure.*

Commitment 2: Outline Mastery Levels on Scaled, Proficiency-Based Science Practices

Science teachers love to measure things objectively. Often a concern (or criticism) in determining proficiency levels is that this is a *subjective* process. Teachers emphasize assigning a score requires *professional judgment supported by evidence.* Teachers are professionals and recognize quality student work. To provide clarity and consistency, teachers need to develop rubrics that differentiate proficiency levels without being so restrictive that they attempt to describe every possible situation that may arise in student work.

Our rubrics include a scaled learning target and description of the success criteria for that particular SEP. The scaled target is intended for classification—assigning a score—and the success criteria are for communication—anchoring feedback to students. Figure 7.2 is an example of our scaled rubric for the SEP construct explanations, along with those success criteria.

Learning Target: Construct explanations			
4—Exceeds Proficiency	**3—Proficiency**	**2—Approaches Proficiency**	**1—Developing Foundational Skills**
I can construct explanations and design solutions using all essential components in unfamiliar contexts or make connections to related science concepts.	I can construct explanations and design solutions using all essential components in familiar contexts.	I can construct explanations and design solutions using some essential components in familiar contexts.	I can construct explanations and design solutions in familiar contexts with support.

Success Criteria:
- The claim is accurate and concise and answers the questions.
- Evidence includes data specifics and context.
- Evidence is sufficient and accurate.
- Evidence includes trends, patterns, or comparisons.
- Reasoning does the following.
  - It describes the significance or meaning of trends or data and explains why the data count as evidence to support the claim.
  - It includes one or more biological principles that are important to the claim and evidence.

Source for standard: NGSS, 2013a, 2013b, 2013c. Source: Adapted from Adlai E. Stevenson High School, 2018.

Figure 7.2: Scaled rubric for the SEP construct explanations.

We maintained consistency in the scaled learning target across all of our science courses—they are the same. This reduces the time teachers or teams need to spend developing the scales, as well as provides consistency as students move through their science coursework. However, the success criteria are flexible, and teams change them to match their course focus and change them for particular assessment events. Within this framework, we have seen a great deal of vertical articulation between our teams across all grade levels and all science disciplines. For example, here are the success criteria for the same SEP of constructing explanations from our AP chemistry team.

Qualities of a well-constructed explanation:

- Applies appropriate scientific principles, ideas, or evidence
- Makes connections between main ideas
- Uses important vocabulary appropriately
- Constructs or uses models to help clarify explanations
- Chooses and uses data as evidence to support explanations
- Applies clear and concise reasoning

The two teams have taken a slightly different approach in defining the success criteria, but they provide a great foundation for learning together and describing what they are looking for in students' work. Both teams will change these criteria over time as they apply them to student work, refine their own thinking, and come to better ways to present these to students.

In our system, a level 3 proficiency ultimately translates to an A letter grade. Teachers look for a pattern in student work that demonstrates proficiency across many samples of work. Biology teacher Tommy Wolfe emphasizes the importance of providing tasks that allow students to engage in these practices, but also notes that teachers are looking not for perfection, but rather for a pattern of proficiency (T. Wolfe, personal communication, January 16, 2019). Ultimately, the teacher is using all of the success criteria, the scaled learning target, and his or her professional judgment to determine that the pattern of evidence shows proficiency with the SEP using the various DCIs students have been asked to practice.

To ensure fairness, teachers need to follow best practices, such as providing anchor samples that typify level 1, 2, 3, and 4 proficiency. These anchor samples are models of student work that show varying proficiency levels, and include how the success criteria guide accurate scoring. It is most helpful when these samples very clearly show the presence or absence of particular success criteria. It is imperative that teachers collaborate and anchor their judgment in exemplars. Visit **go.SolutionTree .com/assessment** for exemplars at various proficiency levels.

One important note: teachers must recognize that a points-based system inherently relies on professional judgment embedded throughout. In traditional grading, determining how many points to assign a problem or how many teacher-generated multiple choice test items they need to determine student understanding is certainly not perfectly valid and reliable either. Rather, points and percentages often provide an illusion of accuracy. This illusion hit me hard when I received the following email from one of my son's teachers:

> Good morning,
>
> Steve got his chapter test back yesterday. He received a 75 percent on it. The grade had nothing to do with his understanding of the material. He forgot to continue the negative sign in two problems and didn't read the question carefully in one question. This test score doesn't reflect his ability or work ethic and I told him that. I know he cares about his grades.

As you might imagine, I was dumbfounded! First, I would like to believe the grade is *not* based on ability or work ethic, but rather on his proficiency in the learning targets. Second, if the grade has "nothing to do with his understanding of the material," then the teacher shouldn't give it! It should be formative, procedural feedback. While the teacher clearly had some sense of confidence that a 75 percent score was worth recording, I saw the teacher's illusion of accuracy and reliability.

Commitment 3: Focus on All Three Dimensions of Science as Called For in the NGSS

The SEPs are the foundation for our learning targets. As students interact with and demonstrate their growing proficiency in the SEPs, they do so within the context of the DCIs, along with the CCCs. This aligns with the performance expectations presented in the NGSS, although we have found multiple ways to combine SEPs, DCIs, and CCCs. As noted, the success criteria then weave in the appropriate aspects of the DCI and CCC called for in that particular task. It is important that students accurately use the DCI and the CCC in their work.

The NGSS appendices inform the success criteria we have developed and use. For example, Appendix F (NGSS, 2013a) has a continuum for expected thinking when engaging in argument that grows from identify arguments (grades K–2), to compare and refine arguments (grades 3–5), to compare and critique two arguments on the same topic (grades 6–8), to compare and evaluate competing arguments (grades 9–12). These insights promote both clarity in the current course and vertical articulation between grade levels (NGSS, 2013a). In addition to defining what teachers expect proficiency to look like, these appendices help them articulate and calibrate expectations with students' experiences *before* taking the class and *after* taking the class.

It is important for teachers to fully understand and be conversant in what the NGSS SEP and CCC call for.

Science and Engineering Practices

The eight SEPs (NGSS, 2013a) follow:

1. Asking questions (for science) and defining problems (for engineering)
2. Developing and using models
3. Planning and carrying out investigations
4. Analyzing and interpreting data
5. Using mathematics and computational thinking
6. Constructing explanations (for science) and designing solutions (for engineering)
7. Engaging in argument from evidence
8. Obtaining, evaluating, and communicating information

Crosscutting Concepts

The seven CCCs (NGSS, 2013b) follow:

1. **Patterns**—Observed patterns of forms and events guide organization and classification, and they prompt questions about relationships and the factors that influence them.
2. **Cause and effect**—Mechanism and explanation. Events have causes, sometimes simple, sometimes multifaceted. A major activity of science is investigating and explaining causal relationships and the mechanisms by which they are mediated. Such mechanisms can then be tested across given contexts and used to predict and explain events in new contexts.
3. **Scale, proportion, and quantity**—In considering phenomena, it is critical to recognize what is relevant at different measures of size, time, and energy and to recognize how changes in scale, proportion, or quantity affect a system's structure or performance.
4. **Systems and system models**—Defining the system under study—specifying its boundaries and making explicit a model of that system—provides tools for understanding and testing ideas that are applicable throughout science and engineering.
5. **Energy and matter**—Flows, cycles, and conservation. Tracking fluxes of energy and matter into, out of, and within systems helps one understand the systems' possibilities and limitations.
6. **Structure and function**—The way in which an object or living thing is shaped and its substructure determine many of its properties and functions.
7. **Stability and change**—For natural and built systems alike, conditions of stability and determinants of rates of change or evolution of a system are critical elements of study.

Commitment 4: Focus on Transferable Science Skills That Provide Lasting Value to Students

Focusing on transferable skills (such as those the SEPs outline) provides value to students in all aspects of life and academic pursuits. There is a great deal of overlap between the SEPs and the CCSS for English language arts and mathematics practices. For example, all three sets of standards call for students to use evidence to support an argument. Figure 7.3 shows some of these connections. For further clarity and over-lap, see a Venn diagram demonstrating this overlap at https://stanford.io/2x7Nirs; Cheuk, 2013). Proficiency-based grading provides a common language for learning across school disciplines, helping students make sense of *why* they are learning.

Science Practices	Mathematics Practices	ELA Practices
SEP 7: Engage in argument from evidence.	Mathematical Practice 3: Construct viable and valid arguments from evidence and critique reasoning of others.	EP1: Support analysis of a range of grade-level complex texts with evidence.
SEP 5: Use mathematics and computational thinking. SEP 2: Develop and use models.	Mathematical Practice 4: Model with mathematics.	—
SEP 8: Obtain, evaluate, and communicate information.	—	EP2: Produce clear and coherent writing in which the development, organization, and style are appropriate to task, purpose, and audience.

Source for standard: CCSSO & English Language Proficiency Development Framework Committee, 2012; NGA & CCSSO 2013b; NGSS, 2013c. Source: Adapted from Cheuk, 2013.

Figure 7.3: Overlap among SEPs and CCSS for English language arts and mathematics.

In addition, transferable skills are useful in all academic work, as well as in life after formal education. For example, teachers have always asked students to write effective conclusions for science lab reports or as a reflection on other learning experiences. However, many teachers do not provide students the explicit structures for doing this work. When educators teach students a clear structure for making a claim, providing specific evidence (such as key values from a lab), and then reasoning from this evidence that is only possible in light of an emerging under-standing of the concept, they are preparing students to write a coherent conclusion. This structure will carry over into students' writing in all coursework. Students begin to say things like, "Oh, you mean you want me to write this like we learned in English class?" Yes, we do!

Commitment 5: Continue Weaving Mastery Into Other NGSS Dimensions

Teachers must understand that moving the focus to skills does not abandon the science content all science teachers love so much. Teaching core ideas (such as the way meiosis leads to genetic diversity, how conservation of matter connects to balanced equations, or how an understanding of the Earth-sun-moon system can explain the phases of the moon) will always be a big part of students becoming scientifically knowledgeable and literate. The move to the NGSS and proficiency-based grading simply calls on students to demonstrate this knowledge by using the SEPs, and to make connections to the CCCs.

Since implementing proficiency-based grading, it is increasingly clear that the knowledge (DCIs) and connections (CCCs) Stevenson educators always valued should become the success criteria to determine how well a student can construct an explanation or ask testable questions (SEPs). Now, however, instead of using the DCIs as the learning target, it becomes the content with which students demon-strate increasing proficiency with the SEP-focused learning targets. Students will continue to be literate in the science vocabulary, and teachers will continue to plan great labs, demonstrations, and activities to develop these understandings. Proficiency-based grading provides a framework within which we can weave these together with instruction, assessment, and reporting. This is the fundamental change our teams have been experiencing with the release of the NGSS and proficiency-based grading implementation.

Incubation: The Unexpected Questions of Proficiency-Based Grading in Science

As teachers progress toward proficiency-based grading implementation, they will uncover some wonderful questions that drive inquiry and implementation. During this second stage, several adopted practices may be working, but teachers may pay a lot of attention to the items that seem to threaten work or that have provided new challenges. This includes the increased complexity of weaving together all three dimensions of the NGSS, providing scaffolded instruction on the science practices, and then collecting enough evidence to accurately assess proficiency on the science practices in addition to the DCIs. With so much new information, it can be hard to not worry that some challenges will never be overcome. The following questions are representative of the incubation stage challenges that require patience and persistence.

Unexpected Question 1: How Do Teachers Coordinate Instruction and Assessment for All Three NGSS Dimensions?

After developing the scaled learning targets, teachers must work to align instruction and assessment practices to these targets. It is one thing to expect students to be able to *do* the science practices, but it is even more important for teachers to *teach* them how to do it. One step in this process is taking an inventory of the current lessons and assessments to see what practices students learn and teachers assess. Some might be surprised at the relative abundance (or relative paucity) of lessons that directly align to teaching the science practices.

Once this inventory is complete, teachers determine which practices most closely align and support particular DCIs. Certainly, the NGSS performance expectations provide some guidance, since each contains one SEP, one DCI, and one CCC. For example, in the NGSS (2013c), HS-LS2-5 asks that students "Develop a model to illustrate the role of photosynthesis and cellular respiration in the cycling of carbon among the biosphere, atmosphere, hydrosphere, and geosphere." However, teachers should not limit themselves to this particular alignment; there are several SEPs that support each DCI. For example, in the preceding performance expectation, you could ask students to construct an explanation; analyze and interpret data; or obtain, evaluate, and communicate information related to the cycling of carbon through photosynthesis and cellular respiration.

As this work proceeds, teachers may also need to let go of some of the science core ideas that students traditionally learn so they can devote more time to fully exploring, practicing, and mastering the SEPs. Many schools faced a similar process when implementing the NGSS. Just as with the backward design framework (Wiggins & McTighe, 1998), teachers must consider the skills that will transfer to students' daily lives and are well beyond the scope of one particular course, or science coursework in general. For example, in backward design, we begin with two or three long-term transfer goals that will drive science teaching and learning. These are the handful of big ideas we hope our students still remember and apply to their lives when they are full-grown adults. From this starting point, we plan the assessments, and then go further backward to create the smaller instructional building blocks that students need.

Stevenson's teams worked to represent the ideal of three-dimensional learning central to the NGSS. While team members talked to many colleagues at other schools about how they accomplish this, it became clear how to use a familiar tool to organize their thinking. This tool, developed by Carol Ann Tomlinson (2005) and commonly referred to as *KUD*, outlines what a student should know, understand, and do. Figure 7.4 (page 202) shows how this links directly to the three dimensions of the NGSS.

Jessica Lemieux, a biology teacher and curricular coach at Champlain Valley Union High School, shared how her school has been using this model with students breaking out of tradition and identifying what they need to know, understand, and do (J. Lemieux, personal communication, January 2019). This clearly aligns with the principles of backward design as well (Wiggins & McTighe, 1998). Stevenson teams have found this to be a useful tool to show how students learn the DCIs, SEPs, and CCCs in a unit.

Unexpected Question 2: How Much Evidence Is Enough for Each Science Practice?

The answer to this question will vary by grade level, the nature of the skill, and the complexity of the final expectations. There are times when you can weave several skills together in one assessment. For example, it might make sense to develop a model and then caption the model as an explanation. This one task could provide some insights into student proficiency on both of these SEPs. Other times, the task's complexity demands more time focused on developing one science practice. For example, a student might need to spend considerable time "Developing a quantitative model to describe the cycling of carbon among the hydrosphere, atmosphere, geosphere, and biosphere" (HS-ESS2-6; NGSS, 2013c). This complex task at the high school level might be broken into multiple steps. However, there should be numerous opportunities for students to both practice and demonstrate their mastery on the science practice skill without teachers always needing to conduct high-stakes formal, recorded assessments. This would certainly include a bare minimum of three assessments that count toward the grade, but would likely range in number from three to ten. Students should have explicit instruction on the skill with opportunities for practice, reflection, and feedback before the teacher starts marking scores in the gradebook and between scored assessments.

As teachers gain expertise in explicit instruction on these skills, they will increasingly be able to identify the learning progression and how to differentiate instruction for students at the various points on the scale. Just like a doctor checks many vital signs, his or her professional judgment will allow the doctor to focus on the evidence most critical to a diagnosis. Certainly, many students will not have fully mastered the SEPs early in the course, so the teacher's descriptive feedback will refine their thinking and lead to mastery later on.

Stevenson teachers often refer to this learning events sequence using a sports analogy. *Practice* events may be teacher led or done collaboratively with other students. In addition, these tasks typically involve gathering student knowledge of the DCIs

Unit 1: Matter and Energy
Guiding question: Where does a tree get its mass?

Know (DCIs)	Understand (CCCs)	Do (SEPs)
1. The eight characteristics all living things share: genetic code (DNA), growth and development, respond to environment, organized as cells, reproduction, homeostasis, use energy, and evolve. 2. The components of the scientific process including hypotheses, independent variables, dependent variables, constants, control group, and experimental group in a scientific experiment, as well as construct and analyze tables and graphs. 3. The structure of an atom and the structure of a molecule. (HS-LS1-6) 4. Factors that affect the rate of photosynthesis. (HS-LS1-5) 5. The purpose of photosynthesis, and the reactants and products of the chemical equation. (HS-LS1-5)	**Energy and Matter:** Explain how energy and matter are conserved in a reaction. (HS-LS1-6) **System Models:** Use models to simulate systems and interactions.	**Summative (reported and in gradebook)** • **Construct an explanation** about factors that affect the rate of photosynthesis. • **Plan an investigation** to determine factors that affect the rate of photosynthesis. • **Model** a combustion reaction. • **Model** photosynthesis. • **Analyze and interpret data** regarding factors that affect photosynthesis. • **Analyze and interpret data** from the term test mouse vitamin scenario. • **Analyze data** from the push-up example between teachers. **Formative (reported, not used in grade)** • **Construct an explanation** about whether viruses are living or nonliving. • **Construct an explanation** of mass or energy conservation (from the combustion reactions). • **Plan an investigation** to determine the ideal condition for mung bean growth. • **Analyze and interpret data** regarding the ideal condition for mung bean growth. • **Model** combustion reactions. • **Interpret data** by having students create or analyze the graph-a-day warm-ups. **Additional Practice (information for teachers only; don't need to share this with students)** • **Model** atoms (paper cutouts), molecules (playdough or gumdrops), chemical reaction (drawing). • **Construct an explanation** by constructing an explanation tool (This is what I see, this is what it means). • **Construct an explanation** around photosynthesis data (Look at and give feedback on the evidence part or the reasoning part of example arguments). • **Construct an explanation** about the connection between a plant and the candle burning. • **Construct an explanation** about whether peas (or mystery organism) are doing photosynthesis, and if this onion is doing photosynthesis. • **Construct an explanation** (claim and evidence only) about causes-of-death data.

Source for standard: NGSS, 2013a, 2013b, 2013c. Source: Adapted from Adlai E. Stevenson High School, 2018.

Figure 7.4: Ideal NGSS 3-D learning.

and using smaller components of the science practice, performing the skill in an isolated setting, doing the skill repeatedly, or demonstrating the skill with support. *Scrimmage* events ask students to pull these components together on their own, but in a truly formative manner to inform them and teachers about proficiency on this SEP with a DCI and a CCC. *Games* are assessment tasks that count toward the grade, just like the games a basketball team plays count toward its overall record. These events occur less frequently than *practices* or *scrimmages*. In addition, just like in athletic competitions, there will be future opportunities to demonstrate these *same* skills students develop in additional practice events and scrimmages throughout the duration of the course. Teachers will challenge students who demonstrate proficiency early with the new core ideas the class will explore later in the course, as well as add complexity to their thinking for future tasks.

Unexpected Question 3: How Will Science Assessments Need to Change?

There might still be a place for multiple choice tests, especially to ensure students have the baseline knowledge to complete the assessment tasks. There are some core ideas teachers want to ensure students know. However, assessment practices can't stop with multiple choice questions, nor should those questions compose the majority of the assessment system. The ultimate goal is for students to do the SEPs using the DCIs.

For example, consider the different types of thinking students need to demonstrate understanding of the core ideas related to cellular respiration. A traditional multiple choice exam might ask the questions in figure 7.5.

---

1. What is the impact of increasing light levels on the rate of photosynthesis?
   a. There is no impact.
   b. There is a direct relationship.
   c. There is an inverse relationship.
   d. It depends on if it is a plant or an animal.
2. How does decreasing temperature affect cellular respiration?
   a. Decreasing temperature increases the rate due to enzymatic activity.
   b. Decreasing temperature increases the rate due to a more optimal enzyme shape.
   c. Decreasing temperature has no impact.
   d. Decreasing temperature slows cellular respiration by decreasing the number of collisions.
   e. More than one of the above are true.

Figure 7.5: Traditional multiple choice exam questions.

Now, compare this to an assessment, developed by Thomas P. Wolfe (2019) and shown in figure 7.6, where students are in the process of demonstrating their understanding of the impact of temperature or light on the rate of cellular respiration at the same time they are developing proficiency in constructing explanations and analyzing and interpreting data. This task differentiates the performance task into level 1 (more scaffolded) or level 2 (less scaffolded) based on the student's self-assessment of his or her proficiency in constructing an explanation. Included in the assessment example are sample answers (italicized and in brackets) that teachers might expect of students on this practice task.

Skill practice: Construct an explanation.

Directions: Decide what level you're on and complete the corresponding practice explanation.

Level 1: You need guiding questions for support while writing your explanation.

Level 2: You feel confident writing your explanation independently.

Practice Explanation 1—Level 1: Answer guiding questions that support you as you provide a claim, evidence, and reasoning.

Question: What effect does light have on cellular respiration?

Claim: How does light affect cellular respiration? Does it cause it to increase, does it cause it to decrease, or does it not have an effect? If you do not know, come back to this question after completing the evidence.

[Light does not affect cellular respiration.]

Evidence: Only provide evidence on CO_2.

1. Tell the story of your graph:
   As _____ increases from _____, the _____ _____ from (or at) _____.
   (X-axis independent variable) (Specific data points) (Y-axis dependent variable) (Increases Decreases Remains constant) (Specific data points)

2. How are the trends in the two graphs similar or different?
   [Both graphs have a similar increase of CO_2 over time.]

3. Tell the story of Graph 1.
   [With no light, as time increases over 5 minutes, the CO_2 increases from 357 ppm to 392 ppm.]

4. Tell the story of Graph 2.
   [In the light condition, as time increases over 5 minutes, the CO_2 increases from 355 ppm to 389 ppm.]

Reasoning: What do your data, patterns, or both mean?

1. How does a trend in carbon dioxide show us aerobic cellular respiration is occurring? Hint: What are the reactants and products of cellular respiration, and what does it mean when they go up or down?

[The increase in CO_2 tells us aerobic cellular respiration is occurring because CO_2 is a product of cellular respiration.]

2. How does a trend in carbon dioxide between the experimental group and control show us aerobic cellular respiration is affected or not affected?

   [Because the amount of CO_2 produced is the same in both conditions, light does not have any effect on cellular respiration.]

3. How do biological concepts explain why this phenomenon occurred? Specifically, what do we know about energy and cellular respiration that can explain the trends we see in our evidence?

   [Light does not have an effect on cellular respiration because it is not involved in the process. It is not a reactant or a product. Light is only a critical component in photosynthesis.]

Practice Explanation 1—Level 2: Provide evidence and reasoning that support your claim.

Question: What effect does light have on cellular respiration?

Claim: _____

[Light does not affect cellular respiration.]

Evidence: Only provide evidence on CO_2.

[Both graphs have a similar increase of CO_2 over time.]

[With no light, as time increases over 5 minutes, the CO_2 increases from 357 ppm to 392 ppm.]

[In the light condition, as time increases over 5 minutes, the CO_2 increases from 355 ppm to 389 ppm.]

Reasoning: What do your data, patterns, or both mean?

1. How can scientific concepts explain why we see the pattern?

   [The increase in CO_2 tells us aerobic cellular respiration is occurring because CO_2 is a product of cellular respiration.]

   [Because the amount of CO_2 produced is the same in both conditions, light does not have any effect on cellular respiration.]

   [Light does not have an effect on cellular respiration because it is not involved in the process. It is not a reactant or a product. Light is only a critical component in photosynthesis.]

   [The decrease in O_2 tells us aerobic cellular respiration is occurring because O_2 is a reactant of cellular respiration and is being used up in the experiments.]

   [A smaller decrease of O_2 in the cold temperature shows that cellular respiration is not happening as fast because O_2 is not being used up as quickly by the process.]

Source: © 2019 by Thomas P. Wolfe.

Figure 7.6: Assessment task differentiated into level 1 (more scaffolded) or level 2 (less scaffolded) based on a student self-assessment.

Unexpected Question 4: How Do Conversations Focus on a *Not Yet* Attitude About Science Learning?

One of the most motivating pieces of transitioning to proficiency-based grading is how it changes conversations with students. Most teachers have had way too many conversations with students who want to debate (or argue) about a point or two on a lab report. Similarly, most have too often been asked, "How many points is this worth?" No teacher likes those conversations. Proficiency-based grading helps shift conversations from points to proficiency for both teachers and students. Certainly, scales of 1, 2, 3, and 4 are not perfect, but they are more reliable and defensible than an 89.3 percent being a solid B+ and not an A-. Teachers use professional judgment to consistently tell the difference between 4, 3, 2, and 1 (or an A and a B), but I've met few teachers who can holistically look at an assignment and meaningfully tell an 86 percent from an 88 percent.

Proficiency-based learning is about *growth progression*. One benefit is that teachers do not reward students simply for learning fast or from prior knowledge. Students must develop and maintain proficiency, and this will happen at different times for different students. This is the *not yet*. Students will recognize that assessments grow from practicing isolated skills with the teacher or peers into combining these skills for independent demonstration. These assessments increase in complexity, but teachers always provide students with opportunities for more practice and future opportunities to demonstrate proficiency. Students who demonstrate proficiency early in the course will need to maintain and demonstrate these same skills later in the course. True proficiency is not a one-and-done experience for the student who has already demonstrated proficiency or for the student who has *not yet* demonstrated proficiency. All students have multiple opportunities to either demonstrate or maintain proficiency throughout the course with varying DCIs and CCCs.

Unexpected Question 5: Does Proficiency-Based Grading Represent the Nature of Science?

Once teacher teams implement a proficiency-based system (or any system for that matter), they should step back and take a broader view of the curriculum, instruction, and assessment system. One of the primary reasons to make this change is to allow educators to more closely align with the nature of science—that is, *doing* the science practices in the context of science core ideas.

Teachers should consider the following question when reflecting on the system they have implemented: Are we giving students an authentic experience, using the science practices that most closely align to the nature of our discipline? This is one of the most important and lasting goals for science instruction and grading, and the grading system should support these ideals. However, any teacher can quickly fall into the trap of refining the minutiae while missing the much larger picture. I was reminded of this while reviewing with my son for his freshman biology final exam. I was forced to retrieve what I would call *biology trivia* I had not even thought about since my college zoology class. Unfortunately, this course appeared to focus on some facts of science rather than the true nature of science. The former will quickly be forgotten, while the latter has the potential to shape students' thinking for the rest of their lives.

Insight: The Essential Insights of Proficiency-Based Grading in Science

As teachers begin to move beyond the initial fears and roadblocks and gain insight, it is vitally important to take some time to look back on and appreciate how the team has passed some intimidating hurdles thus far. Teams should have a clear enough idea of how proficiency-based grading works, and they can play to its strengths as they teach and plan. They begin providing proficiency-based grading with more power instead of just trying to get their balance.

At this point, science teachers might have the following insights: (1) instructional strategies, assessment, and feedback must align to the SEPs and skills, and (2) focusing more intentionally on all three dimensions of science allows for more differentiation opportunities.

Insight 1: Instructional Strategies, Assessment, and Feedback Must Align to the SEPs and Skills

Certainly, teachers already expect students to demonstrate many skills or science practices in classrooms. Instructional strategies, assessments, and feedback must all align. Teachers will need to continually reflect on a pattern of instruction and assessment that focuses first on science practices (skills), is supported by science ideas (content), and ties into the broader CCCs. As noted earlier, this will include a little evolution and a little revolution.

The following sections cover instructional strategies, assessment, and feedback regarding SEPs and skills alignment.

Instructional Strategies

The transition to proficiency-based grading will include teachers identifying current lessons that have embedded science practices and creating new ones to provide adequate opportunity for practice and formal assessments. Many science teachers conducted this process during the transition to the NGSS. Stevenson teams found the move to proficiency-based grading caused teachers to look much more closely at how and when they explicitly teach and assess these practices. Many teachers (over many years) just expected students to already know how to do the practices or figure them out. Just like our students, teachers learned and developed their *own* proficiency with the SEPs throughout their own educational experiences. Even though we might like to think otherwise, teachers didn't always know how to do these practices well.

An instructional progression for the SEP follows the same model we would use for a traditional content-focused learning outcome. We begin by defining the learning target along with the success criteria that will indicate proficiency. For example, with the SEP of *constructing explanations*, we might ask students to interpret some data, state a claim, use the data as evidence to support the claim, and then provide solid science reasoning that supports the explanation. Once we have clearly defined the success criteria, we begin modeling for students how to complete the task. This can include doing a talk-aloud about our own thinking while we complete a similar task ourselves. This can include doing the smaller components of the overall SEP before putting it all together. Students can then practice, both independently and in small groups, to grow their confidence and proficiency. There is value in providing frequent small tasks that allow students to practice (and teachers to model) the SEP. These tasks can be in the form of daily warm-up tasks or in the middle of a class period. They should not be isolated to big assessment events.

Assessment

At times, teachers can include assessment and feedback on the SEP with slight modifications to existing plans, bringing those practices to the forefront of learning. One place for teachers to begin is looking at the current system of assessments in the classroom. When considering which events could be labeled *assessments*, determine the following.

- **Does the task students do and the feedback they receive focus primarily on the DCI or on the SEP?** Focusing primarily on the DCI can build background knowledge to prepare for assessment, but will not directly be used to assess proficiency on the learning target unless it is coupled with proficiency in the SEP. The assessments that determine proficiency will need to be done in class and directly reflect the success criteria outlined in relation to the SEP.

- **Is there an appropriate balance between selecting a correct answer when given a list of options (multiple choice) and demonstrating proficiency on the SEP?** When assessing learning targets that focus on the SEP, use multiple choice questions sparingly.

> While knowledge is important, the real success criteria will be the accuracy and completeness of the scientific thinking as students *do* the SEP.

- **Does the gradebook reflect the ideal balance between students knowing science facts and showing proficiency in doing science?** In proficiency-based grading, the gradebook needs to show proficiency levels reported directly on the SEP-focused learning targets.

There is an emerging body of helpful resources that support science teachers in creating 3-D learning and assessment experiences for students. One extremely practical resource is the set of STEM Teaching Tools (Van Horne, Penuel, & Bell, 2016). In particular, STEM Teaching Tool #30 (https://bit.ly/2yIUegj) outlines potential task formats that teachers can use to modify existing lessons to align them more closely with the SEPs. In these sample task starters, it is clear that nearly all of them begin with a phenomenon to ground students' thinking. For example, for the SEP related to asking questions, you might:

> Present students with a scientific phenomenon to be explained and a scientific question, then ask students to evaluate whether or not the question is relevant to explaining the phenomenon. If the question is relevant, ask students to describe what evidence is needed to answer that question. (Van Horne et al., 2016)

A task related to engaging in argument from evidence might be:

> Present two different arguments related to a phenomenon, one with evidence and one without. Then ask students to identify the argument that is more scientific and ask them why they think that is the case. (Van Horne et al., 2016)

Feedback

Keeping in line with instruction and assessment, the feedback teachers give students—and the feedback students give one another or themselves—needs to be grounded in the SEPs. Students and teachers will use the scaled learning target rubrics to reflect on how the success criteria are (or are not) represented in the work students create. The feedback should cause students to self-reflect on any gaps between their work and the success criteria as well as ways they can improve in the future.

One way students can do this is by using various color highlighters to clearly show where in their work each of the success criteria appears. This often forces students to carefully review the success criteria and to identify gaps between their work and what the teacher expects.

Insight 2: Focusing More Intentionally on All Three Dimensions of Science Allows for More Differentiation Opportunities

Teachers find that proficiency-based grading allows for more differentiation opportunities. When teachers have a solid grasp on where students are in performing a particular skill, it allows them to differentiate lessons that target specific, common issues that arise in that skill development. For example, when students are constructing scientific explanations, many teachers use the claim, evidence, and reasoning (CER) format. It is common for students not to directly state an accurate claim. In this case, the teacher can ask students to clarify and rework their claim. For students who are really struggling, this differentiation might include choosing the best claim from three that the teacher presents.

Still other students might not sift through all the data from an experiment to highlight the most relevant evidence that directly supports the claim. The teacher can ask these students to rank the evidence they have provided from *most directly* to *least directly* supporting the claim. Finally, other students will find it challenging to bring scientific knowledge and theory to bear. Students will find it even more challenging to correctly complete the explanation when the data are incomplete or seem to run counter to the scientific principles they are exploring. In times like these, the teacher can ask students—especially those who have previously demonstrated proficiency—to try more challenging tasks.

Teachers may ask students who are proficient on the science practice early in the course to apply the science practice and connect other DCIs from this course or other science courses. For example, when engaging in making an argument from evidence in a chemistry classroom, students who are proficient could pull evidence from other chemistry units, from biology, or from their daily lives to bolster their argument or to offer possible counterclaims to their argument. Teachers can also construct a task that specifically prompts students to review and complete a more challenging scenario. In our system, level 4 translates to an A+ on the final grade reporting, and these opportunities for a 4 are not presented on every assessment but at times make sense and lend themselves to this extension experience.

One challenge for teachers is knowing *each* student's proficiency level on the SEP he or she is working on on any given day. It is even *more* important that each *student* knows *his or her own* proficiency level. For this reason, assessment should be frequent and small. It is impossible, and not that productive, to score and provide feedback on every one of these smaller assessment tasks. However, this series of assessment tasks will build proficiency, and the students will see patterns emerging in their work.

At the same time, it is important for teachers to make the assessment using a reasonable amount of work and time. This is where creative and masterful teachers shine, realizing there are multiple ways to assess and provide feedback to guide individual students' learning. Certainly, sitting with a student one-to-one and having a conversation or practicing the skill is effective, but not particularly efficient. Other strategies include the following.

- Have students structure their reflection, including comparing their work to the success criteria and reviewing their work with peers.

- Have students videotape their explanations so peers or the teacher can watch it later.

- Have students compare their work to a teacher-generated key that shows complete, thorough, and attainable work. Students can identify similarities and differences between their work, including ways their sample might even be more effective or creative than the key.

In addition, it is valuable and worthwhile to have students consider the effectiveness of the feedback and self-reflections and to explain their thinking. The teacher or peers can provide feedback on the quality of their reflections or the feedback they provided. This feedback—both on the work and on the self-reflections or peer feedback itself—should be clear and stimulate further thinking. This could include a review of the feedback or self-reflection that explores questions like the following. Visit **go.SolutionTree.com/assessment** for a free reproducible version of these questions.

- Was the feedback or self-reflection positive but honest enough to provide actionable steps that could make the work better?

- Did the feedback or self-reflection cause more thinking (preferred) or simply give direction or ideas that led to a single alternative approach (not as helpful)?

- Did the feedback or self-reflection clearly connect back to the success criteria, ensuring the improvements would move the student work closer to proficiency?

Stevenson teams realize that on a four-point scale, a level 2 (approaching proficiency) is broad and includes a wide range of work. Students develop or approach proficiency in many ways and at different rates. Some students cannot achieve and maintain proficiency early in the course. The system must allow for proficiency that develops gradually and not penalize students as they move toward proficiency. This is the *not yet* attitude.

When developing meaningful assessments that focus on SEPs, teachers realize there might be fewer gradebook entries. If a teacher's routine has been to enter every warm-up, homework, exit ticket, lab, quiz, and test in the gradebook, there will certainly be fewer scores—or at least fewer that factor into the grade. Proficiency-based grading uses the practice events to be informative, not just a list of points, as students prepare for a formal assessment. The number of *meaningful* scored assessments in the gradebook will go up, since all entries truly assess core ideas and practices. Teachers will collect more focused and meaningful data to guide students, parents, and interventionists.

Evaluation: The Key Questions of Proficiency-Based Grading in Science

Implementation's beginning stages bring a perspective of evaluation. While professional growth never takes one path, reaching this point allows teams to set a goal of reaching regular practice and to confidently look into ways that the system impacts feedback and grading.

Evaluation can lead science teachers to ask the following key questions: (1) "What type of feedback are teachers giving about proficiency on the SEPs?" (2) "How can teachers involve students in peer and self-assessment to track their progress and make improvement plans?" and (3) "How do teachers ensure consistent scoring and grading when evaluating science proficiency?"

Key Question 1: What Type of Feedback Are Teachers Giving About Proficiency on the SEPs?

Teachers must commit to making sure *students* will receive feedback that addresses learning targets. This feedback should include a recipe for success, whether the feedback is coming from the teacher or a peer, or through self-reflection. This follows with a commitment to providing multiple opportunities for practice, graded formal assessments, and individual feedback and reflection. You can precede or follow these feedback opportunities with examples of how to provide thoughtful, actionable feedback.

For example, if students have designed an experiment to test reaction rates in chemistry, reflected on the quality of their procedure, and then discussed this with peers, the teacher or peers could provide feedback to promote further thinking. If a student hasn't grasped the concept of constants or controlled variables, the teacher might ask a question as direct as "What things do you want to remain the same between the control group and the experimental group?" For students who have demonstrated proficiency, a question might extend their thinking with a slight twist: "If you were not able to manipulate the variable you have chosen, how could you test the reaction rate with a fixed quantity of a chemical at a specific temperature?" The feedback should also point the student back to success criteria: "Use the yellow highlighter to show the controlled variables, a green highlighter to show the independent variable, and a pink highlighter to show the dependent variable."

Bringing students into the reflection and assessment process is critical, particularly as this passes the heavy cognitive lifting of comparing their work to the standards, as well as developing strategies to close learning gaps. Read more about that in Key Question 2: How Can Teachers Involve Students in Peer and Self-Assessment to Track Their Progress and Make Improvement Plans?

Key Question 2: How Can Teachers Involve Students in Peer and Self-Assessment to Track Their Progress and Make Improvement Plans?

Peer and self-assessment can promote social-emotional competencies such as self-awareness, social awareness (when doing peer feedback), and responsible decision making (CASEL, 2017). Teachers find that a proficiency-based system can bring rich reflective conversations with students about their level of mastery and help plan the next steps on their learning journey.

To guide students' thinking in this process, our teams used several tools aligned to scaled learning targets and success criteria. In figure 7.7 (page 214), the left column identifies the teacher-created (with input from students) success criteria. The right column is a set of open-ended questions for students as they reflect on the aspects of quality represented (or missing) in their work. Co-constructed feedback between a teacher and a student promotes the reflection and conversations that bring clarity to students. In the form, the teacher could provide feedback directly in alignment with the success criteria in the left column, record this feedback separately, or save the feedback for a conversation in which the student shares his or her responses to the reflection questions in the right column (either in writing or verbally) to the teacher.

When teachers provide repeated opportunities for students to practice the skill to demonstrate proficiency, it will be virtually impossible for the teacher to evaluate every piece of learning evidence. Students must identify and articulate their current state of understanding and identify ways to close learning gaps. Reflection through co-constructed feedback allows for multiple people to provide feedback on student work. By involving students in self-assessment and peer assessment, more timely feedback familiarizes students with the success criteria and shifts the mindset of both teachers and students about the nature of learning and feedback.

Learning Target: I can analyze and interpret data using all essential components in familiar contexts.

Success Criteria for Graphing Components	Reflections: Specific Examples From Your Work
Accuracy and scaling • Plot correct data on graph. • Create equal scale increments for X-axis. • Create equal scale increments for Y-axis.	**Review your work.** • Check your scaling. Are the first half of the squares on the X-axis the same amount as the last half of the squares? Are the first half of the squares on the Y-axis the same amount as the last half of the squares? • Do any of your data points fall outside the trend of your data? If so, are they outliers or plotted incorrectly?
Labels and legends • Label X-axis with variable and units (IV). • Label Y-axis with variable and units (DV). • Ensure multiple data sets are easily distinguishable (shapes, colors, line style) and the data sets are identifiable (either a label or a key or legend).	**Review your work or the work of a peer.** • How is the purpose of the graph identified by the title and axis labels? • How does the choice of graph type best represent the data? • What can you say about the data presentation?

General graph considerations	Review your work or the work of a peer.
• Write a title for the graph. • Choose the appropriate type of graph based on the data set. • Make the graph as large as possible. • Label X- and Y-axes at the origin (lowest data value).	• How is each set of data identified? • How might the scaling be done differently to better read the data and trends?
Extensions • Use data presented in tables or graphs to make accurate, appropriate predictions and inferences. • Use data presented in tables or graphs to determine logical variable relationships and data trends. • Use all provided information to draw conclusions.	**Review your work or the work of a peer.** • What evidence (data, trends) did your peer use from the graph that you might add to strengthen your predictions or inferences? What did you include as evidence that your peer might add to strengthen his or hers? • What biology principles, concepts, or provided background information did you draw on to draw conclusions?

When reviewing your work (or your peer's), consider the following reflective questions, which you can customize to any of the SEPs.

• Which three success criteria do you think are represented best in your work? Why did you choose these three?

• Which success criteria could you have represented better?

• What is one thing you struggled to incorporate into your work on the assessment?

• If this activity's goal is to both assess proficiency and promote learning, what is one thing you think can improve this activity?

Figure 7.7: Co-constructed feedback example.

Bringing multiple sets of eyes to provide feedback on student work is key, and can include teacher and student, student and student, or even another group of students. In this process, students benefit by receiving feedback, but also gain clarity as they interact with the rubrics and scaled learning targets. Ideally, students will be involved in creating these success criteria (as listed in the left column of figure 7.7, page 214) with teachers and articulate why these criteria demonstrate true proficiency of the skill.

These success criteria can be generated in a variety of ways, including a whole-class discussion and students individually writing what they would look for in a quality work sample. This process can take place before the performance task, and be refined following the task; the task itself will likely generate some ideas.

Key Question 3: How Do Teachers Ensure Consistent Scoring and Grading When Evaluating Science Proficiency?

If a team of teachers does the transition, such as in a Professional Learning Community environment, there will be many conversations about expectations and grading calibration to ensure consistency. Grading student work blindly (without names, or work from other teachers' students) is important. Recently, I was working with a team of chemistry teachers who were discussing trends in the students' work related to the learning target of developing and using models. It became clear the team needed to have more conversations about what is expected and required of students. For example, Does the model need to correctly represent scale and proportion? Does the model need to represent the movement of molecules, or would that be going beyond the target requirements? The resulting conversations led to clearer teacher expectations, as well as to more consistent scoring and grading.

Elaboration: The Core Beliefs of Proficiency-Based Grading in Science

Teachers at the elaboration phase of implementation have reached a mature and clear perspective of using a proficiency-based grading system. They have discovered that the system does not push them out of valued projects, simulations, or other assessments and activities they know help students learn; instead, they see there is depth to be gained from such work, with an underlying and clear focus on skills. With their comfort in this system, teachers are resources for their colleagues and on the cutting edge for new ways to provide more support for and collaboration with their students.

Teachers who successfully implement proficiency-based grading adhere to all seven of the core beliefs explained in chapter 1 (page 9): (1) growth is a central concept, (2) reperformance is essential, (3) building students' reflection abilities is essential, (4) homework has a role, (5) communication with parents and the community is key, (6) culminating experiences like final exams have a different purpose, and (7) behavior can be in or out of the grade. The following sections, which reflect the core beliefs' original numbering, explore the core beliefs that science teachers in particular should never lose sight of.

Core Belief 2: Reperformance Is Essential

Students will need multiple opportunities to demonstrate science skills proficiency. This will occur naturally during the normal course progression, as skills come up again. Students will continue to explore new core ideas and apply the skills to these new understandings. For example, when working with students to develop and use models throughout the year in a chemistry course, the teacher might ask students to develop models that demonstrate the structure of an atom or even to explain the theories of Dalton, Bohr, Thomson, and others. Later in the course, the teachers may build on these prior experiences with atomic models to develop *other* models. They might ask students to "develop and use models to illustrate that energy at the macroscopic scale can be accounted for as a combination of energy associated with the motion of particles (objects) and energy associated with the relative position of the particles (objects)" (HS-PS3–2; NGSS, 2013c).

In this case, the reperformance is not directly repeating the same task, as it would have been if the student simply remade the atomic models. Rather, students have an opportunity to reperform the SEP *develop and use models* later in the course in a different context. This reperformance would follow the same scaled learning target and generally the same success criteria, although the criteria may have changed due to the specific task.

Core Belief 3: Building Students' Reflection Abilities Is Essential

Students will apply the long-term transferable skills to future science courses and other academic pursuits. These are the types of skills they will use in their daily lives and should apply to a rich diversity of science DCIs. In addition to the SEPs, a student's thoughtful reflection on learning progress is one of these skills, something teachers often assume or hope students are able to do. However, teachers eventually realize they also need to *teach* students how to reflect.

Following are several key ideas for making the reflection process meaningful.

- Provide tools for reflection like that in figure 7.7 (page 214). Reflection tools include frameworks, question stems, and prompts to get students thinking and that provide a guide for them to follow.

- Include diverse aspects of student learning, ranging from their mastery on the SEPs and DCIs to the way they interact with peers on a particular learning experience and demonstrate social-emotional learning skills.

- Provide time during class. Students who often need the most support are the least likely to complete tasks outside school. To ensure the most thoughtful reflections and provide support as they work, it is important for the teacher to build this routine in class. Our teams found that effective reflection comes at various times in a lesson, not just right before the bell rings to signal the end of class.

- Model reflective practices and provide examples of what reflection can and should look like. Show your work as you approach a particular assessment task. This example would include a clear connection to the success criteria and how it meets the assessment prompt. In addition, explain (verbally or in writing) how you chose your approach. Likewise, teachers should provide relevant examples of how reflection has led to new insights, both for educators and for students.

Core Belief 7: Behavior Can Be In or Out of the Grade

Some science courses might value something such as environmental stewardship, applying course concepts to modifications around the home to improve energy efficiency. Our teams see this as something to include in students' performance tasks. However, if stewardship is a particular focus for your school, this might be something to include in the conversation about grading and reporting.

Finally, students need to act responsibly in the lab setting, following safe and accepted lab procedures while they work. This is not something to be taken lightly, particularly when dealing with hazards in chemistry, moving objects in physics, or field experiences in environmental science. Again, this is something we do not include in the gradebook, but treat as a non-negotiable. However, some teams might include these behaviors, but must provide students a scaled learning target with success criteria and consistent, specific feedback detailing where students are in relation to these criteria.

Key Points

To ensure full understanding, review the following key points from this chapter.

- To successfully transition to proficiency-based grading, science teachers need to focus instruction, assessment, and classroom practice on the SEPs.

This does not minimize the importance of the DCIs. However, teachers should treat the DCIs as the supporting content, while students interact with and demonstrate proficiency in the SEPs.

- Assessments will change. The nature of science and of this type of learning calls all science teachers to consider how they assess proficiency. While multiple choice and other forced-choice test items may play a supporting role in the assessment process, students should demonstrate their understanding and proficiency using new and novel performance tasks.

- Teachers will need to be very intentional about teaching students *how* to achieve proficiency in the SEPs. This includes identifying and communicating very clear success criteria, as well as teaching students how to reflect, self-assess, and make plans for achieving proficiency.

Bradley Smith is the director of the social studies division at Adlai E. Stevenson High School in Lincolnshire, Illinois. He has been the data assessment manager, advanced placement United States history team leader, teacher association president, and social studies teacher while at Stevenson. He also spent six years as a social studies teacher at International American Schools in Guatemala, Honduras, and Spain.

Brad is a member of the National Council for the Social Studies (NCSS), the NCSS College University Faculty Assembly (CUFA), the Illinois Council for the Social Studies (ICSS), and the Association for Supervision and Curriculum Development (ASCD). He has received training by College Board for AP government and AP United States history, and has served as a reader for AP government and politics.

Brad earned a master's degree in educational leadership from The College of New Jersey, a master of arts in teaching from Colgate University, and a bachelor of arts from Cornell College. Brad is currently pursuing his doctorate in education in curriculum and instruction—instructional systems design at the University of Kentucky.

To book Bradley Smith for professional development, contact pd@SolutionTree. com.

Chapter 8

Implementing Proficiency-Based Grading in Social Science

Bradley Smith

Advocates of citizenship education cross the political spectrum,
but they are bound by a common belief that our democratic republic
will not sustain unless students are aware of their changing cultural
and physical environments; know the past; read, write, and think
deeply; and act in ways that promote the common good.

—National Council for the Social Studies

For students to develop the skills to be critical actors in our civic society, social
sciences teachers must engage students with a mindset that all students can
learn, reflect on their own learning, and grow toward improvement. From these
commitments, teachers can devote their efforts to developing learning systems that
allow time and space for students to develop their own academic consciousness
and efficacy.

There is research and common sentiment in education, social sciences, and
social justice communities about the ills and concerns of traditional learning
models, points-based grading systems, and other traditional approaches to learning (Syverson, 2009). Researchers Robert J. Marzano (2003, 2006), John Hattie

(2012), Grant Wiggins and Jay McTighe (1998), Thomas R. Guskey (2015), and many others call for improved instruction, assessment, curriculum, grading, and reporting practices.

With all of the efforts toward improving learning in the social sciences—civics, political science, government, economics, geography, global or international relations, history, law, philosophy, psychology, sociology, religions, and more—and the myriad of advances teachers make in their classrooms year after year, why do many of us continue to ignore traditional grading practices that divert attention away from the "goal of knowledgeable, thinking, and active citizens?" (National Council for the Social Studies, 2013, p. 82).

In schools and the social sciences, the following four things are common.

1. Students' primary recursive civic interactions in life are their school experiences, which teachers regularly and primarily communicate through a grading system. It is common for students to have one common experience with a social and civic institution—their school. We commonly think of how we educate students as a process of learning of distinct disciplines or socialized behaviors. We have not focused enough on the level of civic empowerment, or lack thereof, that develops from the process of schooling and the primary frame educators use to communicate the official school experience (grading and reporting systems) to children and parents. It is vital to consider what impact this has on developing individuals. When grading and reporting systems are not interactive, achievement based, or connected from experiences or, worse, are arbitrary or inaccurate, students are walking away with the lesson to not engage with large institutions and to not look at themselves as empowered or capable of growth.

2. The type of grading and reporting a school uses can frame an adolescent student's egocentric nature, which is a strong motivator (Schwartz, Maynard, & Uzelac, 2008).

3. The type of grading and reporting a school uses was developed around achievement-based assessment systems reflecting content acquisition learning standards of past decades. These systems now often block efficient and supportive grading and reporting of growth toward skill-based standards, as well as reinforce assessment and instruction practices of teachers toward primarily content acquisition and achievement-based learning.

4. Quite often, the grading style that a school uses is woefully out of sync with the type of learning that promotes student development of academic

and civic efficacy, or growth called for in social studies–specific skills or inquiry skills.

Essentially, school systems are not just missing an opportunity to reinforce but also are often undermining efforts to develop students' academic consciousness and self-efficacy due to an outdated, fixed mindset and points-based systems of grading and reporting. Proficiency-based grading offers a grading approach that reinforces and strengthens the work of teachers and administrators to develop growth-minded, discipline-literate critical thinkers ready and able to engage in the civic, academic, and professional world around them. If the frame of reference that students, parents, and communities use to construct their understanding of learning and student and school effectiveness is through grades, then educators need to have a grading system that reflects the types of learning they espouse today; proficiency-based grading does this.

This chapter explains the reasons to implement proficiency-based grading in social science courses through five phases: (1) preparation, (2) incubation, (3) insight, (4) evaluation, and (5) elaboration (Csikszentmihalyi, 1990).

Reasons to Implement Proficiency-Based Grading in Social Science

When considering proficiency-based grading in a social science classroom, teachers often worry about changes that would undercut values they hold around teaching their subject. These values generally focus on using the specific discipline conceptual skills to create students capable of critical thinking about, and engagement with, contemporary societal issues and long-standing personal or social questions. Concerns around how grading changes may affect social sciences instruction, content, and grading workload are common. Social studies teachers will wonder if they can keep students motivated to do their preparatory work to be able to effectively utilize the conceptual tools and practices without a points system. Will a new system be as effective as current complex point systems at getting students to the grades teachers believe student thinking and application warrants when not funneled through the myriad of complex systems? And, will their communities accept a system of grading and reporting framed around student growth toward inquiry or discipline skills when presented with it? As teachers learn about this grading method (which sounds valuable, but so unfamiliar), they begin to understand the deeper rationale—the *why*—behind proficiency-based grading, and their concerns diminish.

The following sections address how proficiency-based grading supports the skills-based movement, promotes social justice efficacy, supports the core ideas of social science, supports the idea of the whole social sciences student, improves students' citizenship, benefits the community by producing community-minded students, and promotes personal efficacy for learning social science.

Proficiency-Based Grading in Social Science Supports the Skills-Based Movement

History and government AP programs have moved toward skill-based curricula, and the SAT exhorts this movement through assessments of the development of critical reasoning skills, not the acquisition of facts or concepts.

However, efforts to develop discipline-specific inquiry skills require more than just schools adopting revised standards. To fully develop students' skill sets, social science course teachers will need to do more than simply add a few assignments or projects. Increased formative feedback and student reflection as part of a fully integrated approach to developing learner efficacy around discipline-specific conceptual and inquiry skills is what proficiency-based grading brings to the curricular, instructional, and assessment work.

Past approaches of achievement learning alone will not provide students the opportunity to develop the reflective practices needed to consolidate their transferable conceptual skills, such as historical argumentation, source analysis, spatial analysis, or sociological mindset to name a few, or inquiry skills, such as the National Council for the Social Studies (NCSS; 2013) college, career, and civic life (C3) identifies: questioning, use of evidence, discipline concepts, communicating conclusions, and taking informed action. The process of developing meaningful arguments to answer teacher- or student-generated questions using discipline-specific tools to analyze evidence to build and communicate those arguments, and reflecting on one's own growth process toward established levels of proficiency in these practices, is at the heart of all social studies learning.

Growth-focused proficiency-based grading approaches offer a broader perspective for students, but too often devolve into an overwhelming, ineffective, unwieldy number of disparate skills and activities that are far too expansive for developing learners. Proficiency-based grading provides a tighter, recursive, and skill-centered focus on essential disciplinary skills proficiency and offers the opportunity to realize curricular, assessment, and instructional goals of inquiry-based standards reform. A key is the narrow definition of a *target* (desired proficiency level of a standard written in student-friendly language) that a learner recursively reflects his or her work (evidence) against over and over. There may be multiple or many success criteria involved in attaining the proficiency level, target, or both, but the standards and targets should be limited to fewer than seven for the total course.

Proficiency-Based Grading Promotes Social Justice Efficacy

Beyond the direct learning implications for improving both discipline literacy and conceptual thinking skills in the social sciences, there is a series of additional benefits from an adopting proficiency-based grading system. Extensive research from Robert J. Marzano (2003, 2006), Thomas Guskey (2015), and many others demonstrate the practical and societal ills of traditional grading-based educational programs to warrant a social justice advocate's interest in new, different, and empowering forms of grading.

For the social justice–minded educators, convincing students to believe in the power of individuals and institutions to promote social improvement will be far easier when residing in an institution that promotes discipline skills and growth through its system of grading. Further, curriculum director and former science teacher Andrew Jones (2015) warns, "Ultimately the current grading system is not a reliable indicator of student achievement . . . [which] often leads to grades that can be inconsistent and unfair to students." When a teacher seeks to empower self-advocacy and effective communal action, it stands to reason doing so from within an institution that reinforces those practices will help far more than when the institution blatantly counters them in its most high-stakes form of communication—grading and reporting.

Improved efficacy for all learners alone is a social justice goal worth this implementation. The essential elements of proficiency-based grading focus on student performance (and reperformance, as needed) toward discipline-specific skills rather than achievement of sometimes arbitrary content. This creates space for a far more applicable and universal social justice–supporting curriculum.

Proficiency-Based Grading Supports the Core Ideas of Social Science

Reflecting on evidence, setting goals (based on evidence), and collaboratively integrating objective national, state, or district standards for learning help develop individual academic consciousness and learner efficacy in all students, empowering them to be informed critics as well as contributory and efficacious members of any society (Hattie, 2012; Shanahan & Shanahan, 2011; Swan et al., 2013). Additionally, government consolidation around conceptual social science habits of mind (whether inquiry from the NCSS's 2013 *College, Career, and Civic Life C3 Framework for Social Studies State Standards* or disciplinary practices and reasoning skills) can be the focus of instruction, student growth, assessment, student reflection, and grading and reporting in a proficiency-based grading system. Proficiency-based grading systems require instruction, assessment, and student activities to center on essential and recursive conceptual skill growth that often does not naturally fit into traditional grading systems, but does fit with contemporary standards reflected in many arenas like the Illinois social science standards (Illinois State Board of Education, 2013), the NCSS (2013) C3 Framework, and the redesigned AP College Board U.S. (2017b), European (2017a), and world history (2017c) course descriptions.

Proficiency-Based Grading Supports the Idea of the Whole Social Science Student

Developing a proficiency-based grading system around discipline-specific skills focuses all student reflection, grade reporting, communicating, instructional design, and assessment implementation on both the social science skills and ability of students to identify their own capacities and needs for further growth. All academic endeavors will take place in the context of the discipline-specific skills the curricular team determines for how the student is performing toward the performance standard. This allows for both recursive horizontal and vertical focus on student skill development. Just as teachers use essential discipline-specific skill targets to focus learning in a given course, similar discipline courses across the curriculum can and should utilize the same discipline skills, such as mapping and spatial analysis, economic graphing, textual evidence analysis, or thesis-based argumentative writing.

Contemporary standards call for the development of the whole social studies student in ways not explicitly called for previously, and luckily well supported by proficiency-based grading. No longer is it enough to have students pursue discipline content knowledge and measure that knowledge through factual recognition, recall, reports, or occasional essays. Today's students need to be empowered to recognize important questions within disciplines and develop the ability to ask their own informed questions. Students need to practice and be competent at employing the distinct analytical tools each discipline offers for examining questions, evidence, and arguments. We also must train students to communicate their learning in effective ways using the discipline's common practices. In addition, teachers are charged with having students practice taking informed action on what they are learning within some semblance of the public sphere. Growth toward these abilities is enhanced through the use of proficiency-based grading. In particular, the necessary feedback and student reflective processes can help empower students toward developing their own academic consciousness within the discipline and in the pursuit of taking informed action on their own, while furthering individual civic consciousness and sense of agency in the real world.

Proficiency-Based Grading Improves Students' Citizenship

Improved discipline literacies and conceptual skills integration should translate into students' improved civic capacity as well. As previously noted, students will develop a greater sense of both academic and civic consciousness from their ability to recognize how to take meaningful action in society through reflection of their growth toward taking informed action. Not only will students have the greater awareness of opportunities, but they will also practice applying discipline skills in real-world contexts and reflecting on their own capacity to do so. Additional benefits for the community as a whole will also come from increased student collaboration and reflective classroom practices. Increasing SEL empathy, social awareness, and interpersonal communication skills contributes to what Nancy Frey, Douglas Fisher, and Dominique Smith (2019) call a student's *public spirit*.

Hattie (2009) identifies in his meta-analyses the power of student reflection and students identifying their own performance (grade) levels. Within SEL, there are many exciting connections between the development of interpersonal skills through student collaborative work and adult and professional life environments. There are also calls for connections or transference between academic empathy in students and civic empathy in adulthood that can come from potentially both collaborative inter-action and academic study. With proficiency-based grading, students will have many opportunities to co-construct their feedback and reflection to provide meaningful and important growth between peers and not just in an isolated individual setting or a top-down authority-to-subordinate process of teacher to student. Just as effective citizenship requires an individual's ability to communicate and productively interact with others, a proficiency-based grading course requires students to provide feedback with and to one another in accurate, supportive, and meaningful ways.

These goals intertwine with CASEL (2017) SEL standards and collaborative learning practices, such as self-management, self-responsibility, and social awareness. Developing meaningful and effective classroom instruction and student learning in a proficiency-based grading setting requires a focus on both SEL competencies and collaborative student learning. This obviously requires a merging of the individual student-reflection time and space and the teacher's very intentional design to ensure all competing needs are met in the different classroom spaces and student learning practices. Examples include cognitive workshops, co-constructed feedback, and learning plans differentiated by students.

For the proficiency-based grading teacher, the simple reality of *limited time* requires students to individually reflect on their performances in relation to the course standards and to assist their peers. Developing the ability to self-reflect and interact effectively and confidently about social science learning and thinking skills contributes to learner efficacy and individual academic consciousness in all students and citizens.

Proficiency-Based Grading Benefits the Community by Producing Community-Minded Students

While C3 (NCSS, 2013) social science standards call for taking informed action and improving service learning efforts, proficiency-based grading will help reinforce the implementation of such community-benefiting standards. Collaboration with peers is an essential skill for the workplace and even more important in the community. With the decrease of in-person interaction and increase of digital interaction, teachers should increase co-constructed feedback, encourage reflection on learning between peers, and explicitly teach person-to-person interaction. Yes, teachers should already have students work together on academic curricular goals, but the proficiency-based grading dynamics force teachers to expand student interaction by helping one another understand how everyone is performing and could be improving. This kind of positive and supportive interaction in all classrooms— not just social sciences—will improve students' interpersonal abilities and their interconnectedness with others. Both are areas of importance to civic functioning, as political scientist Robert D. Putnam (2000) indicates:

> A society characterized by generalized reciprocity is more efficient than a distrustful society, for the same reason that money is more efficient than barter. If we don't have to balance every exchange instantly, we can get a lot more accomplished. Trustworthiness lubricates social life. Frequent interaction among a diverse set of people tends to produce a norm of generalized reciprocity. Civic engagement and social capital entail mutual obligation and responsibility for action. (p. 21)

Proficiency-Based Grading Promotes Personal Efficacy for Learning Social Science

A proficiency-based grading model requires teachers to develop what we like to call, instead of discipline literacy, *disciplinary habits of mind* for students in the course. These habits of mind are not discipline agnostic, but there is extensive similarity in reflection, goal setting, and collaboration from one course, grade, or division to another. For examples, see figure 8.1 and figure 8.2.

Standard 1: Analyze like an economist.			
Learning Target 1: I can draw an accurate conclusion from unfamiliar scenarios when provided a limited context.			
4—Refined Mastery	**3—Proficiency**	**2—Approaches Proficiency**	**1—Still Developing**
I can draw an accurate conclusion from unfamiliar scenarios without context.	I can draw an accurate conclusion from unfamiliar scenarios with limited context.	I can draw an appropriate conclusion from fully contextualized scenarios.	I can draw an appropriate conclusion from familiar scenarios with support.

Source for standard: Adapted from Adlai E. Stevenson High School, 2016.

Figure 8.1: Example of AP microeconomics learning targets.

Standard 4: Show economic understanding of financial literacy.			
Learning Target 4: I can use economic skills and concepts to make major financial choices.			
4—Refined Mastery	**3—Proficiency**	**2—Approaches Proficiency**	**1—Still Developing**
I can use appropriate economic skills and concepts to make major financial choices in unfamiliar context.	I can use appropriate economic skills and concepts to make major financial choices in familiar context.	I can use economic skills and concepts to make major financial choices when provided support and context.	I can use given economic skills and concepts to make major financial choices when provided support and context.

Source for standard: Adapted from Adlai E. Stevenson High School, 2016.

Figure 8.2: Example of AP economics learning targets.

Preparation: The Commitments of Proficiency-Based Grading in Social Science

Teachers and teams make certain commitments to successfully implement this improved system of assessing and instructing. This can be difficult because teachers often have very personal and intense attachments to specific resources, literature, other curriculum, instruction, and assessment. When a team of teachers is preparing to do this work, there will be worries about losing autonomy and the challenge of adapting teaching and assessment in the near future. That is when making a series of commitments will allow teachers to support each other on the road to success.

The following commitments are discussed in subsequent sections: (1) base social science standards on skills, (2) focus on the standards of learning social science, (3) use the essential standards of learning social science, (4) don't assume all students are natural readers of social science contexts, and (5) pursue the right social science standards.

Commitment 1: Base Social Science Standards on Skills

Before implementing a system of instruction, assessment, curriculum, and grading and reporting, teachers must make a commitment to what is essential for students to learn in the social sciences. This requires a commitment from not only teachers but also learners and the general public on the importance of an understanding of curriculum, instruction, and assessment of student development on discipline-specific skills using rich and accurate discipline-area content.

Luckily, standards for those skills and content are not hard to find and include the NCSS (2013) C3 inquiry standards, Illinois State Board of Education (2013) social studies standards, and AP College Board (2017a, 2017b, 2017c) history course descriptions.

Commitment 2: Focus on the Standards of Learning Social Science

Proficiency-based grading forces teachers to focus on discipline-specific conceptual skills. The NCSS (2013) C3 inquiry skills or the AP College Board program shifts the focus on disciplinary practices and reasoning skills in each course and across disciplines like history to focus on developing what we believe educational leaders Sam Wineburg, Daisy Martin, and Chauncey Monte-Sano (2013) would call *reading like a historian*, or what Nikki Mandell and Bobbie Malone (2007) would call *thinking like a historian* (or like an economist, an engaged citizen, a political scientist, a geographer, and so on).

These standards and approaches to learning in proficiency-based grading support are consistent with discipline literacy theory (Shanahan & Shanahan, 2012) and CCSS (NGA & CCSSO, 2010a). It's easy to say there is widespread acceptance and a calling for discipline-specific skill standards to develop curriculum, instruction, and assessment. Any team and teacher looking to develop the most independent and critically conscious social sciences students must start with these types of standards before developing a specific proficiency-based grading system.

Figure 8.3 is a sample rubric for writing in a traditional point-driven grade 11 U.S. history course. Compare it to the proficiency-based grading rubric for grade 12 political science in figure 8.4 (page 233).

Learning Target: Persuasive writing

4—Excellent	3—Good	2—Satisfactory	1—Needs Improvement
Thesis: What are you arguing?			
My thesis meets all the expectations of "Good" and also . . . • Is sophisticated • Includes a counterargument • Is part of a complete introduction with specific details relating to the time period of the prompt • Is part of a thought-provoking conclusion that begins with the counterargument	My thesis . . . • Takes a clear position and previews body paragraphs • Is part of a complete introduction with general details relating to the time period of the prompt • Is part of a conclusion that enhances my argument by offering insight or building on the argument	My thesis . . . • Is broad or vague and doesn't preview the evidence • Is part of an introduction but context may be vague or underdeveloped or leaves out key information • Is part of a conclusion that only restates the thesis rather than offering insight or building on the argument	My thesis . . . • Is not detectable or apparent • Is not part of an introduction that establishes context • Does not restate or elaborate on my ideas in a conclusion
Evidence: What are the major points to support your argument?			
All of my evidence meets the expectations of "Good" and . . . • Demonstrates an excellent knowledge of the topic	Most of my evidence . . . • Demonstrates expected knowledge of the topic • Is organized into clear body paragraphs	Some of my evidence . . . • Suggests some knowledge of the topic, but is missing key evidence	My evidence . . . • Demonstrates a lack of understanding of the topic • Is not organized into clear body paragraphs

Figure 8.3: Traditional rubric.

continued ⟶

4—Excellent	3—Good	2—Satisfactory	1—Needs Improvement
• Is substantial enough to persuade the audience to agree with my thesis	• Is made clear in the topic sentences of each paragraph • Includes effective use of primary sources	• Is too limited to make a persuasive case to support my thesis • Is somewhat organized into body paragraphs • Includes primary sources	
Analysis and Synthesis: How is your evidence used to build a persuasive argument?			
All of my evidence . . . • Is analyzed precisely and convincingly shows support for the thesis • Builds to form a complete argument over the course of each body paragraph • Is based on primary sources that reflect a perceptive reading of the source	Most of my evidence . . . • Is analyzed, showing how my evidence supports the thesis • Is synthesized or grouped to build a case that supports my thesis • Is based on primary sources that reflect an accurate reading of the source	Some of my evidence . . . • Is analyzed, showing a relationship between facts and the thesis • Is vague or doesn't show I have an understanding of the content	My evidence . . . • Is stated without analysis
Mechanics: Is your writing clear, grammatically correct, and well organized?			
My writing. . . . • Is grammatically error free • Is organized into paragraphs, each with a clear purpose • Contains strong, persuasive vocabulary	My writing . . . • Contains minor grammatical or spelling errors • Is clear, and my sentence structure is correct • Is organized into paragraphs, most with a clear purpose	My writing . . . • Contains many grammatical or spelling errors • Is sometimes confusing at the sentence level • Is organized into paragraphs, but the purpose of each is unclear	My writing . . . • Contains distracting grammatical and spelling errors • Lacks clarity at the sentence level • Is not organized into paragraphs
Additional feedback:		**Grade:**	

The traditional rubric in figure 8.3 has many criteria for many components: thesis, evidence, analysis and synthesis, and mechanics. The proficiency-based grading rubric in figure 8.4 has a single proficiency scale for the same learning target.

Learning Target: Persuasive writing			
4—Refined Mastery	**3—Proficiency**	**2—Approaches Proficiency**	**1—Still Developing**
I consistently write insightful arguments that establish claims, and use evidence, elevated and complex reasoning, and sophisticated language appropriate for the task.	I consistently write arguments that establish claims, and use sufficient evidence, elevated and complex reasoning, and language appropriate for the task.	I write arguments that establish claims, use limited evidence and basic reasoning, and often use appropriate language for the task.	I attempt to establish an argument without establishing a claim or using necessary support, accurate analysis, and appropriate language for the task.

Figure 8.4: Proficiency-based grading rubric.

Commitment 3: Use the Essential Standards of Learning Social Science

Teachers in a proficiency-based grading system choose learning targets and must only focus on student learning. Additional SEL competencies or behavioral reporting can and should exist. But what teachers report and students contribute to the final grade should only be essential learning in the proficiency targets tied to each standard—and nothing more. Teachers can should expect students to uphold proper academic, classroom, and school behaviors, as well as develop an array of explicit SEL competencies. However, unless teachers explicitly integrate them as part of instruction, neither should contribute to the grade determination.

Teachers should report important behavioral and SEL components to students, parents, and support personnel regularly, and on an as-needed basis per student. Teachers collect and report evidence toward all standards plus any SEL or behavioral elements. What contributes to any grade at the end of a course should only reflect the academic learning represented in the identified discipline standards.

Commitment 4: Don't Assume All Students Are Natural Readers of Social Science Contexts

One of the challenges any experienced educator or expert in a field will identify with teaching and learning is understanding the learning needs and learning trajectory of the novice. Teachers must adhere to the principles that students are not all inherently curious about social sciences and, more importantly, not all students possess the ingrained ability to read, think, write, speak, question, analyze, and reflect. This is crucially important in the varied social sciences disciplines. Teachers must recognize that, for example, a student's strength in history often does not translate to similar conceptual skill strength in geography or economics.

Also, a teacher unequivocally recognizes that while a student may not come to a course with a social scientist's habits (or even an academically conscious learner's habits), a student does come to school with the ability to grow and succeed in those skills with help.

Commitment 5: Pursue the Right Social Science Standards

There will a need for teachers to commit to focusing on pursuing the right standards, in the right language, for all students to become autonomous thinkers in social sciences. Team members will repeatedly ask themselves several questions about standards and targets, including "Do our targets achieve autonomous discipline-specific thinking in our students?" The standards and targets tied to national, state, province, and district guidelines should achieve this.

An initial challenge for teachers is crafting the standard and learning target language. Is the language accessible and useful for all students? Does the language result in learning for all? Standards may change due to forces outside the classroom, but effective standards and targets may well adjust due to a myriad of dynamic and evolving student needs as students work with the targets recursively over many years. Teachers need to pay attention to the language they use, particularly when giving feedback. Teachers should examine the language and design of student targets for effectiveness daily throughout the course.

Logically, a key place for teachers to evaluate and question if students are learning to be efficacious learners and thinkers and if the target language is accessible to all students is their formative and summative assessment tools. First and foremost, teachers need to have established a robust and comprehensive formative assessment approach in their courses. Creating meaningful student learning dissonance is a challenge that will require constant vigilance and fine-tuning. Teachers will need to constantly be reflecting on the type and quality of work students are producing to ensure it is meeting the goals of creating evidence for the learning target and context to reflect on it. This is best done in collaborative teacher teams. Teachers need time to not only calibrate student evidence for inter-rater reliability, but to make sure their targets continue asking students for the right kinds of evidence and that their instruction and feedback stimulate student growth.

While counterintuitive to some, this ongoing course evolution is the nature of learning in a diverse and dynamic democracy looking to develop robust efficacy and citizenship.

Incubation: The Unexpected Questions of Proficiency-Based Grading in Social Science

As teachers progress toward using proficiency-based grading, they will uncover some wonderful questions that drive inquiry and implementation. During this second stage, many previously adopted practices may be working, but teachers may pay a lot of attention to the items that seem to create different types of instruction or student work, providing new challenges for both students and teachers. With so much new information, it can be hard not to worry that some challenges will never be overcome. The following questions are representative of the incubation stage challenges that require patience and persistence.

Unexpected Question 1: What Is Assessment's Role in Proficiency-Based Social Science?

Many types of challenges can and will emerge during implementation, with content, assessment, feedback, and student-friendly learning target language generally emerging as places wanting attention. It is hard to tease apart the content and assessment practices topic. If a teacher has been working in a world of traditional summative assessment for content recognition, he or she will need a lot of exposure and training, likely through formal professional development supported by informal mentoring or team support.

To make a jump from forced-choice achievement-based content assessment to a recursive skills based a proficiency model requires the teachers to use different assessment tools (source- or stimulus-based SAT questions, AP questions, various rubrics) when building instruction or providing feedback toward growth. Once teachers can see the types of evidence through formal and informal formative assessments that students create, they can then identify which standards to teach and put into student proficiency target language.

Figure 8.5 (page 236) shows an example of how students produce evidence toward multiple standards, including writing and graphing standards, in a grade 11 and 12 economics course assessment.

Collaborative teacher teams, with support from curriculum coaches, drafted the targets from required state standard language over the course of several meetings during the summer. Teachers employing these types of assessments and proficiency-based grading practices are familiar with formative assessment practices and also possess an understanding of discipline practices and a knowledge of contemporary discipline-specific conceptual skills based standards like the C3, updated AP, or some state or provincial standards.

Directions: Research and create an opinion statement on one of the following categories using the tools of cost-benefit analysis and the production possibility frontier (PPF) in your evaluation.

In the constantly changing and evolving technological and globalized world, there's no shortage of innovation around the way we spend our money. New markets in hotels, music, movies, shopping, learning, and travel have popped up in recent years with huge impacts in the world economy. Your task in this unit one final is to evaluate the statement "Are _____ a good thing?" for one of the following industries. You'll be using the tools of cost-benefit analysis as well as article research, argumentative writing, and PPF graphing in your evaluation.

Topics:

1. Room sharing (Airbnb, hostels)

2. Streaming services (Netflix, Spotify, Amazon Prime Music and Movies, Pandora)

3. Online marketplaces (Etsy, Amazon)

4. Bike sharing (Divvy, Mobike)

5. Virtual schools (LearnDash, Kahn Academy, YouTube)

4—Refined Mastery	3—Proficiency	2—Approaches Proficiency	1—Still Developing
Standard 2: Write like an economist.			
Learning Target 1: I write arguments to support claims with evidence.			
I write an arguable claim with a clear position and fully developed context supported with quality evidence and reasoning.	I write an arguable claim with a clear position on a prompt supported with quality evidence and reasoning.	I write an arguable claim when given a clear position and fully developed context supported with evidence and reasoning.	I write an arguable claim when given a clear position, fully developed context, and evidence and reasoning support.

Standard 3: Graph like an economist.			
Learning Target 1: I accurately illustrate familiar scenarios using all key features.			
I illustrate unfamiliar scenarios using all key features without context.	I illustrate unfamiliar scenarios using all key features with limited context.	I illustrate fully contextualized scenarios using specific key features.	I illustrate familiar scenarios using all key features with support.

Source for standard: Adapted from Adlai E. Stevenson High School, 2017.

Figure 8.5: College prep economics rubric.

Visit go.SolutionTree.com/assessment for a free reproducible version of this figure.

Once those understandings are in place, the teams decide on various assessment strategies. Then, teachers must wrestle with deciding which standards are the most comprehensive, essential, and enduring for their courses, and put those standards into student-friendly proficiency language. Teacher teams need time and space to develop, reflect on, practice, and review the proficiency language they design before implementation. Even once implemented, teachers will calibrate different assessments and evidence. Finding opportunities for teachers to engage in this reflective building and calibration process is also essential to continue for several reasons. From a student perspective, the assurance of equitable assessment is important. There is also great value for teacher growth and learning from collaborating with professional peers. The collaborative, reflective discussions for instruction and remediation will benefit all teachers and students.

Unexpected Question 2: Are Assessments Effective and Collecting the Right Evidence of Learning in This Social Science?

Teachers will not have much trouble if they have background in the discipline and even a modicum of experience working with students in identifying if the student evidence is consistent with meeting the proficiency level they have set. While calibrating with peers takes time, it needs to happen recursively. Teachers use their training and experience to identify whether the evidence is accurately meeting the standards within the discipline. That is only half of a teacher's professional responsibility toward effective assessment process and evidence.

The somewhat newer half that proficiency-based grading requires is to see if the assessment process and evidence are actually allowing for meaningful feedback and reflection by the students to solicit growth toward proficiency. The feedback, reflection, and growth dilemma hits teachers as they see the benefits of aligning their grading and reporting to the discipline skills students need to develop, but the challenge side of using the formative assessment process and evidence in efficient instructional ways that create growth becomes the focus of their individual and collective energies at this point.

Once teachers have an idea of what they will be looking for and how to instruct to build toward it in students, the feedback dilemma hits. If their instructional and assessment practices are already heavily formative and built around skills, giving feedback will be less challenging. However, if these practices are not, then the time and space for this process will be significant. Teachers will realize the need to create time and space for students to receive growth-oriented feedback and to reflect.

One of the big-picture items will be the gradebook and what flexibility or options teachers have with reporting student progress. This will require data reporting programs with creative and interactive capacity. In the classroom, teachers will have to start with a clear understanding of the learning targets and informative feedback on how students are progressing. From there, students will have to be taught to internalize methods of individual and co-constructed feedback, reflection, and goal setting.

Teachers should spend some time collaboratively previewing how they give feedback and what kinds of supports, goals, or action steps students can take in various learning trajectories toward mastering proficiency. As the semester or year proceeds, teachers will need to instruct students how to individually and collaboratively identify and communicate proficiency levels, actionable feedback, and goals. One benefit of this work is a recognition of new time and structures in the classroom. Teachers can find the space in their instruction for the types of student learning they desire—types that traditional approaches for content acquisition often block.

Figure 8.6 is a type of lesson that simply never existed using traditional grading systems. This lesson includes a writing standard and the lessons that build student proficiency.

Insight: The Essential Insights of Proficiency-Based Grading in Social Science

As teachers begin to move beyond the initial fears and roadblocks and gain insight, it is vitally important to take some time to look back on and appreciate how the team has passed some intimidating hurdles thus far. Teams should have a clear enough idea of how proficiency-based grading works, and they can play to its strengths as they teach and plan. They begin providing proficiency-based grading with more power instead of just trying to get their balance.

To what extent does the free market improve standard of living?		
Section 1: Define your argument.		
Circle one: The free market does improve standard of living. The free market does not improve standard of living.		
What three details support your argument?	**What are the strengths of your supporting details?**	**What are the weaknesses of your supporting details?**
1.		
2.		
3.		
Section 2: Show the sources for your claim. Go back to your readings and seek other texts to find evidence to back your claims.		
Source:	**How credible is this source? Why is it believable or convincing?**	**What evidence from this source supports your argument?**

Section 3: Make a counterclaim using convincing arguments for the other side.			
What was the most convincing argument for the other side?	What evidence supports the counterargument you chose?	Why was the argument convincing?	How might you respond to this argument in your paper?

Source: Adlai E. Stevenson High School, 2017.

Figure 8.6: Writing lesson for college preparatory economics.

*Visit **go.SolutionTree.com/assessment** for a free reproducible version of this figure.*

At this point, social science teachers might have the following insights: (1) developing social science proficiency is the goal, (2) social science instruction includes reflection, and (3) all students need differentiation to successfully set goals.

Insight 1: Developing Social Science Proficiency Is the Goal

One of the first aha moments that emerge from teachers as they design lessons and instruction is when they begin developing in-class activities that allow for students to review feedback, reflect on their own growth, and then set goals. Not only are teachers seeing a simplified, clear, and direct alignment between learning skill, standard, assessment, and grading system, but so will students. That "aha!" can trigger a teacher's desire to increase the time and space for activities.

Previously, teachers often allowed students only to reflect after a test or at the end of a lesson; it is often the first thing omitted from most daily learning experiences for students. In a proficiency-based grading system, the process will unravel if there is no reflection. Building student reflection abilities is core belief 3 (page 14). Making reflection around essential skill standards the primary, recursive focus of instruction, assessment, reflection, and grading allows students' experience to become more like an apprenticeship model. That aligns with promising social studies research on cognitive apprenticeship models (De La Paz et al., 2017).

Insight 2: Social Science Instruction Includes Reflection

Author Bruce A. VanSledright (2010) discusses the importance and power of student self-assessment as an essential ingredient toward reinforcing the development of student investigative and critical thinking skills in *The Challenge of Rethinking History Education: On Practices, Theories, and Policy*:

> Becker has gathered powerful evidence for the efficacy of his approach, of the growing level of responsibility his students assume over their own learning process once he opens the assessment terrain and invites students onto it as co-participants . . . This would only reinforce the strength of the feedback loop his assessment theory entailed. He also interpreted such moves as evidence of his students becoming the self-assessors he prized most especially. (pp. 169–170)

For the many teachers struggling for student buy-in, proficiency-based grading is a dream come true. The teacher can divorce discussion from the points-based reflection and focus students exclusively on the conceptual or discipline skill. Possibly more valuably, in a schoolwide proficiency-based grading system, all teachers in all classes learn students' reflective practices and efficacy throughout their school experience. This knowledge doesn't just occur in one division or another, or randomly throughout students' time in school.

Teachers will come to realize they need to integrate and space for metacognition in all lessons daily. Then, there is the second reflection space, which is broader or more holistic and awakens the teacher's awareness to a student's general lack of skills in learning reflection and goal setting. Teachers will adjust their instructional approach to increase clarity, time, and space for students to see what skill or learning target they are working on at introduction, providing clear proficiency-level feedback during instruction, and again time to reflect on performance.

During this process, students need various practices, collaborative and peer-to-peer feedback protocols, and resources to help them individually see their own performance in comparison to the proficiency level actively sought or teachers design. Some common examples are peer editing, weekly goal setting, assessment reflections journals, and target-tracking spreadsheets. At times, teachers may recognize that student needs or understandings are evolving and adjust instruction, remediation, or success criteria language. That is yet another reason collaboratively calibrating assessment evidence and instruction, remediation, and reflection practices works.

Over time and with multiple success criteria, teachers will realize the need to create time and space for students to reflect on the whole body of their progress and set longer-term goals. Identifying the space will also require developing additional protocols or tools for students to use. It will also become evident that the teacher cannot provide formal detailed feedback for every single student for every reflection. Reflections will need to be done collaboratively with peers and teachers, as well as individually by effectively trained students. Teachers need an effective means of monitoring these processes, but learning ownership rests with the students.

Student training on how to reflect is a second part of the "reflection wall" I see teachers hit. Students and parents raised on traditional points-based grading systems tend to not naturally walk in with an expectation, or prior training, on how to reflect on their own growth and development in a course. Nor do they usually have the skills to set academic goals beyond possibly creating daily schedules for themselves to get their homework done or to study for tests. It is not surprising that students would need explicit instruction and supports with not only understanding what a standard and its proficiency levels are but also how to examine their own individual progress toward proficiency and set meaningful growth goals toward proficiency.

This is where the analogy to literacy skills is strongest. Experienced teachers have spent a lot of time reflecting on the learning trajectories of their course outcomes even if they have not used that terminology. They can see and have internalized what a certain grade or points performance means and what steps students need to take to improve performance on both a short- and long-term process. Generally speaking, most students and parents need help with the reflective practices and feedback language.

Parent training and support work best if done as a school- or districtwide effort and all content areas use common reporting platforms and language. That said, with practice, teachers will become more comfortable explaining their targets, what evidence of proficiency looks like, and how to grow toward it. Some of the most valuable practice is during the collaborative teacher team process of developing proficiency-based grading systems, with teachers asking questions. Teachers come to realize they will need to find time not just to allow students to reflect and goal set but also to sustain instruction and support to help students do this.

Insight 3: All Students Need Differentiation to Successfully Set Goals

If teachers want to empower all students to find their own pathways to individual success, they must teach students how to accurately reflect on their own learning and goals set for their specific course and based on their proficiency. I have found teachers spend a lot of time collaborating with one another about how to help students reflect and goal set during their first semester of implementing proficiency-based grading.

Teachers coming out of this process come to identify *developing accurate and effective student metacognition* as the most meaningful differentiated learning they encounter in the classroom. Student reflection in a proficiency-based grading system means dozens of individualized learning plans for each class period, with students identifying their own strengths and weaknesses, setting purposefully differentiated goals to improve, and then executing that plan. That then triggers reinforcement of having the right types of learning targets and activities for students to focus their own needs.

Writing an essay (historical analysis, written communication, or the like) is a common example of the work students reflect on feedback from to plan ways of improving their proficiency. Teachers can structure a series of activities that release students to doing more and more of the feedback and reflection on their own. Early in a term, teachers might provide exemplars for students to review and contrast against a projected example that the teacher then models. Later, students get opportunities to co-construct feedback with partners or small groups and submit it to the teacher for a quick review (or give it to the teacher after the work has been assessed but not physically marked). Individual blind feedback can be done then in round-robin formats with students as well.

With practice and additional activities, students should begin internalizing the proficiency levels and success criteria and recognizing possible individualized goals they should pursue. A learning target around evidence interpretation or discipline analysis can also provide this through something as simple as annotating. There are dozens of assessment types a historian, geographer, economist, sociologist, or political scientist could focus on, depending on the type of evidence (primary, secondary, or tertiary text; political cartoon; type of map, chart, or graph).

Evaluation: The Key Questions of Proficiency-Based Grading in Social Science

Implementation's beginning stages bring a perspective of evaluation. While professional growth never takes one path, reaching this point allows teams to set a goal of reaching regular practice and to confidently look into ways that the system impacts feedback and grading.

Evaluation can lead social science teachers to ask the following key questions: (1) "How important is individual student reflection in social science courses?" (2) "What type of feedback do teachers give in proficiency-based grading social science courses?" and (3) "How do social science teachers structure student reflection in class?"

Key Question 1: How Important Is Individual Student Reflection in Social Science Courses?

The first question teachers in the social sciences should ask themselves is "Are my students learning to think like social scientists—historians, psychologists, political scientists, economists?" This focus keeps a course aligned with the discipline literacies and skills unique to each profession. Students will become better at thinking, reading, analyzing, and writing while developing their own discipline lenses through internal conversations or conversing with peers and teachers. They need the practice, feedback, and explicitly structured time for reflection to develop these unique capacities. Teachers must make certain the standards and targets reflect this in language and execution. Teachers integrate much of this at the level of success criteria, and through the feedback reflection and goal-setting stages of learning. This instructional experience around disciplinary habits of mind leads to a cognitive apprenticeship or social science lab-type experience.

In the end, teachers need to be confident and clear that students are not just learning to be generic thinkers but also expanding and improving their individual academic consciousness by becoming autonomous discipline-specific thinkers. Focusing students on the critical analysis of concepts as well as their own learning is evident in the rubric in figure 8.7 (page 244).

Standard: Think like an economist.			
Learning Target: I draw an accurate conclusion from unfamiliar scenarios with limited context.			
4—Refined Mastery	**3—Proficiency**	**2—Approaches Proficiency**	**1—Still Developing**
I draw an accurate conclusion from unfamiliar scenarios without context.	I draw an accurate conclusion from unfamiliar scenarios with limited context.	I draw an appropriate conclusion from fully contextualized scenarios.	I draw an appropriate conclusion from familiar scenarios with support.
Success Criteria	**How Well Am I Doing?**	**Teacher Comments**	
• Vocabulary application • Formulas • Calculations • Comparisons • Data • Models • Contrasts • Connections to graphs			

Figure 8.7: AP microeconomics rubric.

Key Question 2: What Type of Feedback Do Teachers Give in Proficiency-Based Grading Social Science Courses?

The first key question—How important is individual student reflection in social science courses?—provides the basis for the subsequent questions, including the following.

- Do your assessments lead to effective feedback for student learning?

- Are you creating assessments around the evidence that students and teachers need to identify proficiency levels and attainable short- and long-term goals, and that allow differentiated student focus?

Teachers and students come together in their need for assessment information that is not about achievement but that provides a practice-feedback-practice-feedback loop adjusted for all learners' needs. For some assessments, this might simply require adjusting student feedback—for example, grading homework or reading notes no longer for completion but rather for the proficiency it shows. Another example is graphing accuracy in economics with success criteria of properly naming or illustrating the X- and Y-axis.

For multiple choice tests, it is no longer about the score or points; it must be an opportunity to demonstrate and identify the level of knowledge or type of analysis a student is capable of in a content area. The challenge is not so much recognizing this; it is more challenging to adhere to the consistency of these assessment practices as the year progresses and prior assessment habits emerge. It is also a great challenge for teachers when confronted with an external assessment (AP or provincial) that does not assess in the same format, or possibly for more content acquisition or achievement, rather than growth or skill performance. Here again is one of the benefits to team calibration. Teachers can reflect and test their own fidelity to the target proficiency they set, and then monitor outside factors, past practices, or assessment misalignment to keep it from influencing their classrooms.

With time, experience, and reflection, teachers will see that assessing students on the goal of developing the skill sets for being efficacious learners and thinkers in specific disciplines will continue to meet student performance levels on external assessments.

Key Question 3: How Do Social Science Teachers Structure Student Reflection in Class?

A student reflecting on his or her learning efficacy in a history course versus a geography course, an economics course, or any other course will use question stems, thought processes, and analysis tools unique to each course and discipline standard. While a general or common level of reflection and collaboration is likely meaningful prior to ninth grade and certainly important for developing abilities in this area, as students age and take courses with increasing specification, it both expands their educational consciousness and serves the goals of more complex disciplinary study to see the habits of mind unique to each discipline or course.

Obviously as a school is implementing proficiency-based grading, there will be a heightened need for clarity; students will not be familiar with the overall process of self-reflective learning through an analysis of evidence against a standard. However, even once students are familiar with the concept in general and have experienced multiple classes, the importance of this clarity will remain on a course-by-course basis. Students, particularly those who struggle and their supporters, will need to clearly know the standards, what proficiency looks like, and what steps they can take to develop proficiency and produce evidence of it.

Figure 8.8 shows an example of an economics preassessment that helps develop student reflection skills.

Directions: Before the unit two test, it's important to reflect on graphing and determinants. Please go through your supply, demand, and equilibrium graphs to write down what mistakes you continue to make. Are you missing the title? Is your title incorrect? Are you not shifting the correct curve or direction? Spend time practicing determinants before Friday.

1. What mistakes do I continue to make on my graphs?

2. What step can I take before Friday to fix these mistakes?

3. On a scale of 1–10, how confident am I in the determinants? Circle one.

    1   2   3   4   5   6   7   8   9   10

4. Why did I select that number?

5. What step can I take before the test to move closer to 10?

Figure 8.8: College prep economics example of reflection on graphing.

Elaboration: The Core Beliefs of Proficiency-Based Grading in Social Science

Teachers at the elaboration phase of implementation have reached a mature and clear perspective of using a proficiency-based grading system. They have discovered that the system does not push them out of valued projects, simulations, or other assessments and activities they know help students learn; instead, they see there is depth to be gained from such work, with an underlying and clear focus on skills. With their comfort in this system, teachers are resources for their colleagues and on the cutting edge for new ways to provide more support for and collaboration with their students.

Teachers who successfully implement proficiency-based grading adhere to all seven of the core beliefs explained in chapter 1 (page 9): (1) growth is a central concept,

(2) reperformance is essential, (3) building students' reflection abilities is essential, (4) homework has a role, (5) communication with parents and the community is key, (6) culminating experiences like final exams have a different purpose, and (7) behavior can be in or out of the grade. The following sections, which reflect the core beliefs' original numbering, explore the core beliefs that social science teachers in particular should never lose sight of.

Core Belief 1: Growth Is a Central Concept

As teachers in the social sciences embrace the discipline skills that develop authentic inquiry in all courses, there is no better partner than proficiency-based grading. The system provides a conceptual and pragmatic system of coherent focus on student growth and progress toward the types of standards and skills social scientists seek to set for students. A schoolwide system of proficiency-based grading, where student learning experiences are a growth model and all classes help to develop student individual academic efficacy, reinforces the social science goals of civic efficacy and social justice. Focusing on proficiency empowers students to see that they themselves can grow and impact change, and that the primary institution they experience—school—also facilitates their growth and understanding. As they recognize and explicitly develop their own academic efficacy, this approach will reinforce the social science goals of constructive civic interaction and collaborative and individual efforts to taking informed action.

No longer will social science teachers have students explore their disciplines for efficacy and social justice but then be forced into limited assessment and reporting models that undermine student metacognition, skill growth, responsibility, and efficacy. Simply put, in proficiency-based grading, students have a grading system that allows them to continually and exclusively focus on the discipline literacy and conceptual skills teachers set for them, all the while becoming increasingly autonomous thinkers and learners.

Core Belief 3: Building Students' Reflection Abilities Is Essential

Teachers and teams would do well to ask themselves the following questions.

- "Are we empowering autonomous student self-reflection?"
- "Do the analytical skills and self-reflection practices students develop at our schools, and uniquely in each of our courses, transfer to their lives beyond our classroom?"
- "Can students maintain the individual academic consciousness and learner efficacy we seek when they are not in school?"

- "Do the skills we teach students transfer to the workplace, higher learning environments, or the public sphere?"

The backbone of effective learning from feedback also requires students to improve their capacity to reflect and use constructive feedback from teachers, peers, and even themselves to identify goals and action steps toward improving skills like thesis writing, identifying change over time, analyzing economics, and being sociologically mindful. This reflection ability supports an understanding of the sometimes slow processes behind any type of change, be it individual or collective. Most of all, graduates' improved collaboration and reflection skills will strengthen their ability to build and recognize the bonds between others in our communities large and small. Empathy, social awareness, self-regulation, and many other SEL skills are directly tied to civic engagement. The academic study as well as the instruction, feedback, and reflective practices required in a proficiency-based grading system make this possible.

Core Belief 7: Behavior Can Be In or Out of the Grade

Many social science teachers recognize the importance of a collaborative learning environment for developing civic competencies, as well as instructional practices as simple as co-constructed feedback. Teachers often identify SEL competencies as essential for course success and easily recognizable as profoundly important factors for future success in academia and the workforce, and for civic contribution in adulthood. Social science teachers should incorporate SEL competencies into academic standards and targets as appropriate success criteria. They should teach, assess, and report on—but not include in student grades—otherwise stand-alone SEL skills.

Key Points

To ensure full understanding, review the following key points from this chapter.

- Proficiency-based grading is essential for developing academic efficacy, which supports civic efficacy.

- Proficiency-based grading improves instructional integration at the same time it helps social science teachers focus on skills—making historical arguments, graphing like an economist, being sociologically mindful, analyzing sources, and taking informed action as examples—intrinsic to their courses.

- Teachers using proficiency-based grading will find the greatest change in their instruction is developing authentic and regular reflective space for students.

 **Justin Fisk, MEd,** is the director of world languages and English language learning at Adlai E. Stevenson High School in Lincolnshire, Illinois, where he supports close to forty teachers and paraprofessionals. Justin has taught both Spanish and German at a number of high schools in the Chicago area and in Montgomery County, Maryland, where he began his education career in 2002.

Justin's concerted focus on professional development, team-driven instructional innovation, and the creation and implementation of programming that drives all students toward success has seen him and his colleagues create high levels of success for his district's multilingual learners. One example of this success is that over 20 percent of district graduates have been recognized through the Illinois State Seal of Biliteracy.

Justin is a member of the American Council on the Teaching of Foreign Languages, the National Association of District Supervisors of Foreign Languages, the National Association for Bilingual Education, Learning Forward, the Association for Supervision and Curriculum Development, the Illinois Association of Multilingual Multicultural Education, and the Illinois Council on the Teaching of Foreign Languages. He has presented at state, regional, and national conferences and written for *The Language Educator*.

Justin earned a bachelor of arts in Spanish for international service and a master of arts in Spanish literature from The Catholic University of America. He earned a master of arts in teaching in secondary Spanish education from Johns Hopkins University and a master of education in teacher leadership and English as a second language from Loyola University Chicago.

To book Justin Fisk for professional development, contact pd@SolutionTree.com.

Chapter 9

Implementing Proficiency-Based Grading in World Languages

Justin Fisk

> Knowledge of languages is the doorway to wisdom.
>
> —*Roger Bacon*

For teachers who have made the leap to a proficiency-oriented approach to language instruction, and for those whose performance assessments rightly hold greater importance than fill-in-the blank grammar and vocabulary drills, there is already a deep understanding that the traditional grading system is incontrovertibly broken. The random and haphazard assignment of points just doesn't jive with the way teachers know students learn and grow in a language. And while "If it ain't broke, don't fix it" doesn't work here since educators acknowledge the system is, in fact, broken, there can be an undercurrent of "It's good enough and students are learning." This type of thinking disinvites the type of innovation, such as our collective pivot toward proficiency-based assessment, that has seen second language acquisition pedagogy move resolutely away from the grammar-translation method. The progress made demands teachers move forward, and the proficiency-based approach provides the framework for these efforts. That said, many language teachers are understandably fearful that any sort of paradigm shift, as it necessarily questions our current best practices, might disrupt the progress we've already collectively made.

This chapter explains the reasons to implement proficiency-based grading in world languages through five phases: (1) preparation, (2) incubation, (3) insight, (4) evaluation, and (5) elaboration (Csikszentmihalyi, 1990).

Reasons to Implement Proficiency-Based Grading in World Languages

When considering proficiency-based grading in a world languages classroom, teachers often worry about changes that would undercut values they hold around teaching. World languages teachers might wonder, Will this system support a communicative approach? How can I maintain my autonomy and creativity? Concerns around how this may affect world languages instruction, content, and grading workload are also common: Will a shift in focus affect my students' success? Will I need to change everything I do? Will I have time to do anything other than grade? As teachers learn about this grading method (which sounds valuable, but so unfamiliar), they begin to understand the deeper rationale—the *why*—behind proficiency-based grading, and their concerns diminish.

The following sections address how proficiency-based grading develops self-efficacy in learning languages, values the proficiency development in communicating with a new language, teaches students to be language users, and makes students active agents on their language proficiency journey.

Proficiency-Based Grading Develops Self-Efficacy in Learning Languages

The most successful language learners are resilient individuals who embrace the need to constantly redefine understanding; they throw themselves into new contexts. Successful learners not only build on prior knowledge, but forge new understanding by confronting challenge and cognitive disequilibrium; they are intrinsically motivated. As psychologist Albert Bandura (1986) says, "persons who have a strong sense of efficacy deploy their attention and effort to the demands of the situation and are spurred by obstacles to greater effort" (p. 394). A language learner innately knows where he or she would like to be by observing the native speaker or viewing authentic target language media.

The effective language learner also knows there are plenty of obstacles between one's current proficiency and that desired state. It is by navigating these difficulties that students gain knowledge, skill, and proficiency. A proficiency-based grading system insists on the self-efficacy this path demands. While you might find glimmers of this efficacy in good instructional practice in a traditional system, the linear, one-way-only path of points accumulation that defines traditional grading is ultimately incompatible with the development of self-efficacy. When a student measures his or her progress by amassing points, the learning process itself and any indication of next steps are completely veiled by a system that decouples measurement from desired outcomes. It takes great effort on the student's part to determine what a score of 24 out of 26 on an assessment says about what his or her next steps should be.

Proficiency-Based Grading Values the Proficiency Development in Communicating With a New Language

For anyone who has ever taught a language class, whether at the novice or advanced level, there can be no doubt that language learning is a nonlinear process. Students' control of any number of elements of language will vary at any given point from full to partial to conceptual. Time, experience, prior knowledge, and any number of other factors all play a role in students' individualized language journeys. With this being the case, establishing specific learning targets affords students the opportunity to continually fine-tune their progress toward the desired outcome. Students can constantly adjust their understanding as they grow closer to that desired state. One way to envision students' proficiency journey is to use the analogy of sound dampening. If you strike a chord on a guitar, the sound wave itself will slowly deintensify until it is flat. This kind of dampening is an integral part of proficiency-based grading. In the same way a sound wave oscillates across time until it falls flat and a new chord is ready to be struck, we must expect students to vary from proficiency expectations during the learning process.

Traditional models, again, are far too linear in their approach and don't account for students' need to zero in on a proficiency expectation by moving from conceptual to partial to full control in language development (see figure 9.1). To use the dampening analogy, we can say that traditional grading will assess students' proficiency before a chord can be fully played. Proficiency-based grading insists on allowing a more sustained time frame in which students can grow, make mistakes, and ultimately hit the right note—demonstrate proficiency.

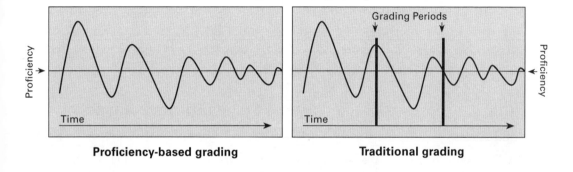

Figure 9.1: Proficiency-based grading provides more time for proficiency development.

Many schools insert arbitrary grading periods that can cut students' learning journeys short and not provide many students adequate time to approach desired proficiency. While ultimately a course must exist in the confines of an academic term (such as a semester), traditional grading models that further subdivide grading terms into quarters, trimesters, or six weeks are curtailing students' opportunities to show and experience growth as language learners.

Proficiency-Based Grading Teaches Students to Be Language Users

While it should go without saying that the goal should be to form students into language users, I can't state strongly enough how important it is to remain focused on this. The goal is to empower students to be language users—people who can converse, write, read, and understand spoken language. Despite this understanding, many teachers come into proficiency-based grading from a traditional classroom model with gradebooks full of quizzes on discrete grammar and vocabulary that don't reflect the whole picture of where students should be—it's as if the goal is to engage students in learning the essential skills of linguists or translators. While many language teachers resolutely espouse a proficiency-based approach, the assessment process itself often harkens back to grammar translation.

Assessments must shift so that proficiency is front and center. It is essential to avoid clinging to the vestiges of holding students accountable by pretending that grammar and vocabulary quizzes are actually some sort of interpretive reading assessments. The folly of this belief becomes apparent very quickly, as it is difficult to scale students' success on something they understand or don't understand. This becomes a very pronounced aha moment for teams and will eventually spur more innovative approaches to supporting students' acquisition and contextualized use of these building blocks. What's the upshot? Teams must quickly relegate grammar and vocabulary to supporting content or success criteria. Feedback can still take place through homework or quick, infrequent quizzes on discrete skills that can't be part of the formalized gradebook; importantly, however, it will also occur through performance-based assessments, during which the student and teacher can address contextualized vocabulary and grammar. Contextualized, authentic performance assessment has to be the exclusive lens through which teachers gather evidence of students' growth as language users.

Proficiency-Based Grading Makes Students Active Agents on Their Language Proficiency Journey

While educators have used terms like *student-centered pedagogy* or *student-centered learning* since the time of John Dewey (1938), these terms are often boiled down to mean something akin to *avoid lecturing students* or *use cooperative learning strategies*. While there's great value in cooperative learning strategies and they should definitely play an integral role in any proficiency-based classroom, proficiency-based grading calls for a deeper and more transformative approach to learning: students need to co-construct their learning with their teacher or, importantly, with their peers. Authors Bonnie Adair-Hauck, Eileen W. Glisan, and Francis J. Troyan's (2013) *Implementing Integrated Performance Assessment* provides an excellent framework for what this looks like in practice. The authors exhort teachers to engage *with* students in the assessment process.

Proficiency-based grading insists that teachers not limit student involvement to formal assessment practices, but should rather integrate it throughout students' learning experience. Longitudinal learning targets and success criteria permit students the opportunity to regularly and routinely examine their performance through the lens of individual success criteria as they relate to a targeted proficiency level. In a third-year German classroom, for example, students might record a conversation with a partner in which they discuss their preferences and opinions about social media. They'd then reflect individually on things that students understand and "produce in order to perform the functions of the level" (American Council on the Teaching of Foreign Languages, 2012) or engage in a dialogue with peers about communication strategies in the conversation. This process requires intensive, focused instructional modeling before students can do it on their own, of course, but it results in student-driven metacognitive and meta-task discourse that not only intimately informs students of where they are and need to be but also points to steps to improve their performance. Students will grow tremendously through this process and ultimately take greater ownership of their learning as they begin recognizing pathways to improvement on their own.

While external indicators such as scores and attainment rates in a Seal of Biliteracy program certainly bear out the success of this proficiency-based approach, I'd offer that students' self-efficacy and agency will also grow. As a language teacher, I think that this is ultimately far more important for students: self-efficacy is what makes learning last and what drives our students to continue their proficiency journeys. Figure 9.2 (page 256) shows an example of a rubric that facilitates co-constructing assessments and that serves as a tool for the conversation between teacher and student during the co-constructed feedback process. This rubric has components that make it an effective tool for co-construction with students.

- The learning target itself drives the conversation and is featured prominently at the top of the rubric.
- It has agreed-on success criteria.

- It has space for students to note evidence that speaks to the success criteria. During face-to-face feedback, this provides a tangible reference point for the conversation.

- As a single-point rubric, the feedback sheet does not create a forced choice, which can happen with a traditional rubric. This single-point rubric invites exploration and discussion of the evidence.

Learning Target 2A: I engage in conversation.

4—Refined Mastery	3—Proficiency	2—Approaches Proficiency	1—Still Developing
I independently maintain a conversation using above-level language.	I independently maintain a conversation using level-appropriate language.	I independently maintain a conversation using level- and non-level-appropriate language.	I independently maintain a conversation using non-level-appropriate language.

Success Criteria	Student Evidence
Language Function • How did you satisfy all parts of the prompt? • If you did not, what was missing? • How did you create with language?	
Text Type • How are you expanding your message (discourse level)? (word → phrase → sentence → connected sentences → paragraph)	
Communication Strategies • How did you participate in the conversation? • What questions did you ask? • What strategies did you apply when you weren't understood or when you had difficulty understanding your partner? (spoken performance)	
Comprehensibility • How might you have been difficult to understand?	

• How might you have had to rephrase or repeat your message? (spoken performance)	
Language Control • What types of grammatical structures are present in this performance? • What examples of thematic vocabulary are present? • What errors do you need to correct, and how will you correct them?	

Source: Adapted from Adair-Hauck, Glisan, & Troyan, 2013.

Figure 9.2: Single-point rubric with feedback space.
Visit go.SolutionTree.com/assessment for a free reproducible version of this figure.

Preparation: The Commitments of Proficiency-Based Grading in World Languages

Teachers and teams make certain commitments to successfully implement this improved system of assessing and instructing. This can be difficult because teachers often have very personal and intense attachments to specific resources, literature, other curriculum, instruction, and assessment. When a team of teachers is preparing to do this work, there will be worries about losing autonomy and the challenge of adapting teaching and assessment in the near future. That is when making a series of commitments will allow teachers to support each other on the road to success.

The following commitments are discussed in subsequent sections: (1) use a proficiency-based framework of language acquisition and (2) effectively communicate learning targets and standards for learning a language.

Commitment 1: Use a Proficiency-Based Framework of Language Acquisition

When a team decides to dive into the proficiency-based grading pool, one of the first fundamental questions members must ask themselves is "What do we want our students to learn?" More often than not, if a language team is implementing proficiency-based grading, team members are not only early adopters, innovators, and risk takers but also a team that has already firmly embraced the following (American Council on the Teaching of Foreign Languages [ACTFL], 1996).

- World-readiness standards for learning languages, or *5Cs*, goal areas: (1) communication, (2) cultures, (3) connections, (4) comparisons, and (5) communities

- The three modes of communication: (1) presentational, (2) interpersonal, and (3) interpretive

Without hesitation and from the get-go, such a team might decide to base its standards on these goals and modes. The benefit of committing to longitudinal, proficiency-based standards to frame students' learning, as opposed to more granular, context-bound targets such as *I can* statements or *model performance indicators* (MPIs), is multifaceted. If a daily or unit content target, or *can do* statement, is *I can describe an experience that shaped my life in several well-developed paragraphs*, for example, teachers should view students' reflection around their general success at this task through the overarching lens of students' presentation writing skill development. Those granular, context-bound targets can be important ways for teachers to contextualize overarching standards in specific learning on a daily or unit-by-unit basis, but students need to have their eyes on the larger learning journey by doing the following. With communication at the core of language learning, the ACTFL (2012) three standards of communication—(1) presentational, (2) interpersonal, and (3) interpretive—stand ready to serve as foundational standards.

- **Students chart their progress across a course and program:** Providing students and teachers with a limited number of focused, essential, and transcendent targets makes it possible for students to track their learning with action-minded accuracy. Make no mistake, *I can* descriptors and statements are still important for instructional planning, but a focus on transferable skills leads students *through* specific content experiences. Take the case of an interpersonal speaking task in which students are asked to discuss weekend plans. While the authentic context and goal orientation of the task are important, it is students' ability to generalize and reflect upon the relative communicative success of the assessment event that gives the event a learning value. When students reflect and then chart their relative success in the context of broader skills, the reflective experience transcends the specific conversation and helps concretely orient students in their proficiency journey.

- **Feedback and reflection transcend an individual event:** While context-specific teacher feedback is necessary, focus on targeted student proficiency tied to mutually understood learning targets ensures growth.

- **Assessment becomes a process of opportunities for evidence, part of a greater whole:** When teachers integrate assessment into all learning, each event is part of the big picture and the process is coherent.

Discrete grammar and vocabulary sets are important supporting skills and building blocks for learners to make meaning, but the meaning-making itself matters more. The first foundational commitment, therefore, needs to be a commitment to a proficiency-based and communication-oriented framework. As language and instruction professors Eileen W. Glisan and Richard Donato (2017) remind, "language learning is fundamentally a social process" (pp. 92–93).

That first team to dive in might embrace this reality fairly easily, but by no means will it necessarily be a readily digestible fact of life for all teachers. As work progresses, more than a few teachers may see content accountability as an essential part of the work. Yes, students who are exposed to massed practice, or cramming, in the form of conjugation drills can conjugate really well (at least on the test that comes right after the drill work). What this creates, however, is a false sense of perceived mastery that reinforces a belief in the power of drill work. As Brown and associates (2014) note in *Make It Stick*, the "rapid gains produced by massed practice are often evident, but the rapid forgetting that follows is not" (p. 47). The solution to this flawed belief in the primacy of the discrete, granular building blocks is an assessment paradigm that firmly places competency over content.

Commitment 2: Effectively Communicate Learning Targets and Standards for Learning a Language

Teachers must meaningfully communicate meaningful expectations. Providing clarity around learning expectations for stakeholders is fundamental to the success of proficiency-based grading. Effectively communicating learning targets and standards is non-negotiable. Gobble et al. (2017) offer three questions to consider:

1. Do students understand the expectations?
2. Do parents understand the expectations?
3. Do colleagues understand the expectations? (p. 107)

We'll explore how teachers in the world languages context can leverage rubrics, standards, and the collaborative process to create clarity.

Do Students Understand the Expectations?

Students using the learning targets language and success criteria is an important gauge of their understanding (Gobble et al., 2017). By purposefully modelling and co-constructing these criteria with students, teams can ensure students actively and routinely use this language in the classroom. The common language of

Adair-Hauck et al.'s (2013) Integrated Performance Assessment (IPA) performance rubrics offers implementation tools. It follows that if teachers want to use the IPA Interpersonal Speaking rubric's success criteria of text type, language function, communication strategies, comprehensibility, and language control as success criteria in the proficiency-based grading system, students need to understand what these criteria are.

Importantly, the learning targets also point to the purpose and intention of *why* students are learning. As director of education at American Council on the Teaching of Foreign Languages Paul Sandrock (2010) rightly implores, "Motivate students by providing clear learning targets—and clear purposes behind the tasks" (p. 69). *Authentic* experiences, *authentic* tasks, and *authentic* assessment—events that allow students to experience language in a realistic setting—should all point to (and come from) authentic learning targets.

Do Parents Understand the Expectations?

One advantage of learning languages lies in the clarity of the standards; in many ways, the three communicative standards (presentational, interpersonal, and interpretive) speak for themselves as inherent and integral elements of communication and, by extension, language learning.

However, a proactive outreach to parents is essential. In 2008, the National Education Association laid out the benefits of clear communication with parents, explaining that "community support of the educational process is considered one of the characteristics common to high-performing schools" (p. 1). Whether teams craft and collectively sign letters explaining the approach to assessment and grading or host an informational website, it is imperative for parents to have access to the expectations and the rationale behind them. Open house and other community outreach events are prime opportunities for communication.

When communicating expectations, at a minimum it is important to include what the standards of learning are (the three communicative standards), a clear rationale for the change, and a thorough explanation of the grading and reporting system (including how parents will follow their students' learning journey).

Do Colleagues Understand the Expectations?

Teams must commit to regular and meaningful calibration of expectations. Specifically, teachers must engage in frequent assessment calibration with the aim of ensuring *inter-rater reliability* as they evaluate (or co-construct) student evidence. A successful systems-level implementation demands that proficiency expectations be the same for all teachers on a curricular team and necessarily requires articulation of expectations across course levels. Calibration within teams can be accomplished through regular and transparent analysis of student data, as well as collaboratively grading student work (with individuals grading a series of exemplars and then comparing during collaborative discussion). Teachers using discipline-specific language to articulate learning targets and proficiency scales (intermediate high for a fifth-year course, for example) is essential to this process: teachers need to know what targeted proficiency levels are.

Incubation: The Unexpected Questions of Proficiency-Based Grading in World Languages

As teachers progress toward using proficiency-based grading, they will uncover some wonderful questions that drive inquiry and implementation. During this second stage, several adopted practices may be working, but teachers may understandably pay a lot of attention to the items or practices that have the potential to derail a team's progress or that have been challenging. With so much new information, it can be hard not to worry that some challenges will never be overcome. The following questions are representative of the incubation stage challenges that require patience and persistence.

Unexpected Question 1: What Is Assessment's Role or Process in Proficiency-Based Language Courses?

IPA can prove to be foundational inspiration for this work. Its emphasis on assessment as a learning *process* is a huge part of what makes it such a beautiful tool for proficiency development and such a great fit for proficiency-based grading, which focuses on growth. As assessment author, expert, and consultant Dylan Wiliam (2018) reminds, assessment is the "bridge between teaching and learning" (p. 56). Teams must understand there is more to assessment than formative and summative, quiz, or unit test. Beyond this understanding, however, lies what teams ultimately come to realize: assessment must be both a *system* and a *process*.

As a system, assessment must provide for logical, ordered evidence of learning. There must be a progression—an order—to students' experiences with assessment that serves to tell students concretely where they've been, where they are, and where they're heading. In other words, students must experience assessment as the story of their proficiency development. The interconnectedness of performances both in and across communication modes must be clear to students. Having a set of standards and learning targets that reflects this and that permits students to chart their learning across time and proficiency levels helps tremendously. See Insight 1: Self-Regulated Language Learning Is the Goal (page 266) for more about student charting.

Assessment must also be a process. It can't begin when the student puts pen to paper or end when the student hits Stop on the recorder; it must have a *through line* like that in figure 9.3.

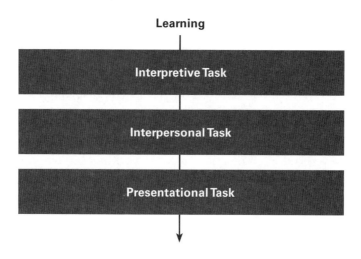

Figure 9.3: Integrated learning and assessment require a through line.

Adair-Hauck et al. (2013) say IPA is designed to provide students with *washback*, or valuable information that points to next steps in learning. Likewise, preparatory or anticipatory IPA tasks can precede the actual assessment event to both strengthen the link of assessment to learning and *prime the pump* so learners can more fully immerse themselves in the process. If novice or intermediate students are asked to interpret an infographic that describes ecotourism, for example, including an anticipatory conversation about their personal travel preferences would draw students into the assessment experience by deepening and personalizing the context. It is through a deep literacy of this process that teacher teams can collaboratively design experiences that empower students to take ownership of their learning.

Unexpected Question 2: Are Teachers Collecting the Right Evidence to Determine a Grade in Proficiency-Based World Language Courses?

The learning targets define the right evidence. It's quite simple: performance tasks in authentic contexts need to drive evidence. Any student work—discrete grammar practice, for example—that doesn't rise to this level teachers needn't dismiss summarily as invaluable, but teachers cannot position this work as valid proficiency evidence. Basing students' grades on uncontextualized, specific practice around individual success criteria is akin to rating a baseball player solely on his ability to lay down sacrifice bunts during night games in September against left-handed pitchers named Larry: it can't contribute to the narrative of the whole story. This is no more ridiculous than choosing to isolate a student's ability to conjugate *tener* in a first- or second-year Spanish class.

Unexpected Question 3: If Language Skill Proficiency Supersedes Content, What Must the Learning Targets Be?

Once we accept that we can't perseverate on granular and isolated elements of language (such as specific grammar concepts), it follows that we must acknowledge that the three ACTFL communicative standards necessarily form the core of our work and that the modes of communication must represent our learning targets.

As teams collaborate on learning targets, they will find that the answer to *What must our learning targets be?* will serve as a key to many other questions. Once teachers lay out what they want students to learn, quite a bit will naturally follow. For many who engage in this work, assessments and learning targets prior to diving into proficiency-based grading might be incredibly granular and focus on supporting content—or grammar and vocabulary. With the shift to proficiency-based grading, it is important to avoid the pitfall of elevating success criteria to the level of learning targets. Grammar and vocabulary, while important building blocks students use to make meaning, are just that: building blocks. Teachers can't grade or make judgments on students' success with manipulating these building blocks any more than they might rate a child who had picked all the right pieces to build a LEGO set. It's putting the blocks together to create meaning that matters.

Feedback on grammar and vocabulary can flow naturally through a well-sorted feedback instrument, such as the one in figure 9.2 (page 256). Likewise, choosing learning targets based on granular tasks or very specific language functions (including thematic unit-specific *I can* statements) makes longitudinal feedback and reflection for students impossible. A set of learning targets that are scalable across levels and languages is possible when we permit students and teachers to build the expectations together for what success looks like. In figure 9.4 (page 264), the targeted proficiency level (3—Demonstrates Mastery) uses the relative term *level-appropriate* (and *non–level appropriate*) for the first four learning targets. This approach forces students to contextualize what they're doing *currently* within the big picture of proficiency. What this might look like in practice is discussed in greater detail in the section Key Question 2: Do Students View the Evidence of Language Proficiency From the Same Perspective Teachers Do? (page 269).

Presentational Speaking: Learners present information, concepts, and ideas to inform, explain, persuade, and narrate on a variety of topics using appropriate media and adapting to various audiences of listeners, readers, or viewers.

4—Refined Mastery	3—Proficiency	2—Approaches Proficiency	1—Still Developing
Learning Target 1A: I can create an original spoken message. (Presentational speaking)			
I can independently create a spoken message using above-level language.	I can independently create a spoken message using level-appropriate language.	I can independently create a spoken message using level- and non-level-appropriate language.	I can independently create a spoken message using non-level-appropriate language.
Learning Target 1B: I can create an original written message. (Presentational writing)			
I can independently create a written message using above-level language.	I can independently create a written message using level-appropriate language.	I can independently create a written message using level- and non-level-appropriate language.	I can independently create a written message using non-level-appropriate language.

Interpersonal Communication: Learners interact and negotiate meaning in spoken or written conversations to share information, reactions, feelings, and opinions.

4—Refined Mastery	3—Proficiency	2—Approaches Proficiency	1—Still Developing
Learning Target 2A: I can engage in conversation. (Interpersonal speaking)			
I can independently maintain a conversation using above-level language.	I can independently maintain a conversation using level-appropriate language.	I can independently maintain a conversation using level- and non-level-appropriate language.	I can independently maintain a conversation using non-level-appropriate language.
Learning Target 2B: I can engage in written interpersonal communication. (Interpersonal writing)			
I can independently maintain a written interpersonal communication using above-level language.	I can independently maintain a written interpersonal communication using level-appropriate language.	I can independently maintain a written interpersonal communication using level- and non-level-appropriate language.	I can independently maintain a written interpersonal communication using non-level-appropriate language.

Interpretive Skills: Learners understand, interpret, and analyze what they hear, read, or view on a variety of topics.			
Learning Target 3A: I can interpret an audio or visual source. (Listening and viewing)			
I can accurately demonstrate literal and interpretive comprehension of an audio or visual source with insightful details and reasoning.	I can demonstrate literal and interpretive comprehension of an audio or visual source.	I can demonstrate basic comprehension of an audio or visual source.	I can demonstrate minimal comprehension of an audio or visual source.
Learning Target 3B: I can interpret a written passage. (Reading)			
I can accurately demonstrate literal and interpretive comprehension of a text with insightful details or reasoning.	I can demonstrate literal and interpretive comprehension of a text.	I can demonstrate basic comprehension of a text.	I can demonstrate minimal comprehension of a text.

Figure 9.4: Presentation learning targets that focus on communicative proficiency.

Unexpected Question 4: If Evidence Drives the Grade, What's Enough of the Right Evidence for Language Proficiency?

Proficiency-based grading demands for evidence to propel both students' and teachers' understanding of proficiency and points to where a student is along his or her path to proficiency. Experience seems to point to a *minimum* of around four pieces of evidence for each of the three standards. It bears mentioning that many teams will feel obligated to gather evidence much more frequently.

Can there be too much evidence? Perhaps. It is important that not every performance event be high stakes. Students must have ample opportunity for self-reflection in lower-stakes situations. While teacher and peer feedback remains an essential part of the assessment process, students need time and space to develop proficiency and receive focused feedback on specific success criteria without judgment.

Can there be too little evidence? Definitely. Take, for instance, a team that found itself on a trajectory to only have three pieces of evidence in the presentational standard by the end of the semester: one piece six weeks in, another twelve weeks in, and a final event toward the very end of the semester. As the team discussed what this might mean for students, they realized this evidence wouldn't allow for sufficient opportunities for students to use the assessment process to grow toward competency in the standard. Students might work on the standard informally, but they only had two points in the semester to get a concrete look at their progress. With six weeks remaining, the team added one more graded evidence opportunity to their plans. The following year, they added one more formal graded event on top of that. This example demonstrates that teams should plan on building a semester course with at least four pieces of evidence per standard.

Insight: The Essential Insights of Proficiency-Based Grading in World Languages

As teachers begin to move beyond the initial fears and roadblocks and gain insight, it is vitally important to take some time to look back on and appreciate how the team has passed some intimidating hurdles thus far. Teams should have a clear enough idea of how proficiency-based grading works, and they can play to its strengths as they teach and plan. They begin providing proficiency-based grading with more power instead of just trying to get their balance.

At this point, world languages teachers might have the following insights: (1) self-regulated language learning is the goal, (2) co-constructed language learning is important, and (3) every moment is a viable moment for evidence generation.

Insight 1: Self-Regulated Language Learning Is the Goal

Language learning greatly benefits from student engagement in the actual process of learning. While it sounds obvious that a learner be an active agent in his or her own learning, teachers often underprioritize or completely ignore this focus in practice. Passive learning is, unfortunately, too often the norm. The most so-called student-centered classroom that doesn't challenge students to look within, reflect on where they are, and build a path toward where they need to be doesn't actually focus on individual students at all. As Bandura (1986) notes, "People not only gain understanding through reflection, they evaluate and alter their own thinking" (p. 21). Full ownership lives with the learner and must be a reflective process. Proficiency-based grading provides a framework for this self-regulated learning. When students have the chance to identify specifically what went well in a performance assessment and where their areas for continued growth lie, they can think specifically about how to improve. Figure 9.5 provides an example of what this student self-reflection might look like in practice.

Learning Targets:

1A: I can create an original spoken message. (Presentational speaking)

1B: I can create an original written message. (Presentational writing)

2A: I can engage in conversation. (Interpersonal speaking)

2B: I can engage in written interpersonal communication. (Interpersonal writing)

3A: I can interpret an audio or visual source. (Listening and viewing)

3B: I can interpret a written passage. (Reading)

Assessment Event	Outcome	Reflection and Feedback What went well? In what areas do I need to grow?	Next Steps What will I do to improve?
3A—Unit I	2	Plus = main idea Delta = inferences	I will use 3modes.org and will work with a peer tutor to review authentic audio.
2A—Unit I	3	My text type was solid (paragraph-length discourse), but I need to work on asking clarifying questions.	I will practice changing yes/no questions into open-ended questions.
1B—Unit I	3	I did a great job narrating in the past, but I still have some conjugation issues that don't interfere with comprehensibility.	I will keep journaling about my weekend experiences and completing my cultural blog.

Figure 9.5: Student reflection sheet for a curricular unit.

*Visit **go.SolutionTree.com/assessment** for a free reproducible version of this figure.*

Insight 2: Co-Constructed Language Learning Is Important

Since students are the ultimate owners of the learning process, what does this leave for the teacher? The teacher is not only the arbiter of evidence but also an essential partner in students' construction of meaning (Adair-Hauck et al., 2013). A co-constructive process drives language learning: teachers empower students to interact with others to build a firmer understanding of where they are, where they need to be, and how to get there. As a teacher dialogues with a student around a performance, both teacher and student are partners in this process. The student can no longer be a passive recipient of feedback, but must actively participate. This is necessarily a process that positions the teacher as co-facilitator of students' learning.

Insight 3: Every Moment Is a Viable Moment for Evidence Generation

The IPA process has an underlying motif that I need to emphasize here: assessment must be a process that drives all elements of instruction and, as a result, student learning. Set-piece summative assessment—the unit tests of yore—deny both students and teachers the opportunity to use the assessment process meaningfully. Without washback, an assessment is nothing more than an autopsy of where a student was. Teachers have the responsibility to work with students to help point them to where they need to be. Importantly, this means that students can engage in assessment in any moment. When *all* tasks are aligned to meaningful outcomes, as is the case with IPA, then it stands to reason that teachers can invite students to consider their own progress at any point. This invitation can range from informally checking for understanding on an authentic reading ("What contributed to your understanding of the main idea of this text?") to a more formal co-constructed reflection on a persuasive essay. What's important is that both teacher and students are able to use any learning experience to orient the student toward proficiency.

Evaluation: The Key Questions of Proficiency-Based Grading in World Languages

Implementation's beginning stages bring a perspective of evaluation. While professional growth never takes one path, reaching this point allows teams to set a goal of reaching regular practice and to confidently look into ways that the system impacts feedback and grading.

Evaluation can lead world language teachers to ask the following key questions: (1) "Are teachers effectively communicating expectations of language learning?" and (2) "Do students view the evidence of language proficiency from the same perspective teachers do?"

Key Question 1: Are Teachers Effectively Communicating Expectations of Language Learning?

If the desire is to position evidence front and center in students' experience within the assessment process, teachers and students stand to gain much from the active use of a *single-point rubric* (or a single set of success criteria). A single-point rubric invites students to find evidence that speaks to success criteria. As educator Jarene Fluckiger (2010) plainly states, "[this] is an ethical tool to assist students with their responsibilities of goal setting and self-assessment of their own education" (p. 18). By asking students to be part of this process, their involvement automatically rises to the level of metacognition, and they become active agents in figuring out their next steps. A well-structured feedback sheet based on a single-point rubric like that in figure 9.5 (page 267) makes this possible. Teachers may ask students, for example, to use evidence from their performances to identify what language functions they successfully elicited, how they showed language control through specific language elements, or what sort of text type they may have produced (such as lists, sentence strings, paragraph-length discourse, and so on). If, for example, a student is asked to narrate a past event in writing, he or she might note specific instances of temporal adverbs in his or her text as evidence for language control. Students gain a far more intimate understanding of what is expected of them when teachers ask them to evaluate their own evidence against expectations. An effective feedback sheet also leaves room for a teacher to take notes or add comments as part of their commitment to this process.

When a student provides examples of temporal adverbs, the teacher, as the expert voice in a reflective conversation, can challenge the student to explain why he or she chose the particular adverbs. The teacher, for her part, must use dialogue to drive a student's introspection. It is only when students know *how they did* that they can think through *how they can improve*. They can do this goal-setting process with the teacher or engage in it as a long-term process.

This is not to say students needn't be aware of what expectations might be in individual proficiency levels or of what performance doesn't meet expectations. As Sandrock (2010) notes, a rubric "needs to describe the characteristics of the language performance that does not yet meet the proficiency target and the characteristics that exceed the proficiency target" (p. 55). Students must be aware of what can move them from one level to the next. IPA rubrics are an excellent reference sheet for the proficiency range for a course. A single-point feedback sheet requires students to look to their own evidence and situate that evidence according to the success criteria; it very actively pulls students into the assessment process.

Key Question 2: Do Students View the Evidence of Language Proficiency From the Same Perspective Teachers Do?

It is essential that both teachers and students have a common understanding of what constitutes *proficiency*. While the general categories of success criteria—language function, text type, communication strategies, comprehensibility, and language control—won't change from one interpersonal speaking performance assessment to the next, the learning context will absolutely change the criteria (Adair-Hauck al., 2013). What success *actually* looks or sounds like when students compare their school days and when they try to come to agreement on plans for a future celebration will be quite different.

The teacher and students must co-construct the specific, leveled expectations in a classroom. This can involve individual student brainstorming, group discussion, and then whole-class discussion and agreement on context-specific success criteria. If students are to engage in an interpersonal speaking task by discussing weekend plans with a partner, for example, they might collaboratively brainstorm what expectation for language control makes sense for the task. What they anticipate will be based on their common understanding of proficiency expectations in the context of the performance (in this case, partial control of the future tense).

Working with students to identify tools to help them achieve success is also important. Pre-speaking activities (akin to pre-reading strategies) are an approach elaborated by Chantal P. Thompson and Elaine Phillips (2013). They are an excellent example of a way to engage students in meaningful thought around the supporting structures, cohesive devices, and other communication tools as they prepare to perform. As students prepare to engage in a speaking task, they individually and then collectively think through vocabulary, cohesive devices, and supporting structures. Figure 9.6 includes a simple example of what a pre-speaking organizer might look like as students prepare to discuss summer plans.

Directions: Fill in the left column with topics to discuss and the right column with vocabulary and structures to support your conversation.	
Topic	**Vocabulary and Supporting Structures**
July 4th plans	• Fireworks, barbeque, baseball game, parade • modals: will, can, should
Beach	• Swim, sand, bathing suit, towel • Questions: Do you . . . ? When? With whom?
What cohesive devices can you use? because, however, while, but, first, then	

Figure 9.6: A pre-speaking tool for students.

*Visit **go.SolutionTree.com/assessment** for a free reproducible version of this figure.*

If we accept that it is essential that both teachers and students have a common understanding of what constitutes *proficiency*, we must insist that all teachers on a curricular team also share a common understanding. It bears emphasizing here: since teachers are working with single-point rubrics in which success criteria are contextualized, teachers must be on the same page not only with students but also with each another. This can only happen through purposeful and constant calibration through collaborative team efforts, ideally during face-to-face meetings using actual student exemplars.

Elaboration: The Core Beliefs of Proficiency-Based Grading in World Languages

Teachers at the elaboration phase of implementation have reached a mature and clear perspective of using a proficiency-based grading system. They have discovered that the system does not push them out of valued projects or other assessments and activities they know help students learn; instead, they see there is depth to be gained from such work, with an underlying and clear focus on skills. With their comfort in this system, teachers are resources for their colleagues and on the cutting edge for new ways to provide more support for and collaboration with their students.

Teachers who successfully implement proficiency-based grading adhere to all seven of the core beliefs explained in chapter 1 (page 9): (1) growth is a central concept, (2) reperformance is essential, (3) building students' reflection abilities is essential, (4) homework has a role, (5) communication with parents and the community is key, (6) culminating experiences like final exams have a different purpose, and (7) behavior can be in or out of the grade. The following sections, which reflect the core beliefs' original numbering, explore the core beliefs that world languages teachers in particular should never lose sight of.

Core Belief 1: Growth Is a Central Concept

Students can predict their growth on their ability to *act* on feedback. The co-constructed feedback process not only asks students to reflect on where they can improve but also *demands* students chart how they're going to improve on a specific learning target, such as our interpersonal speaking: *I can independently maintain a conversation using level-appropriate language.* Students can provide evidence of continued growth two ways: (1) retake an assessment experience in a thematic unit to provide an additional piece of evidence or (2) perform anew for the same learning target in the next thematic unit.

Regarding retakes, it's important the assessment speak to the same target and theme, but not be the same event as the first opportunity. Within a thematic unit on travel, for example, a student's original assessment event may have taken the form of an extemporaneously written persuasive essay weighing the benefits of study-abroad programs. A reperformance can live within the same theme (travel, in this case), but must represent a different event and, therefore, a unique and authentic opportunity for a student to exhibit independent proficiency. In this case, the student's potential reperformance opportunity might be writing a persuasive essay around a different topic (say, the advantages of ecotourism). In both cases, we must assume that students have access to the same rhetorical and content tools as they write. Of course, if students are engaged in process writing (such as a research paper), then feedback and reperformance opportunities are built into the drafting process itself.

Core Belief 5: Communication With Parents and the Community Is Key

It is essential for all stakeholders—teachers, students, parents, and the community—to understand both the rationale and the urgent need that drives proficiency-based grading implementation. In world languages, a crucial part of these efforts resides in the narrative about standards. The National Standards Collaborative Board's (2015) *World-Readiness Standards for Learning Languages* and, specifically, the three communication standards lay out the case. Framing effective communication as the ultimate outcome with students goes a long way in justifying the need for proficiency-based grading. Figure 9.7 is the kind of letter that can communicate with parents and guardians. An important aspect of this letter is that it includes an open invitation to reach out to the teacher.

Dear parents and guardians,

Your child will be part of a world language or English learning (EL) course that uses proficiency-based grading. What does this grading look like in a world language or EL course?

The three academic standards, or the three modes of communication, follow.

1. **Interpretive:** Listening and reading

2. **Presentational:** Writing and speaking to an audience

3. **Interpersonal:** Conversational speaking

These three standards will form the core of our work and drive the conversations around our students' growth as language learners. Additionally, our division has a website that students can visit for additional practice around the three standards.

We will communicate with our students around how they are progressing in the three academic standards. At the end of each semester, a student's course grade is determined by his or her body of work with consideration to growth.

You can monitor your child's progress on our school website. There, you can see your child's progress toward mastery in each standard. The site will show adequate growth (AG), minimal growth (MG), incomplete (I), or failing to grow (FG) for each progress report. At different times throughout the semester, we will report your child's projected letter grade on the website.

It is *essential* that both students and parents refer to the website. That way, they have an accurate picture of a student's overall progress in the course and progress toward mastery for each standard.

The website shows individual scores (4, 3, 2, or 1) for each assessment in each standard.

- **4** indicates exceeding mastery.
- **3** indicates demonstrating mastery.
- **2** indicates approaching mastery.
- **1** indicates still developing mastery.
- **M (Missing)** indicates the student did not take the assessment. In that case, the student needs to make a plan to take the assessment within five school days of the original assessment. If assessments are not taken, the student runs the risk of failing.
- **N (noncompliant)** indicates the student did not make a plan to take a missing test or refused to take the test. If a pattern of *M*s or *N*s exists, the student runs the risk of failing.

The social-emotional learning standards of self-management, relationship skills, and responsible decision making will be reported as necessary throughout the year. This standard *will not* be used to determine a letter grade in the course.

Working together with you, as partners, we can best meet all our students' needs. If you have any questions or concerns regarding proficiency-based grading or your child's language experience, please contact me anytime.

Figure 9.7: Example communication to parents and guardians about proficiency-based grading.

Alongside the framing and rationale, a tenacious and ongoing communication effort must be part and parcel of this work. Dedicated resources, such as a district or departmental website, provide ready access to both the explanation of process and the rationale for parents, students, and community members. The explicit connection of outside assessments and recognitions based on a standards–rooted approach, such as a Seal of Biliteracy (https://sealofbiliteracy.org) program, provides an additional lens or angle for communication.

Core Belief 7: Behavior Can Be In or Out of the Grade

Consistent target language use is undeniably a foundational behavior for student success in classrooms. The question becomes whether teachers should instruct target language maintenance in and of itself as a fundamental competency, or if it is simply a compliance-oriented expectation or habit. Consider the following questions, recognizing that the answers will vary based on the individual courses or programs.

- Is target language use in and of itself a fundamental competency in your course or program?

- If target language use *is* a competency and not simply an act of compliance, can it be assessed and form part of the gradebook?

- If target language use enters the grade calculation, are the team and teachers committed to instructing it, collecting evidence on it (assessing it), and providing actionable feedback? For those looking to assess target language use, Judith L. Shrum and Eileen Glisan's (2016) TALK rubric provides one avenue.

Additionally, as teams and districts rightly look to incorporate SEL competencies in their collective work, it remains important to consider whether the SEL competencies are an integral, instructed, and assessed part of the course. The previous questions for target language use can just as easily apply to discussions around SEL.

Key Points

To ensure full understanding, review the following key points from this chapter.

- Longitudinal learning targets connected to proficiency outcomes permit learners to chart their own growth. Learners need to know where they are and where they're headed and need time and space to reflect on their learning journey.

- Effective implementation of proficiency-based grading for world languages means curricular teams, students, and parents all have a firm understanding of what proficiency-rooted learning outcomes are and how teachers will assess them; moreover, all participants understand that a language *learner* is a language *user* who builds meaning socially and dialogically with others.

- An effective approach to proficiency-based grading within the world languages context will situate the learner as an active agent in his or her own learning; in the same way, language learning itself is an inherently social and communicative process, so learner and teacher must also co-construct the process of assessment.

Epilogue

Building Efficacious Learners

Anthony R. Reibel and Eric Twadell

We find that focusing on proficiency is the key to our continuous improvement efforts. More and more teachers are talking about their expectations for proficiency, and for students, and can articulate the way they assess students for proficiency. In this book, the subject matter experts focus on the content area–specific proficiencies that should be the focus of curriculum, the frame for instruction, the basis of assessment, and the indicator for grades.

Traditionally, lesson planning has focused on a one-size-fits-all model, *teaching* content and rarely varying from the lesson plan to consider whether students are actually *learning*. In this book, the authors suggest instructional practices should focus on how the teacher, student, and class constantly monitor and reflect on the skills that demonstrate proficiency and learning growth.

To learn from an experience, a learner must have had earlier experiences that mirror the ultimate experience. These earlier events are where students had the opportunity to consolidate elements of thoughts and skills into long-term ability or judgment. Teachers know this as *formative assessment*. However, many current lessons do not create a consistent thread of experiences that allow learning consolidation and reflection (Brown et al., 2014). While this is not inherently detrimental to learning, try to envision lesson components as interconnected moments of a singular expected state—proficiency in a specific skill.

In a proficiency-based classroom, the warm-up, quiz, debate, project, and test must create a similar experience as it relates to the proficiency-based learning target. For example, if a teacher wants students to develop presentational speaking skills, that teacher may ask students to present to peers as a warm-up, film a short video presenting at home as a project, complete a homework assignment of watching people presenting, join a small group that presents ideas to group participants, and end with a final presentation and a possible reperformance.

While traditional lessons are usually an array of (albeit) well-organized, well-planned activities, still no experience thread carries through all tasks related to a learning target. We call these *activities without a purpose*. Many times there is nothing more than an illusion of threading, but in these cases the activities only thematically align, such as a unit of study based on equations, World War I, or *Macbeth*. In a proficiency-based environment, this cannot be the case.

Proficiency threading creates an "interconnected networks of knowledge that bolster and support mastery" (Brown et al., 2014, p. 83). Teachers see this concept play out with their collaborative team, which thought that they had a wonderful lesson by mixing up the way students engage with the vocabulary. Students speak it, listen for it in context, and repetitiously write and recite the words to engrain them in their memory. Ultimately, the team's final exam asks the students to write a multipage narrative about the historical context using details and vocabulary to make an argument. In the end, the team members realize they never gave the students an opportunity to write this way at all during prior instruction. The team thought that practicing in a variety of ways would prepare the students for the final exam, but the practicing was unrelated to the proficiency experience that the exam required.

The teacher team realizes they would have been better off thinking about it this way: if a student is developing presentational skills, then a teacher must plan lower-stakes, digestible versions of a *presentation* throughout the unit. Brown et al. (2014) state it well: "the kind of retrieval practice that proves most effective is one that reflects what you'll be doing with the knowledge later" (p. 57). Proficiency-based grading insists on this.

At this point, some may wonder if that means they are just teaching to the test. To this we, the authors, simply say, "No, it is teaching proficiency." Think about it this way: Would you have your student row a boat in order to learn how to ride a bike? In a proficiency-based teaching and learning classroom, all components of a lesson must strive to collect evidence of an expected desired state of competency. Without this structure, a teacher runs the risk of creating a series of disparate academic events that gather minimal evidence of proficiency and lead to short-term recall at best.

Learning, not just remembering, is what we are after. Helping students develop self-efficacy is the way to get there. To develop efficacy, however, students need to be in competency experiences as much as possible so they can build the skills for accurate self-assessment. The goal of assessment, then, is to promote this process, and grading's goal is to evaluate the level to which a student is self-reliant and competent. It can be said that proficiency-based grading is truly "trusted adults observing competencies" (Wagner & Dintersmith, 2015, p. 227) and then grading the evidence of student learning.

The traditional grading mindset has been earning points or, for the sake of this analogy, gold coins. In points-based classrooms, students earn a gold coin for what they do right. At the end of a certain period, teachers give grades based on the size of the student's pile of gold coins. Students build several piles at the same time. They manage these piles throughout the year. If one pile is big enough, they move on to get more coins in another class. And worst of all, if all their piles are big enough to earn the grade they desire, they tend to stop caring about learning, justifying, "My pile is big enough; why earn any more?"

Proficiency-based grading challenges this practice and replaces it with an entirely different perspective. We ask teachers to assess and grade based on proficiency attainment throughout a certain time period. Instead of coins, or points, students earn skills that transfer to other courses and beyond school itself.

This perspective equates to what we call *spinning plates on poles*. Each pole and plate is proficiency, and the student must get the plate spinning and keep it spinning to earn the grade. Piles of gold coins aren't what they rely on to tell them what they are earning.

With no coins to compile, a student must manage anywhere from five to ten learning targets per class, which equates to between twenty-five and fifty targets for a school year. Managing a dynamically changing archive of evidence is a much different skill than managing piles of points. When they manage points, students get a sense of permanent status despite it being temporary success—kind of like earning a prize at a carnival. On the other hand, the more rigorous work of managing proficiency evidence (instead of points) demands reflection abilities, self-evaluative skills, and personal agency.

A proficiency-based approach—to instruction, feedback, assessment, and grading—must help students navigate this mindset change. Eating your vegetables is not easy, but it is really good for you. It's the same with proficiency-based grading. It may require more intention, focus, reflective stamina, self-regulation, and emotional growth—but is that a bad thing? We think not.

References and Resources

Adair-Hauck, B., Glisan, E. W., & Troyan, F. J. (2013). *Implementing integrated performance assessment*. Alexandria, VA: American Council on the Teaching of Foreign Languages.

Adlai E. Stevenson High School. (2017). *MTH 1N1 / MTH 1N2—Algebra 1 collaborative*. Accessed at https://docs.google.com/document/d/1R62XCE5Zmh9Q5TNGpr01fPGdVlbsnrFEEn4KMaZmmBc/edit on October 12, 2018.

Allen, D., & Fraser, B. J. (2007). Parent and student perceptions of classroom learning environment and its association with student outcomes. *Learning Environments Research, 10*(1), 67–82.

American Council on the Teaching of Foreign Languages. (1996). *World-readiness standards for learning languages*. Accessed at www.actfl.org/sites/default/files/publications/standards/World-ReadinessStandardsforLearningLanguages.pdf on November 26, 2018.

American Council on the Teaching of Foreign Languages. (2012). *ACTFL performance descriptors for language learners*. Alexandria, VA: Author.

Arkansas State University. (2016). *3 main types of communication*. Accessed at https://degree.astate.edu/articles/undergraduate-studies/3-main-types-of-communication.aspx on February 11, 2019.

Association for Career and Technical Education. (n.d.a). *CTE today!* Accessed at www.acteonline.org/wp-content/uploads/2018/03/CTE_Today_Fact_Sheet2.pdf on October 10, 2018.

Association for Career and Technical Education. (n.d.b). *What is "career ready"?* Accessed at www.acteonline.org/wp-content/uploads/2018/03/Career_Readiness_Paper_COLOR.pdf on April 2, 2018.

Bailey, K., & Jakicic, C. (2017). *Simplifying common assessment: A guide for Professional Learning Communities at Work™*. Bloomington, IN: Solution Tree Press.

Bandura, A. (1986). *Social foundations of thought and action: A social cognitive theory.* Englewood Cliffs, NJ: Prentice Hall.

Bandura, A. (1997). *Self-efficacy: The exercise of control.* New York: Freeman.

Boughton, D. G. (2004). Assessing art learning in changing contexts: High-stakes accountability, international standards and changing conceptions of artistic development. In E. W. Eisner & M. D. Day (Eds.), *Handbook of research and policy in art education* (pp. 585–606). Mahwah, NJ: Erlbaum.

Boughton, D. G. (2016). Assessment of performance in the visual arts: What, how and why? In A. Kárpáti & E. Gaul (Eds.), *From child art to visual language of youth: New models and tools for assessment of learning and creation in art education* (pp. 119–142). Bristol, England: Intellect.

Brown, P. C., Roediger, H. L., & McDaniel, M. A. (2014). *Make it stick: The science of successful learning.* Cambridge, MA: Belknap Press.

Buffum, A., Mattos, M., & Malone, J. (2018). *Taking action: A handbook for RTI at Work.* Bloomington, IN: Solution Tree Press.

Buffum, A., Mattos, M., & Weber, C. (2009). *Pyramid response to intervention: RTI, professional learning communities, and how to respond when kids don't learn.* Bloomington, IN: Solution Tree Press.

Buffum, A., Mattos, M., & Weber, C. (2010). The why behind RTI. *Educational Leadership, 68*(2), 10–16.

Centers for Disease Control and Prevention. (2017). *Overcoming barriers to physical activity.* Accessed at www.cdc.gov/physicalactivity/basics/adding-pa/barriers.html on October 11, 2018.

Centers for Disease Control and Prevention. (2018). *Physical activity basics.* Accessed at www.cdc.gov/physicalactivity/basics/adding-pa/barriers.html on October 11, 2018.

Chappuis, J. (2009). *Seven strategies of assessment for learning.* Portland, OR: Assessment Training Institute.

Charles A. Dana Center at the University of Texas at Austin & Collaborative for Academic, Social, and Emotional Learning. (2016). *Integrating social and emotional learning and the Common Core State Standards for mathematics: Making the case.* Accessed at www.insidemathematics.org/assets/common-core-resources/social -emotional-learning/a__integrating_sel_and_ccssm_making_the_case.pdf on October 10, 2018.

Cheuk, T. (2013). *Relationships and convergences among the mathematics, science, and ELA practices.* Palo Alto, CA: Stanford University.

Clayton, J. B. (1957). The white circle. In *The strangers were there.* London: Macmillan.

Collaborative for Academic, Social, and Emotional Learning. (2017). *Core SEL competencies.* Accessed at https://casel.org/core-competencies on October 10, 2018.

The College Board. (2012). *Child development and arts education: A review of current research and best practices.* New York: Author.

The College Board. (2017a). *AP European history.* Accessed at https://apcentral .collegeboard.org/pdf/ap-world-history-course-and-exam-description .pdf?course=ap-world-history on February 14, 2019.

The College Board. (2017b). *AP United States history.* Accessed at https://apcentral
.collegeboard.org/pdf/ap-us-history-course-and-exam-description.pdf?course
=ap-united-states-history on February 14, 2019.

The College Board. (2017c). *AP world history.* Accessed at https://apcentral
.collegeboard.org/pdf/ap-world-history-course-and-exam-description
.pdf?course=ap-world-history on February 14, 2019.

The College Board. (2018). *AP studio art scoring guidelines.* Accessed at https://secure
-media.collegeboard.org/ap/pdf/ap18-studio-art-sg.pdf on February 4, 2019.

Compliance. (n.d.). In *Merriam-Webster online.* Accessed at www.merriam-webster
.com/dictionary/compliance on March 13, 2018.

Conti, G. J. (1989). Assessing teaching style in continuing education. In E. Hayes
(Ed.), *Effective teaching styles* (pp. 87–91). San Francisco: Jossey-Bass.

Conti, G. J. (2015). Identifying your teaching style. In M. W. Galbraith (Ed.), *Adult
learning methods: A guide for effective instruction* (3rd ed., pp. 73–91). Malabar, FL:
Krieger.

Conzemius, A. E., & O'Neill, J. (2014). *The handbook for SMART school teams:
Revitalizing best practices for collaboration* (2nd ed.). Bloomington, IN: Solution Tree
Press.

Cooper, R., Mishra, G. D., & Kuh, D. (2011, October). Physical activity across
adulthood and physical performance in midlife: Findings from a British birth
cohort. *American Journal of Preventive Medicine, 41*(4), 376–384.

Costa, A. L., & Kallick, B. (2008). *Learning and leading with habits of mind: 16
essential characteristics for success.* Alexandria, VA: Association for Supervision and
Curriculum Development.

Council of Chief State School Officers. (2012). *Framework for English language
proficiency development standards corresponding to the Common Core State Standards and
the Next Generation Science Standards.* Washington, DC: CCSSO.

Couros, G. (2014). *The innovator's mindset: Empower learning, unleash talent, and lead a
culture of creativity.* San Diego, CA: Dave Burgess Consulting.

Csikszentmihalyi, M. (1990). *Flow: The psychology of optimal experience.* New York:
Harper & Row.

Danielson, C. (2013). *Framework for teaching.* Accessed at www.danielsongroup.org
/framework on February 11, 2019.

De La Paz, S., Monte-Sano, C., Felton, M., Croninger, R., Jackson, C., & Worland, K.
(2017). A historical writing apprenticeship for adolescents: Integrating disciplinary
learning with cognitive strategies. *Reading Research Quarterly, 52*(1), 31–52.

Dewey, J. (1938). *Experience and education.* New York: Macmillan.

Dickens, C. (1859). *A tale of two cities.* New York: Penguin Random House.

DuFour, R., DuFour, R., & Eaker, R. (2008). *Revisiting Professional Learning Communities
at Work: New insights for improving schools.* Bloomington, IN: Solution Tree Press.

Dweck, C. S. (n.d.). *What is mindset?* Accessed at https://mindsetonline.com/whatisit /about/index.html on October 10, 2018.

Dweck, C. S. (2006). *Mindset: The new psychology of success.* New York: Ballantine Books.

Fisher, D., & Frey, N. (2014). *Better learning through structured teaching: A framework for the gradual release of responsibility* (2nd ed.). Alexandria, VA: Association for Supervision and Curriculum Development.

Fitzgerald, F. S. (1925). *The great Gatsby.* New York: Scribner.

Fluckiger, J. (2010). Single point rubric: A tool for responsible student self-assessment. *Delta Kappa Gamma Bulletin, 76*(4), 18–25.

Forsyth, A. D., & Carey, M. P. (1998). Measuring self-efficacy in the context of HIV risk reduction: Research challenges and recommendations. *Health Psychology, 17*(6), 559–568.

Fostering Math Practices. (n.d.). *Avenues of thinking.* Accessed at www .fosteringmathpractices.com/avenues-of-thinking on October 10, 2018.

Frayer, D. A., Frederick, W. C., & Klausmeier, H. G. (1969). *A schema for testing the level of concept mastery: Report from the Project on Situational Variables and Efficiency of Concept Learning.* Madison: Wisconsin Research and Development Center for Cognitive Learning.

Frey, N., Fisher, D., & Smith, D. (2019). *All learning is social and emotional: Helping students develop essential skills for the classroom and beyond.* Alexandria, VA: Association for Supervision and Curriculum Development.

Glisan, E. W., & Donato, R. (2017). *Enacting the work of language instruction: High-leverage teaching practices.* Alexandria, VA: American Council on the Teaching of Foreign Languages.

Gobble, T., Onuscheck, M., Reibel, A. R., & Twadell, E. (2016). *Proficiency-based assessment: Process, not product.* Bloomington, IN: Solution Tree Press.

Gobble, T., Onuscheck, M., Reibel, A. R., & Twadell, E. (2017). *Pathways to proficiency: Implementing evidence-based grading.* Bloomington, IN: Solution Tree Press.

Golding, W. (1954). *Lord of the flies.* London: Faber and Faber.

Gomez-Pinilla, F., & Hillman, C. (2013). The influence of exercise on cognitive abilities. *Comprehensive Physiology, 3*(1), 403–428.

Guskey, T. R. (2015). *On your mark: Challenging the conventions of grading and reporting.* Bloomington, IN: Solution Tree Press.

Guskey, T. R., & Bailey, J. M. (2010). *Developing standards-based report cards.* Thousand Oaks, CA: Corwin Press.

Guskey, T. R., & Jung, L. A. (2013). *Answers to essential questions about standards, assessments, grading, and reporting.* Thousand Oaks, CA: Corwin Press.

Hartley, C. A., & Somerville, L. H. (2015). The neuroscience of adolescent decision-making. *Current Opinion in Behavioral Sciences, 5,* 108–115.

Hattie, J. (2009). *Visible learning: A synthesis of over 800 meta-analyses relating to achievement.* London: Routledge.

Hattie, J. (2012). *Visible learning for teachers: Maximizing impact on learning.* New York: Routledge.

Hillocks, G. (2011). *Teaching argument writing: Supporting claims with relevant evidence and clear reasoning.* Portsmouth, NH: Heinemann.

Hoffman, N. (2018). *10 equity questions to ask about career and technical education.* Accessed at www.jff.org/points-of-view/10-equity-questions-ask-about-career -and-technical-education on November 14, 2018.

Holcomb, E. L. (2009). *Asking the right questions: Tools for collaboration and school change* (3rd ed.). Thousand Oaks, CA: Corwin Press.

Hyslop, A. (2007). Create system incentives and supports for connection of CTE and high school redesign efforts. *Techniques: Connecting Education and Careers, 82*(4), 33–35.

Illinois High School Association. (n.d.). *IHSA music percussion solo/ensemble adjudication form.* Accessed at www.ihsa.org/documents/mu/SE%20Adjudication%20Forms .pdf on February 4, 2019.

Illinois State Board of Education. (n.d.). *Learning standards: Social/emotional learning standards.* Accessed at www.isbe.net/pages/social-emotional-learning-standards .aspx on November 17, 2018.

Illinois State Board of Education. (2013). *Illinois social science standards.* Accessed at www.isbe.net/Documents/K-12-SS-Standards.pdf on February 14, 2019.

Jacobson, L., & Mokher, C. (2009). *Pathways to boosting the earnings of low-income students by increasing their educational attainment.* Accessed at https://files.eric.ed.gov /fulltext/ED504078.pdf on November 13, 2018.

Jain, D., & Reibel, A. (2018). Creating competence in the classroom. *The Assessor, 5,* 16–17. Accessed at www.assessormag.com/uploads/2/1/9/6/21969098/assessor _edition_5.pdf on April 11, 2019.

Jakicic, J. M., Davis, K. K., Rogers, R. J., King, W. C., Marcus, M. D., Helsel, D., et al. (2016). Effect of wearable technology combined with a lifestyle intervention on long-term weight loss: The IDEA randomized clinical trial. *Journal of the American Medical Association, 316*(11), 1161–1171.

Jones, A. (2015, September 8). *Why a paradigm shift around classroom grading practice is necessary: Moving towards standards-based grading and reporting* [Blog post]. Accessed at https://rowlandfoundation.wordpress.com/2015/09/08/why-a-paradigm-shift -around-classroom-grading-practice-is-necessary-moving-towards-standards -based-grading-and-reporting on October 11, 2018.

Kelemanik, G., Lucenta, A., & Creighton, S. J. (2016). *Routines for reasoning: Fostering the mathematical practices in all students.* Portsmouth, NH: Heinemann.

Kraft, M. A., & Dougherty, S. M. (2013). The effect of teacher-family communication on student engagement: Evidence from a randomized field experiment. *Journal of Research on Educational Effectiveness, 6*(3), 199–222.

Mandell, N., & Malone, B. (2007). *Thinking like a historian: Rethinking history instruction.* Madison, WI: Wisconsin Historical Society Press.

Marzano, R. J. (2003). *What works in schools: Translating research into action.* Alexandria, VA: Association for Supervision and Curriculum Development.

Marzano, R. J. (2006). *Classroom assessment and grading that work.* Alexandria, VA: Association for Supervision and Curriculum Development.

Marzano, R. J. (2009). *Designing and teaching learning goals and objectives.* Bloomington, IN: Marzano Research.

McCaskey, S. J., & Crowder, C. L. (2015). Reflection on one's own teaching style and learning strategy can affect the CTE classroom. *CTE Journal, 3*(1), 2–12.

Moss, C. M., & Brookhart, S. M. (2012). *Learning targets: Helping students aim for understanding in today's lesson.* Alexandria, VA: Association for Supervision and Curriculum Development.

National Board for Professional Teaching Standards. (2014). *Career and technical education standards* (2nd ed.). Accessed at www.nbpts.org/wp-content/uploads /EAYA-CTE.pdf on November 19, 2018.

National Coalition for Core Arts Standards. (2014). *National core arts standards.* Accessed at www.nationalartsstandards.org on February 12, 2019.

National Council for the Social Studies. (2013). *Social studies for the next generation: Purposes, practices, and implications of the College, Career, and Civic Life (C3) Framework for Social Studies State Standards—NCSS Bulletin 113.* Silver Spring, MD: Author.

National Council of Teachers of Mathematics. (2014a). *Principles to actions: Ensuring mathematical success for all.* Reston, VA: Author.

National Council of Teachers of Mathematics. (2014b). *Procedural fluency in mathematics.* Accessed at www.nctm.org/uploadedFiles/Standards_and_Positions /Position_Statements/Procedural%20Fluency.pdf on February 13, 2019.

National Education Association. (2008). *Parent, family, community involvement in education: An NEA policy brief.* Washington, DC: Author. Accessed at www.nea .org/assets/docs/PB11_ParentInvolvement08.pdf on February 3, 2019.

National Governors Association Center for Best Practices & Council of Chief State School Officers. (2010a). *Common Core State Standards for English language arts and literacy in history/social studies, science, and technical subjects.* Washington, DC: Authors. Accessed at www.corestandards.org/assets/CCSSI_ELA%20Standards on October 11, 2018.

National Governors Association Center for Best Practices & Council of Chief State School Officers. (2010b). *Common Core State Standards for mathematics.* Washington, DC: Authors. Accessed at www.corestandards.org/assets/CCSSI_Math%20 Standards.pdf on October 11, 2018.

National Research Council. (2001). *Adding it up: Helping children learn mathematics.* Washington, DC: National Academies Press.

National Research Council. (2012). *A framework for K–12 science education: Practices, crosscutting concepts, and core ideas.* Washington, DC: National Academies Press.

National Standards Collaborative Board. (2015). *World-readiness standards for learning languages* (4th ed.). Alexandria, VA: Author.

NCD Risk Factor Collaboration. (2016). Trends in adult body-mass index in 200 countries from 1975 to 2014: A pooled analysis of 1698 population-based measurement studies with 19.2 million participants. *The Lancet, 387*(10026), 1377–1396.

Next Generation Science Standards. (n.d.). *Three dimensional learning.* Accessed at www.nextgenscience.org/three-dimensions on April 10, 2019.

Next Generation Science Standards. (2013a). *Appendix F: Science and engineering practices in the NGSS.* Accessed at www.nextgenscience.org/sites/default/files /Appendix%20F%20%20Science%20and%20Engineering%20Practices%20in%20 the%20NGSS%20-%20FINAL%20060513.pdf on October 12, 2018.

Next Generation Science Standards. (2013b). *Appendix G: Crosscutting concepts.* Accessed at www.nextgenscience.org/sites/default/files/Appendix%20G%20-%20 Crosscutting%20Concepts%20FINAL%20edited%204.10.13.pdf on October 12, 2018.

Next Generation Science Standards. (2013c). *DCI arrangements of the Next Generation Science Standards.* Accessed at www.nextgenscience.org/sites/default/files/NGSS% 20DCI%20Combined%2011.6.13.pdf on November 25, 2018.

O'Callaghan, F., O'Callaghan, M., Williams, G., Bor, W., & Najman, J. (2012). Physical activity and intelligence: A causal exploration. *Journal of Physical Activity and Health, 9*(2), 218–224.

Perkins Collaborative Resource Network. (n.d.). *Employability skills.* Accessed at https://cte.ed.gov/initiatives/employability-skills-framework on October 11, 2018.

Proficiency. (n.d.) In *Merriam-Webster online.* Accessed at www.merriam-webster.com /dictionary/proficiency on March 13, 2018.

Putnam, R. D. (2000). *Bowling alone: The collapse and revival of American community.* New York: Simon & Schuster.

Ratey, J. J., & Hagerman, E. (2013). *Spark: The revolutionary new science of exercise and the brain.* New York: Little, Brown.

Reibel, A. (2018). The three purposes of assessment. *The Assessor,* 12–13.

Robson, R., & Latiolais, M. P. (1999). *Standards-based education and its implications for mathematics faculty.* Accessed at www.maa.org/standards-based-education-and-its -implications-for-mathematics-faculty on October 11, 2018.

Rubric. (n.d.). In *Merriam-Webster online.* Accessed at www.merriam-webster.com /dictionary/rubric on March 13, 2018.

Sandrock, P. (2010). *The keys to assessing language performance: A teacher's manual for measuring student progress.* Alexandria, VA: American Council on the Teaching of Foreign Languages.

Schoemaker, P. J. H. (2011). *Brilliant mistakes.* Philadelphia, PA: Wharton Digital Press.

Schimmer, T. (2016). *Grading from the inside out: Bringing accuracy to student assessment through a standards-based mindset.* Bloomington, IN: Solution Tree Press.

Schonert-Reichl, K. A., & Hymel, S. (2007). Educating the heart as well as the mind: Social and emotional learning for school and life success [Abstract]. *Education Canada, 47*(2), 20–25. Accessed at https://eric.ed.gov/?id=EJ771005 on April 10, 2019.

Schwartz, P. D., Maynard, A. M., & Uzelac, S. M. (2008). Adolescent egocentrism: A contemporary view. *Adolescence, 43*(171), 441–448.

Shakespeare, W. (1973). The tempest. In G. B. Evans , H. Levin, H. Baker, A. Barton, F. Kermode, H. Smith, M. Edel, & C. H. Shattuck (Eds.), *The Riverside Shakespeare* (pp. 1606–1638). Boston: Houghton Mifflin.

Shanahan, T., & Shanahan, C. (2012). What is discipline literacy and why does it matter? *Topics in Language Disorders, 32*(1), 7–18.

Shrum, J. L., & Glisan, E. W. (2016). *Teacher's handbook: Contextualized language instruction* (5th ed.). Boston: Cengage Learning.

Society of Health and Physical Educators America. (n.d.). *Literacy in PE + HE.* Accessed at www.shapeamerica.org/events/healthandphysicalliteracy.aspx on February 1, 2019.

Society of Health and Physical Educators America. (2013). *National standards for K–12 physical education.* Accessed at www.shapeamerica.org/standards/pe on February 11, 2019.

Steverman, B. (2017). *Why you're paying so much to exercise: Millennials are turning the fitness industry upside down.* Accessed at www.bloomberg.com/news/articles /2017-01-30/why-you-re-paying-so-much-to-exercise on October 11, 2018.

Stiggins, R. (2008). *Assessment FOR learning, the achievement gap, and truly effective schools.* Accessed at www.ets.org/Media/Conferences_and_Events/pdf/stiggins .pdf on December 21, 2018.

Sultan, S., & Muhammad, S. (2014). Impact of perceived teachers' competence on students' performance: Evidence for mediating/moderating role of class environment. *i-manager's Journal on Educational Psychology, 8*(1), 10–18.

Swan, K., Barton, K. C., Buckles, S., Burke, F., Charkins, J., Grant, S. G., et al. (2013). *The College, Career, and Civic Life (C3) Framework for Social Studies State Standards: Guidance for enhancing the rigor of K–12 civics, economics, geography, and history.* Silver Springs, MD: National Council for the Social Studies.

Syverson, M. A. (2009). Social justice and evidence-based assessment with the learning record. *Forum on Public Policy,* 1–27.

Thompson, C. P., & Phillips, E. M. (2013). *Mais oui! Introductory French and Francophone culture.* South Melbourne, Victoria, Australia: Heinle Cengage Learning.

Tomlinson, C. A. (2005). *Educators at work: Differentiating curriculum and instruction.* ASCD Annual Conference.

Tomlinson, C. A. (2017). *How to differentiate instruction in academically diverse classrooms* (3rd ed.). Alexandria, Virginia: Association for Supervision and Curriculum Development.

Truman, H. S. (1945). *Special message to the Congress recommending a comprehensive health program.* Accessed at www.trumanlibrary.org/publicpapers/index.php?pid=483 on November 25, 2018.

Van Horne, K., Penuel, W. R., & Bell, P. (2016). *Integrating science practices into assessment tasks.* Accessed at www.stemteachingtools.org/assets/landscapes /NGSSTaskFormats_June2017_v2.pdf on October 12, 2018.

VanSledright, B. A. (2010). *The challenge of rethinking history education: On practices, theories, and policy.* New York: Routledge.

Wagner, T., & Dintersmith, T. (2015). *Most likely to succeed: Preparing our kids for the innovation era.* New York: Scribner.

Webb, N. L. (1997). *Criteria for alignment of expectations and assessments in mathematics and science education* (Research Monograph No. 6). Madison: University of Wisconsin, National Institute for Science Education.

Webb, N. L. (1999). *Alignment of science and mathematics standards and assessments in four states* (Research Monograph No. 18). Madison: University of Wisconsin, National Institute for Science Education.

Wiggins, G., & McTighe, J. (1998). *Understanding by design.* London: Pearson.

Wiliam, D. (2018). *Embedded formative assessment* (2nd ed.). Bloomington, IN: Solution Tree Press.

Wineburg, S., Martin, D., & Monte-Sano, C. (2012). *Reading like a historian: Teaching literacy in middle and high school history classrooms—aligned with Common Core State Standards* (2nd ed.). New York: Teachers College Press.

Wollenschläger, M., Hattie, J., Machts, N., Möller, J., & Harms, U. (2016). What makes rubrics effective in teacher-feedback? Transparency of learning goals is not enough. *Contemporary Educational Psychology, 44–45,* 1–11.

Zins, J. E., Weissberg, R. P., Wang, M. C., & Walberg, H. J. (Eds.). (2004). *Building academic success on social and emotional learning: What does the research say?* New York: Teachers College Press.

Index

Pathways to Proficiency
Troy Gobble, Mark Onuscheck, Anthony R. Reibel, and Eric Twadell

This book provides the pathway for implementing evidence-based grading practices in schools through a straightforward, five-phase creative model. Readers will follow a hypothetical curriculum team's challenging journey through each phase of this process.
BKF682

Proficiency-Based Assessment
Troy Gobble, Mark Onuscheck, Anthony R. Reibel, and Eric Twadell

With this resource, teachers will discover how to close the gaps between assessment, curriculum, and instruction by replacing outmoded assessment methods with proficiency-based assessments. Learn the essentials of proficiency-based assessment, and explore evidence-based strategies for successful implementation.
BKF631

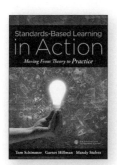

Standards-Based Learning in Action
Tom Schimmer, Garnet Hillman, and Mandy Stalets

Get past the knowing-doing gap and confidently implement standards-based learning in your classroom, school, or district. Each chapter offers readers a well-thought-out action plan for implementation and effective communication strategies for getting student and parent buy-in.
BKF782

Collaborative Common Assessments
Cassandra Erkens

Reignite the passion and energy assessment practices bring as tools to guide teaching and learning. Strengthen instruction with collaborative common assessments that collect vital information. Explore the practical steps teams must take to establish assessment systems, and discover how to continually improve results.
BKF605

Solution Tree | Press

a division of
Solution Tree

Visit SolutionTree.com or call 800.733.6786 to order.

"Excellent engagement
in what truly matters
in **assessment**.

Great examples!"

—Carol Johnson, superintendent,
Central Dauphin School District, Pennsylvania

 PD Services

Our experts draw from decades of research and their own experiences to bring you
practical strategies for designing and implementing quality assessments. You can choose
from a range of customizable services, from a one-day overview to a multiyear process.

Book your assessment PD today!
888.763.9045

Solution Tree